W9-AXI-756

The Idea Edge

Transforming Creative Thought
into Organizational Excellence

Bob King

and

Dr. Helmut Schlicksupp

The Idea Edge: Transforming Creative Thought into Organizational Excellence
Bob King and Dr. Helmut Schlicksupp

© 1998 by GOAL/QPC. Any reproduction of any part of this publication without the written permission of GOAL/QPC is prohibited.

Developmental editing: Michael Brassard and Lynne Levesque
Copy editing: Francine Oddo and Michael Clark
Cover design: Lori Champney
Book design, graphics, layout: Deborah Crovo
Icons, graphics: Michele Kierstead

GOAL/QPC
13 Branch Street, Methuen, MA 01844-1953
Toll free: 1-800-643-4316
Phone: 978-685-3900 Fax: 978-685-6151
E-mail: service@goal.com
Web site: http://www.goalqpc.com

First Edition
10 9 8 7 6 5 4 3 2 1

ISBN 1-57681-019-4

Contents

Appendices

Acknowledgments

Many individuals made significant contributions to this book. Their efforts are very much appreciated. Thanks go to the following groups and individuals.

The creative, patient, and determined project team at GOAL/QPC that persevered through many months to help create a greatly improved final product:

Michael Brassard	Technical Review & Contributing Author (Chapter 12)
Michael Clark	Editor
Deborah Crovo	Book Design, Graphics, & Layout
Michele Kierstead	Icon Design & Graphics
Lynne Levesque	Project Manager & Developmental Editor
Fran Oddo	Editor
Dorie Overhoff	Marketing
Bob Page	Business Development

Other GOAL/QPC staff who supported this effort:

Lee Alphen, Anna Beliveau, Lisa Boisvert, Steve Boudreau, Paul Brassard, Elaine Curtis, Jim Denoncourt, Debbie Elderkin, Lisa Gilliland, Susan Griebel, Rick Hartung, Dona Hotopp, Barbara LaPointe, Larry LeFebre, Stan Marsh, Mona McGovern, Elizabeth Morrison, Richard Morrison, Diane Ritter, Sheryl Roberge, Peter Routhier, Larry Smith, Claire Vigeant.

Individuals who took time to apply their particular expertise to technically reviewing chapters in this publication:

Barry Bebb and Donald Clausing for Chapter 12
Michael Brassard for Chapters 13, 14, and 15

Acknowledgments

Individuals who contributed examples and their experience from training:

Diane Ritter, GOAL/QPC

Tina Sung and other members of the Federal Quality Consulting Group in Washington, D.C.

Tracey Schmidt, Tennessee Valley Authority

A special thanks to Janice Marconi for her practical insights and examples.

The organizations and individuals who agreed to be on the readers' panel. These individuals made a significant contribution by helping us to design a product based on the needs of the customer:

Aberdeen Area Indian Health
Jerome DeWolfe

Chilton Memorial Hospital
Deborah Zastocki

City Year
Ariana Hoy
Jeff Paquette
Stephanie Wu

Computing Devices Hastings Limited
Siân Anderson

Deere & Company
Hollis Hohensee

Donnelly Corporation
Paul Doyle

Ford Motor Company
Larry Smith

Harvard Pilgrim Healthcare
Kathy Mahaney

Hewlett-Packard
Doug Daetz
Joe Podolsky

Mckesson Corporation
Mark Taylor

Milestone
Robert Taraschi

National Naval Medical Center
Elizabeth Niemyer

Puget Sound Naval Shipyard Nuclear Quality Division Process Management Branch
Steven Cicelski
Jeffrey Cizek
Grant Clark
Terri Cordes
Robert Forrest
Ken Gholston
Mary Sieler

Raytheon Systems Company
Jack B. Revelle, Ph.D.

Senco Products Inc.
Ravi Chinta

Shield Inn
Louis Isaacson

Tamarack Consulting
Rick Osterhaus

Tennessee Valley Authority
Tracy Schmidt

Unisys Schweiz Ag
Thomas Fehlmann

University Hospital
Sharon Beck

U.S. Air Force, Center for Quality & Management Innovation
William Friday

Preface

Our stories both began roughly 20 years ago—mine in the United States, and Helmut's in Germany. GOAL/QPC, where I work as CEO, was first established almost 20 years ago. Since that time, it has become a world leader in creating and providing educational products and services to involve all employees in participative planning and problem solving in their organizations. GOAL/QPC's publications, including *The Memory Jogger Plus+*® and The Memory Jogger™ system of pocket reference guides, have been translated into 12 different languages and used by thousands of organizations and millions of people around the world.

Many of GOAL/QPC's efforts over the last two decades have focused on studying and adapting the incremental process control and process improvement methods learned from the Japanese. Today, however, businesses are facing deep changes and increasing pressures to make more rapid and dramatic breakthroughs. Incremental improvements are often not enough. In increasing numbers over the last 10 years, GOAL/QPC's customers have asked for additional tools for making faster and more dramatic improvements.

With a growing awareness of the value of creativity and innovation in the business world and in response to customer demands, I began a search several years ago to fill the need for tools to use when continuous improvement processes are too slow to meet required goals. This search led to an investigation of what was available in the United States. Several approaches were explored, but I did not find them to have the detailed, systematic rigor that organizations have grown to expect because of their experience with using the Quality Control and Management and Planning Tools.

I continued my search by traveling outside the borders of the United States and conducted a more global quest for the appropriate tools. Finally, almost by accident, I found the answer in the work of Dr. Helmut Schlicksupp. For his part, Dr. Schlicksupp had begun his research in creativity methods and techniques while working with a subsidiary of the Battelle Institute in Germany just over 20 years ago. His research there and subsequently in business organizations, led him to the definition of 42 distinct creativity methods. To provide a more manageable set of tools for teams and team leaders, he grouped the different techniques into seven sets of tools. From each of these sets, he has selected the most representative and most versatile tool for use in this book. The tools described in this book have been shown to provide the right techniques to stimulate creative thinking to tackle some of the toughest business problems.

Recognizing that customers need more than idea generation tools, Helmut and I decided to join forces. While the creativity tools are important for generating new ideas, teams also need tools to help them select and then implement the best alternatives. Thus, working together, Helmut and I have enhanced the offering of the creativity tools with tools for idea selection and implementation. Thus, teams and team leaders have in this book the tools and techniques needed to generate ideas, to select from the best of them, and to successfully implement the chosen solutions to create breakthroughs for the organization.

Helmut and I decided to collaborate on this book because we believe that creativity and innovation are the most important ingredients for organizational growth and success. The tools and techniques in this book will bring out the creative and innovative skills of the employees who take the time to learn them. When these tools and techniques are applied to organizational challenges, they can provide breakthrough solutions in problem solving, process improvement and standardization, planning, and product and service development.

I trust that this book and the other activities being undertaken by GOAL/QPC and Dr. Schlicksupp will significantly expand organization-wide creativity and innovation. Helmut and I hope that these efforts will enhance the lives of all who read the book and that the application of these tools will significantly strengthen the future prosperity of organizations and, ultimately, of all society.

Bob King

The Idea Edge

Introduction

"To grow, organizations, like individuals, require the stimulus of challenge and innovation."

D. Leonard Barton

This introduction has three parts: "Setting the Stage for a Systematic Approach to Creativity," "Preparing to Use the Creativity Tools," which begins on page xiv, and "How to Get the Most from this Book and the Tools," beginning on page xxv.

Setting the Stage for a Systematic Approach to Creativity

Understanding creativity can be complex and confusing, and therefore its definitions vary considerably. However, there is a general consensus that creativity is the ability of people to generate new designs, products, or ideas that, until the moment of generation, are completely unknown to the creator. These ideas may be an outcome of imaginative thinking, or the combination of thinking and forming new patterns, or they may come out of a group's experiences. The result is more than the sum of what is already known. The creative product or result must be useful and capable of being implemented, it can't just exist forever in someone's imagination. The creativity process is more than just dreaming. It must eventually result in a tangible product or service, though not necessarily flawless and complete.

Creativity and innovation are often used synonymously, and this can contribute to the confusion of understanding what creativity is. In this book, for the sake of clarity, the more conventional definitions are used. The term "creativity" refers to the process of idea generation. The term "innovation" describes the process of idea selection and the translation of the idea into reality.

Creativity and innovation involve the efforts of an individual or team who, individually and collectively, have unique personalities, backgrounds, and sets of traits and abilities. While anyone, anywhere has the ability to be creative, a person's creativity can be enhanced by being aware of how he or she is creative and by working in an environment that supports and nourishes creativity. A person's creative abilities can be further developed through heightened use and practice, formal and informal training, and support from colleagues and managers. The tools described in this book, when used appropriately, will definitely bolster these creativity and innovation processes.

What is Creative Thinking?

Creative thinking is a process that can lead individuals and teams to more creative results. Tried and true ways of thinking, based on experiences of the past, do not always produce the desired results in today's world of dynamic change. Organizations need creative thinking to successfully solve problems that are uncommon or that require solutions that are different from those used in the past.

Creative thinking is fascinating and somewhat mysterious. It involves ambiguity, contradiction, randomness, and play. The creative mind generates ideas but the underlying sources remain hidden and often cannot be totally controlled or consciously directed. Creative thinking assumes that there are no definite "givens" about a problem. As a result, creative thinking involves experimentation, hypothesis, speculation, and trial and error. Creative thinking is often described as divergent thinking. It emphasizes the rich creation of possibilities and one-of-a-kind ideas. While the process is not completely understood, the output is often new and uncovers interesting ways of doing business, seeing problems, and relating to people.

Key Success Factors for Creative Thinking

A wide variety of tools and techniques can help stimulate and accelerate creative thinking and eliminate restrictions on how people think they should be thinking. However, while tools and techniques can help people access their creativity, just putting people together in one room is not enough to make sparks fly. For a team to successfully solve problems, improve processes, develop new products and services, and plan for the future, it needs its creative thinking to be supported by these key factors:

A. A climate of freedom and openness.

B. Effective teamwork.

C. The use of a standard problem-solving approach.

D. The selection of the right set of tools.

A. A climate of freedom and openness.

There are many possible blocks to creative thinking. Some of these blocks come from concerns about using new techniques and from fears that unusual ideas will be rejected. Creative thinking involves experimentation and speculation. Because creative thinking produces different ideas and perspectives, it may generate criticism. People often check unusual ideas and thoughts with tough self-criticism before they allow their ideas to emerge. A person's ideas are also subjected to criticism from team members or peers. The creative mind finds too little freedom. Yet it is that very freedom that enables "seeds" of ideas to mature into valuable results.

To effectively practice creative thinking, people need to find ways to squelch self-criticism and the effect of criticism from others, open their minds and rid themselves of the fear of making mistakes, let their ideas flow, and hold off evaluation of ideas until a later time. This is why a safe, supportive, and open environment is so important to successful, productive creativity and innovation.[1]

B. Effective teamwork.

The amount and variety of knowledge, experience, and skillsets that team participants have will affect the team's potential for generating creative results. While almost all of the creativity tools can be applied by an individual, more synergy results from their use in well-performing teams. Teamwork is of increasing importance to organizations primarily because:

- The reasons for cooperation are more frequent as more and more activities exist within cross-functional, cross-organizational, and even cross-geographic boundaries.

- A single individual cannot achieve such significant results as quickly or as thoroughly as can a well-harmonized team. Teams can create a considerable amount of synergy, greatly surpassing the potential performance of their most effective individual members working alone. This is largely due to a team's diverse views on the problems, the broader knowledge several individuals can add, and the unique contribution of each team member's mental activities and processes.

---

1. A more in-depth discussion on creating a climate of freedom and openness has been written by Dr. Schlicksupp. The article "Leadership for the Development of Company-wide Creativity" was published in the *Journal of Innovative Management*, Spring 1996, 64–71.

To achieve these benefits, teams must be trained to function effectively and given the support to carry out their training. Anyone who has had the opportunity to work with a well-functioning team knows how a positive group experience can stimulate much more individual knowledge than can solitary thinking. Such effectiveness can be measured by the quality of the goals set, the level of cooperation among members, and the sharing of responsibilities and contributions. High-functioning teamwork often becomes self-sustaining because of the quality of the results.

While this book assumes the use of these tools by teams and team leaders, it does not provide guidelines for achieving high-performance teamwork. References for such information are available in "Recommended Resources" at the back of this book (Appendix C).

C. The use of a standard problem-solving approach.

The use of a systematic, organization-wide process for problem solving has been found to be highly effective in promoting creative thinking and learning. Within the framework of a common set of steps to follow and a common language for solving problems, the team can more effectively use the idea generation and selection tools.

There are several different problem-solving processes that teams can choose to use. Many organizations have adopted a standardized process with specified phases for defining the problem, analyzing data, generating alternative solutions, and selecting and implementing the solution.

While a standard problem-solving process is important, tools are needed to both generate and select ideas or solutions within each step or phase. Within a typical problem-solving process, most idea generation tools currently used are applied in the phase of generating alternative solutions. This effort usually occurs after the problem has been defined, facts have been established, and possible alternative solutions are needed.

Often, however, the definition of the problem can lead the team in different directions. Therefore, the best idea generation tools are those that can deal with the challenges of every phase of a problem-solving process. For example, the tools are needed to support the team when it is creatively examining the definition of a problem to allow the team to make subsequent redefinitions. These tools should also promote the team's ability to recognize conflicting facts and various solution alternatives. All the tools described in this book are designed to work with any problem-solving technique. Chapter 13 has more information on how the methods for generating and selecting ideas can be applied to problem solving.

D. The selection of the right set of tools.

A final ingredient for successful creative thinking is having a set of tools and techniques that will support and promote it. Such tools help teams and team leaders to exercise creative ways of thinking, which for many people are underdeveloped. Many people have been taught that thinking logically and analytically is a more highly valued way of thinking. This type of thinking needs to be used in combination with creative thinking techniques to help people convert their knowledge, logic, and analytical skills into new, creative concepts. Creativity tools support this new way of thinking because they:

- Enable flexibility in thinking about a problem and in coming up with new insights.

- Challenge existing structures and their underlying assumptions.

- Support thinking in analogies or making associations from one field or discipline with another.

- Break complex patterns down into single key elements.

- Promote variations or rearrangement of the elements of the problem.

- Encourage combinations of previously unrelated elements.

These and similar operations to support creative thinking are built into the creativity tools in different ways. All the tools are designed to open up a free space for thoughts—a space in which team members can allow their creative ideas to emerge and grow, without the threat of embarrassment or ridicule.

Once the team has generated new ideas and alternatives, it needs to have tools and techniques to help select and implement the best ideas. The tools described in Section II can provide teams with the methods they need to select and implement their new ideas. These idea selection tools have been used for many years by GOAL/QPC and other organizations to make decisions and to manage and plan for implementation of new products and solutions.

Both the creativity and the idea selection tools will improve the probability of reaching a high quality solution because they:

- Offer the most powerful techniques for incorporating the operations of creative thinking.

- Offer versatility and power.

- Have a history of proven effectiveness through extensive research and application.

- Allow for the fullest generation of creative ideas and the selection of the best of them.

- Can be used at any phase of any problem-solving process.

- Help teams resolve a wide variety of problems and challenges faced in the workplace today.

- Address the many different individual learning and problem-solving styles among team members.

Of the many tools and techniques available, the tools described in the following chapters have been selected because they have been proven to be the most effective and they meet the criteria listed above. They are easy to learn and don't require significant commitment of training time for the team. These tools will fit in with the time pressures of today's world. While there is no one right method to enhance creativity and innovation, these tools will provide significant benefits in more creative problem solving, process improvement and standardization, planning, and product and service development.

Preparing to Use the Creativity Tools

The tools in this book have been selected for two reasons: their versatility and their power to produce results. They provide team leaders with alternatives to help their teams achieve breakthroughs in the organization's business processes. Team leaders are more likely to actualize the power and value of the tools if they plan ahead for the creativity tool session and know how to use and implement the tools appropriately. This section will help team leaders understand what they need to do to prepare for a creativity tool session, what steps are basic for holding the session, and in what ways they should follow up on the session.

Questions to Consider when Planning for a Creativity Tool Session

The team leader should begin by selecting a problem, challenge, opportunity, or issue with which to apply one or several of the tools. The team leader should give some thought to who should attend the session and how it should flow. Questions to consider include:

- Who should participate? What skills, expertise, and perspectives are required to creatively address the problem?

- What are the personalities of the participants?
- What is the nature of the problem? The issues surrounding it? Any controversies involved?
- Should the session be formal or informal?
- What tools should be used?

The following discussion, "Eight Basic Steps for Holding a Successful Creativity Tool Session," gives team leaders suggestions on how to address these questions and ideas for making the session a success.

Eight Basic Steps for Holding a Successful Creativity Tool Session

Step 1. Select a problem, challenge, opportunity or issue.

In every organization there are many different problems and tasks, most of which are routine. Such problems are similar to those handled in the past and a team can usually solve them fairly quickly and quite adequately with the team's accumulated knowledge. Even these routine problems occasionally require new ideas and alternative approaches and can certainly benefit from the application of the tools described in this book.

Given the need to prioritize time and activities, however, a team leader should consider applying these methods for idea generation and selection first to problems or projects where:

- current solutions aren't working.
- the problem is so critical that it needs a new and innovative solution.
- new products and approaches are needed.

A team usually cannot deal with such situations with just logic and routine approaches. Instead, the team needs new techniques for generating a wealth of ideas. The team leader should consider organizing a creativity tool session to deal with the kind of challenges that require new and innovative perspectives, insights, and solutions.

Step 2. Select the team.

After the problem, challenge, opportunity, or issue has been selected, the team leader needs to decide who should be involved in the session and what setting is appropriate. The team leader should consider the following points when choosing team members:

- Participants should be selected for their knowledge, expertise, skills, and ability to work together. The team leader should not expect that participants will have identical levels of knowledge and experience; instead they should have skills and experiences that complement one another, in breadth and depth.

- The team should include both men and women, and a mix of cultures and styles. People of different ethnic backgrounds, educational levels, skills, and backgrounds have different perspectives, which can trigger more interesting solutions.

- Participants agree to support creative thinking approaches and its principles.

- The team has had sufficient training in teambuilding and teamwork skills as well as in the application of the idea generation and selection tools. (While a good facilitator can help to overcome the lack of these skills and experiences, the time scheduled for the session may need to be revised to take this issue into account.)

- All participants should understand and support the ground rules of brainstorming, which are outlined in Chapter 2. It is very important for everyone to agree that all participants are equals and that no differences in organizational rank or status will be recognized. Otherwise, superiors may tend to dominate the session.

In selecting the participants for the creativity tool session, the team leader should consider that the right combination of individuals will produce a more efficient and effective session than a random selection of participants. The creativity tool session, which brings individuals together to work as a team, is intended to stimulate the full creative potential of the participants. This team approach allows participants to push on their creative potential because:

- The problem will be considered from many different perspectives. A single individual is always in danger of looking at a subject only from a very personal and limited point of view. In addition, several individuals can apply a broader range of knowledge to the problem, a range most individuals do not possess on their own.

- The members of a team will provide mutual stimulation of ideas. They will trigger a wide variety and range of associations, which would rarely emerge from a single individual.

- Collaborative thinking keeps brain activities at a high level for a longer period of time. The phases of intense intuitive and spontaneous thinking are distinctly shorter when practiced alone.

- A high-performing team will generate a greater number of ideas and thus has a higher probability of exploring and finding an acceptable, high-quality solution within a shorter period of time. The effort and time involved in expensive development work will be reduced.

- The members of the team will personally identify with the decisions and plans that they have all participated in creating, thus facilitating implementation. Once a decision is made, it will find broader acceptance and will usually be carried out with less resistance. This will be especially true if those persons who represent key functions within the organization have been members of the idea-generation and problem-solving team.

Step 3. Select the right tool.

The team leader should work with the facilitator to be sure that the right tools are selected for the creativity tool session. There are several considerations in picking the most appropriate tool for the given problem. These considerations include the nature and significance of the problem, situational variables, creative thinking development plans for the team, and the quality of the solution desired.

Nature and Significance of the Problem

The nature and significance of the problem may call for specific tools to be applied. For example, one way of classifying problems is by the amount of mental energy required to solve the problem. From this perspective, there are five different types of problems:

- Problems requiring analysis

- Problems requiring a search for alternative solutions within the known field or technology

- Problems requiring a new concept or a reconfiguration
- Problems requiring logical deduction
- Problems requiring selection from a known list

The last two categories, problems that require using logical deduction or making a selection from a known list, are by nature well-structured problems. They usually do not require use of the creativity tools. The other three types of problems can, however, benefit significantly from the application of the creativity tools. Team leaders, of course, need to understand that problems arising in practice are usually so complex that they contain all of the above-named types of problems—sometimes several of each. Thus, if a team leader wants to use a creativity tool to solve a problem, he or she must first break the complex problem down into its component parts and then identify each of these components as problems of structural analysis, an alternatives search, or new concept generation.

Figure I-1 outlines the suitability of the creativity tools for the solution of different types of problems.

The Idea Edge

Type of Problem	Example	Tool	Chapter
Problems requiring analysis	What functional requirements must the lamp meet? (e.g., must it be adjustable to different positions or to different degrees of brightness?)	•Heuristic Redefinition •Morphological Box	1 7
Problems requiring a search for alternative solutions within a known field or technology	What sources can be used to produce the light?	•Brainwriting 6-3-5 •Classic Brainstorming •Imaginary Brainstorming •Word-Picture Associations and Analogies	3 2 4 5
Problems requiring a new concept or a reconfiguration	What is a concept for a mechanism to adjust the lamp in different positions?	•Classic Brainstorming •Imaginary Brainstorming •Morphological Box •TILMAG •Word-Picture Associations and Analogies	2 4 7 6 5
Problems requiring logical deduction	What is the calculation of the degree of effectiveness of X as a source of light?	•None needed.	
Problems requiring solutions from a known list	What is the best material to use in terms of resistance to temperature changes and price?	•Any of the idea selection tools.	8 9 10 11

Figure I-1: Choosing a Tool Based on the Nature/Significance of the Problem

Situational Variables

While the problem itself can influence the choice of a creativity tool, certain conditions in which the group finds itself can also influence tool choice, as Figure I-2 indicates.

Type of Situation	Options	Tool	Chapter
Available time	–Limited	• Brainwriting 6-3-5	3
		• Classic Brainstorming	2
	–Ample	• Morphological Box	7
		• TILMAG	6
		• Word-Picture Associations and Analogies	5
Size of the problem-solving group	–1 to 4	• Heuristic Redefinition	1
	–5 to 8	• Morphological Box	7
		• Brainwriting 6-3-5	3
		• Classic Brainstorming	2
		• Imaginary Brainstorming	4
		• Word-Picture Associations and Analogies	5
Relationship between team members	–History of working together	• All the creativity tools	1–7
	–Relatively new group	• Brainwriting 6-3-5	3
Tensions within the group	–No	• All the creativity tools	1–7
	–Yes	• Brainwriting 6-3-5	3
Experience with the creativity tools	–Limited	• Brainwriting 6-3-5	3
		• Classic Brainstorming	2
		• Word-Picture Associations and Analogies	5
	–More extensive	• Heuristic Redefinition	1
		• Morphological Box	7
		• TILMAG	6
Team members' knowledge of the problem	–Significant expertise	• Heuristic Redefinition	1
		• Morphological Box	7
		• TILMAG	6
		• Word-Picture Associations and Analogies	5
	–Limited expertise	• Brainwriting 6-3-5	3
		• Classic Brainstorming	2
		• Word-Picture Associations and Analogies	5
Need to identify person who had idea	–Significant need to link idea back to the person who thought of it	• Brainwriting 6-3-5	3
	–Identifying the person is not a concern	• All the creativity tools	1–7

Figure I-2: Choosing a Tool Based on Situational Variables

The Idea Edge

Creative Thinking Development Plans for the Team

Another consideration for the use of the tools is their role in releasing creative thinking and imaginative solutions.

Classic Brainstorming and Brainwriting 6-3-5 are tools designed to create the conditions that are appropriate for thinking and working together. They are often the preferred tools because everyone finds them simple and easy to use. They have also been around for 50 years and have stood the test of time. However, they do not have specific operations or mechanics that cause team members to think differently or change their thought patterns. They do not necessarily help team members who are new to creative thinking develop their creative abilities further.

There are a couple of other considerations for using the creativity tools that go beyond Classic Brainstorming and Brainwriting 6-3-5. One consideration is the plan for developing team members' creativity. Once the team is comfortable using the more basic creativity tools, they should intentionally use Imaginary Brainstorming, Word-Picture Associations and Analogies, TILMAG, and the Morphological Box in order to continue to develop their creative thinking abilities. It is important for the team leader and/or facilitator to push the team on for more learning and for better solutions. Don't stop at the first good new idea; there will be so many more good new ideas if the facilitator pushes the team!

Quality of Solution Desired

The final consideration for using tools beyond the basic tools is the type of solution desired. When team members are dealing with problems that have no easy answers and that require them to break out of their established thought patterns, they need additional support to find new or multiple solutions. That is when the tools described in Chapters 4–7 can be especially helpful.

Step 4. Define roles and responsibilities.

There are several roles that should be assigned when the team leader arranges a creativity tool session. These include the problem sponsor (usually the person responsible for the problem resolution), the team leader (who may or may not be the problem sponsor), the recordkeeper, and the facilitator. The roles and responsibilities of the team leader, recordkeeper and facilitator are described in the next section "How to Get the Most from this Book and the Tools." The responsibilities of the participants for knowing and abiding by the ground rules for the session are discussed in Chapter 2. The last set of responsibilities, that of the problem sponsor, are described below.

Problem Sponsor

The problem sponsor is the individual who owns the responsibility for the resolution of the problem. While the sponsor can delegate his or her responsibility to the team leader to manage the problem resolution effort, the sponsor usually has the most at stake in having the problem resolved. The sponsor is the individual who knows the most about the problem and can provide the best information on the background of the problem.

In the event that the problem sponsor is not the same as the team leader, the two individuals need to work together to engage a facilitator and to ensure there is sufficient, mutually shared information about the problem and the goals for the session. During the session, the problem sponsor needs to ensure that the participants are briefed appropriately on the issues, that questions get answered, and that any necessary background information is provided.

Step 5. Schedule/plan the session.

The team leader faces a particularly challenging task in determining how much time to schedule for a creativity tool session. It is critical that a team has enough time to accomplish the goal of the session. Yet, oftentimes, there is not enough time scheduled and the team too quickly and superficially defines and explores the problem. As a result, team members have to frequently interrupt the subsequent phase of creative idea generation with additional questions. If the team has to evaluate and make decisions under time constraints, the outcome may be less than optimal.

To address these issues, the team leader should be sure that the agenda and schedule of the creativity tool session are flexible and contain too few issues rather than too many. Each session is a trip into the unknown. Experience shows that a group is more likely to open up new fields for exploration rather than find shortcuts.

In addition, when arranging the schedule, the team leader needs to plan for sufficient rest breaks, since creative thinking can be a very strenuous activity. Arrangements should also be made for food deliveries, such as snacks and/or lunches, to streamline the use of the group's time.

Other factors that could affect the successful use of the team's time include:

- Skills and experience of the facilitator
- Review of any available background material by the participants before the session
- A clear and well-defined goal for the session that has been clearly communicated to the participants

The team leader should also consider which setting is most appropriate—formal or informal. Often a more informal session is more conducive to idea generation. Whatever the setting, it should be one where participants will be free from distractions and disturbances in order to allow them to concentrate on the activities at hand.

The team leader needs to consider all of these factors *before* holding the session.

Step 6. Obtain the appropriate resources.

Successful completion of a creativity tool session requires not only enough time, but also sufficient tools, aids, and working conditions. Before the session the team leader should review the list of required resources in the next section "How to Get the Most from this Book and the Tools." He or she should update that list with any particular resource requirements called for by the specific problem or situation at hand, such as any special space requirements, equipment, and supplies.

Step 7. Open the creativity tool session.

The team leader should open the session by:

- repeating the purpose of the session so that everyone is clear on the goals and objectives.

- restating the guidelines for the session and asking for additional suggestions and questions.

- discussing expectations for the outcome of the meeting, e.g., rough ideas that will require additional work or a highly polished, finished product), to set the right tone for the session.

- introducing the facilitator and recordkeeper and explaining their roles during the session.

- introducing all the other participants with an "ice-breaker" exercise that sets a relaxed and fun tone for the session.

Step 8. Close the creativity tool session.

A creativity tool session seldom ends with a complete solution that can be implemented immediately. It is more likely that the session will result in rough ideas that are quite promising but require further research and development. Every session should end with a list of what to do next. The team should develop an appropriate action plan, with a list of tasks to be completed, assignment of responsibilities, dates for completion, and any reporting requirements.

Giving feedback to the participants is also important for the team leader to do. This feedback from the team leader can help everyone understand the results of the session and the progress on the action plan. Such feedback helps participants understand the impact of their efforts and promotes an appreciation and interest in the organization-wide application of the tools. An additional step in the action plan could be for the team leader to set a schedule for providing feedback to participants, and to assign a person to be responsible for communicating this feedback.

Summary

A systematic plan for organizing a creativity tool session is a critical factor in ensuring the success of such a session. By following the steps described above, a team leader will have a better chance of helping the team to look at the problem in new ways and to find innovative solutions.

How to Get the Most from this Book and the Tools

This book has been written for team leaders who are responsible for these core business processes: problem solving, process improvement and standardization, planning, and product or service development. This approach has been chosen because of the importance of teams in the world today. However, the book can also be easily used by other managers and supervisors who are charged with a variety of responsibilities.

This book has been developed in the same "easy to use and apply" tradition as other publications from GOAL/QPC, such as *The Memory Jogger Plus+*® and the Memory Jogger™ system of products. *The Idea Edge*, like the Memory Jogger™ products, provides team leaders with easy to follow, step-by-step instructions on how to successfully apply the tools to solve real problems. The instructions make it easy for team leaders to quickly learn and use the tools with their associates, team members, and other teams. Illustrations and diverse examples are included to heighten the learning experience. The examples provide evidence of how much value the tools can add to core business processes. Additional chapters explain how the tools for generating and selecting ideas can enhance and improve the processes of problem solving, process improvement and standardization, planning, and new product or service development.

This section introduces the team leader to some key concepts, such as definitions, roles and responsibilities of team members, and resources required for using the tools. This section also includes the overall organization of the book.

Introduction

Definitions

Term	Definition
Team leader	Individual with management or leadership responsibility for a group of subordinates and/or colleagues. Can include the level of responsibility, known as "supervisor," "project manager," or "department manager."
Team members	A group of individuals with collective responsibility for a set of results. Can refer to a group or department.
Problem	A discrepancy between an existing situation and a desired state of affairs. Includes the concepts of "challenge," "opportunity," "task," "issue," and "process improvement."
Product	The outcome or result, tangible or intangible, of the project or team's effort. Can include "service" or "process."

Figure I-3: Basic Definitions

Roles and Responsibilities

If team leaders want to ensure that tool training is successful, they need to define for team members the roles and responsibilities that are expected of them, and to have available the resources that are needed for any specific tool. Some roles, responsibilities, and resources are generic to all the tools in this book, while there are others that are specific to one tool (which are included in the Helpful Hints section of the chapter.)

Use the role/responsibilities chart and the list of resources on the next page as a guide for using any tool in this book, keeping in mind that a team is at liberty to refine or modify their expectations of these roles according to the team's needs and team members' abilities.

Role	Responsibilities
Team leader	– Sets up the session. – Assigns the roles of facilitator and recordkeeper. The team leader can take on one of those roles, if properly trained. The team leader, however, may want to consider that the facilitator and recordkeeper do not usually participate in the session. – Ensures the team has the appropriate diversity to provide different perspectives and the appropriate levels of expertise on the problem.
Facilitator	– Be knowledgeable in the use of the tool. – Be proficient in managing group dynamics. These skills include knowing the right questions to explore assumptions as well as techniques for handling conflict. – Be able to keep the group moving forward and to manage the heated arguments that can occur. – Knows how to deal with possible impatience or frustration of team members with the process. – Handles the possible attempt of experts to take over the session. – Can jump start the team when it gets stuck. – Sets the agenda and time schedule. – Ensures the agenda and schedule are followed.
Recordkeeper	– Writes down all ideas verbatim. – Avoids interpretation, editing or paraphrasing. – Reaches agreement with the team as to how the notes will be kept. For example, the recordkeeper can use flipcharts, note cards, Post-it™ Notes, or software.
Team members	– Agree to participate in the learning and application process, to share knowledge and perspectives, and to be open to the input of other team members. – Commit to avoid getting frustrated with a process that may seem foreign and uncomfortable at times.

Figure I-4: Team Roles and Responsibilities

Resources Recommended

- Flipcharts or large sheets of paper
- Masking tape or pins
- Pens and markers
- Index cards and Post-it™ Notes

- Room large enough for a comfortable session
- Whiteboard
- Pinboards
- Acetates/Transparencies
- Sufficient time. Different tools require a certain amount of time, depending on the level of training and experience with the tool, as well upon the complexity of the issue. Whatever the time requirements of the tool, the team leader should be sure to allow for sufficient time to apply the tool to the problem at hand.
- Tables and chairs for the participants
- Any forms that may be needed for the particular tool
- Access to research facilities and/or experts, as required by the particular tool

Organization of the Book

The book is divided into three sections on the tools and their application, and three appendices.

Sections I and II

Section I describes the creativity tools, which help teams to generate ideas. Section II describes the idea selection and implementation tools, which help teams select the best ideas and understand how to implement them. In each chapter of Sections I and II, the book provides the team leader with the following information to help in understanding and applying the tools:

- Definition of the Tool
- Use of the Tool
- Overview of the Tool Process
- Outline of Steps
- Step-by-Step Instructions (with examples to illustrate the steps)

- Summary of the Tool
- Helpful Hints
- Frequently Asked Questions
- For Further Study (additional resources for the team leader)
- Additional Examples of Tool Usage (provides the team leader with further illustration of the use of the tools)

Examples

Throughout Sections I and II, a variety of examples are used to illustrate the use of the tools. These examples illustrate the value of the tools in many different applications, such as marketing, product development, process improvement, and general uses across a diverse group of industries. To provide the team leader with an understanding of how the tools can be used together, some of the examples used are extensions of examples from earlier chapters.

Section III

Section III provides information on integrating the tools into the organization's core business processes. This section also contains a chapter on suggestions to help team leaders implement the tools within their organizations. A summary chapter concludes the section.

Appendices

The appendices are intended to provide additional material for team leaders to:

- provide a brief introduction to the Basic Quality Control and Management and Planning Tools (Appendix A) for those unfamiliar with these tools.
- provide information on an additional creativity methodology known as TRIZ (Appendix B).
- help team leaders further their understanding of the tools, creativity and innovation in general, and issues around their application by providing a list of Recommended Resources (Appendix C).

"Every time a man puts a new idea across,
he faces a dozen men who thought of it before he did.
But they only thought of it."

Oren Arnold

Section I:
The Creativity Tools

Teams need tools to boost creative thinking and to generate new and different ideas. Such tools also:

- establish an environment where creativity can really flourish.
- create a common vocabulary for generating new and creative ideas.
- provide new ways to understand all the elements of a problem so that breakthrough solutions can be found.
- incorporate the ideas and talents of everyone on the team.
- inject enthusiasm and energy into the process of solving tough business problems.

The creativity tools are described in the following chapters:

1. Heuristic Redefinition
2. Classic Brainstorming
3. Brainwriting 6-3-5
4. Imaginary Brainstorming
5. Word-Picture Associations and Analogies
6. TILMAG
7. Morphological Box

*"Knowledge is the only instrument of production
that is not subject to diminishing returns."*

J.M. Clark

Heuristic Redefinition

Introduction

How would you proceed if you wanted to climb to the summit of a mountain that doesn't have any trail signs? You probably wouldn't randomly choose any route because it might lead you into difficult ground. Instead, you might consider the best route by looking at the features of the mountain from a distance, and studying the mountain's terrain on a map. When you look at the mountain as a whole, you could start to investigate its shapes, topography, and the nature of its surfaces, which would help you to select the most convenient, possible ascent to the summit.

From this example, it may seem obvious that it's essential to first define the challenge or problem before trying to solve it, but teams often forget to do this! Teams often don't recognize that a "good" definition of a problem in itself contains the seeds of the solution. The definition leads the team to ideas that can be especially efficient and advantageous.

People often block some parts of their creativity with a fixed view of the problem. Some people believe that problems can only be approached in one definite way, and they stick hard to their own point of view. They may as well be wearing blinders on the sides of their heads.

The Heuristic Redefinition tool can free teams from such fixations, helping them to see problems and their contexts as flexible and multifaceted. As in climbing a mountain, different routes can be pursued in solving a problem.

"It's amazing what ordinary people can do if they set out without preconceived notions."

Charles Kettering

Chapter 1

In the abstract, a problem can be understood as a system, consisting of a multitude of elements that are all interrelated. Solving a problem involves changing the system's structure by altering one or more of its elements. Depending on the kind of relationships that connect these elements within the system, the altered elements can be either greatly or minimally effective in achieving a new structure.

Every recognized possibility to alter an element toward the new structure can be understood as an approach to the problem. Finally, one approach to the problem should be selected because it holds the most promise for the greatest effect for the smallest effort.

Definition of the Tool

Heuristic Redefinition is a method of looking at a system in which a problem exists and for picking an approach that promises the greatest effect with the smallest effort. Possible approaches are identified and ranked by applying criteria that are appropriate to the problem.

Use of the Tool

In general, this tool should be used with any creative problem-solving process as a stepping stone to generating ideas for solutions. It helps a team understand the problem in the context of the whole system as well as the complete range of *potential* approaches to the desired solution. By forcing a team to visualize all the parts of the problem or challenge, it ensures that a team won't overlook promising new ways to solve a problem in the rush of initial thoughts. It is especially valuable for the individual problem-solver who is not supported by the creative synergy of a team.

This tool is particularly helpful when a problem or challenge is not well-defined. It is also useful when the team needs to explore a problem as part of a whole system. By allowing the team to examine the components and their interrelationships, this tool can help the team focus its creativity on those parts that lead to exciting solutions.

Overview of the Tool Process

To understand all the directions in which a problem can be approached, that is, all the possible definitions of the problem, it is most advantageous to visualize the problem and all its elements and sub-elements in a pictorial or symbolic presentation such as a drawing, flowchart, or arrow diagram. Then, one by one, the team or individual goes through all the components and asks what must be done to approach the goal. The question is in the format, "How can we ensure that…?" Each question now represents a problem statement. For further work, the team chooses the problem statement with the most promise for problem-solving success. The criteria needed to select the most promising problem statement might include the probability of success or the amount of effort required. The specific criteria depends on the team's priorities.

The creativity tools in the following chapters are used to generate ideas using the most promising problem statement. If the team has selected the right statement, then the problem will be effectively and permanently resolved.

In the following section, the Heuristic Redefinition tool is explained in detail, with an example regarding the watering of flowers in a dry area. The problem exists within the system of the natural environment. This includes the components rain, sun, soil, air temperature, and so on. The problem may be defined as, "How do we ensure that plants in the flower and vegetable garden get enough water to flourish and grow?" Heuristic Redefinition can provide effective approaches to achieve this goal.

Applying the Tool

Outline of Steps

Step	Activity
1.	State the problem or opportunity in terms of the goal.
2.	Visualize the problem as part of a system. Include major components.
3.	Label and understand the impact of each component.
4.	State the links of the components to the goal.
5.	Construct a matrix for rating problem statements against the designated criteria.
6.	Compare each problem statement against the criteria; assign ratings; figure totals.
7.	Discuss and choose the one or two preferred problem statements, based on their potential for directing the team toward a successful solution.

Step-by-Step Instructions

Step 1. State the problem or opportunity in terms of the goal.

The team should limit the statement to a sentence and state it in positive terms. Negative terms, e.g., what the goal should *not* be, tend to limit the team's thinking about the problem, and can pre-define the solution. Also, by framing the statement in terms of the overall goal, team members can break out of old ways of thinking and can avoid being locked into a particular solution. Every problem statement provides a different direction in which to look for ideas for solutions. Teams should carefully consider the difference between "directions" and solutions.

Example

A team is trying to figure out how to keep plants from dying as a result of lack of rain. One team member suggests defining the problem as "How do we keep plants from dying because of a lack of rain?" A few team members realize that this statement is phrased in negative terms, so the team keeps on trying. The team ends up with this: "How do we ensure that plants in the flower and vegetable garden get enough water to flourish and grow?" This statement, everyone agrees, will open up many more opportunities for creative solutions than the initial statement would have.

Step 2. Visualize the problem as part of a system.

The team describes the problem in the context of the complete system. The designated artist, or the facilitator, begins to create a simple picture or illustration of the problem and the system, using flipchart paper or other display board.

The team needs to be sure that each major component of the system is included and illustrated. If team members have trouble defining the components or parts of the system, they can ask questions like:

- What is happening?
- Where does it happen?
- When does it happen?
- Why does it happen?
- How does it happen?
- To whom does it happen? Or who causes it to happen?

The team members might also review these questions when they have completed the drawing so they can be sure they have included all of the components of the system.

"Intelligence is the ability to see many points of view without going completely bonkers."

Douglas Adams

Chapter 1

Example

Figure 1-1 is a drawing of the system and all the components within it that influence the water supply for the plants. The components of the system are the clouds, the basic parts of the plant that help it absorb water, the air, the sun, and the soil.

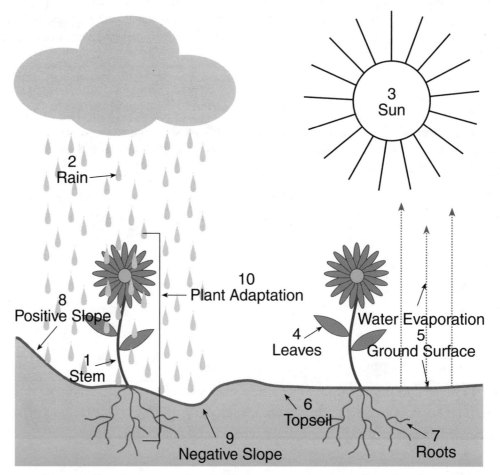

Figure 1-1: How do we ensure that the plants get enough water to flourish and grow?

Step 3. Label and understand the impact of each component.

Team members now explore the results of their efforts. To be sure they have captured all of the key components and that they understand the problem and the system, they address issues such as:

- How are the parts or components of the system related?

- What are the influences or relationships between the components?

- Are there any laws that apply to describe the relationships of the components in the system?

After this discussion, and any revisions to the drawing, the team then labels each part, component, or sub-component with a number.

The team then asks, for each component:

- What does the component do that affects the goal (either positively or negatively)?

Example

Now that the team has a visual representation of the problem and its place within the system, it is easier to see the relationships between the components of the system: clouds produce rain, raindrops fall to the ground and are absorbed into the soil, the sunshine and higher air temperature increase the rate of water evaporation on the plant and in the soil, and the roots, stem, and leaves provide water to the plant.

For each labeled component, the team asks the question: "What does the component do that affects the goal of ensuring that plants in the flower and vegetable garden get enough water to flourish and grow?" For example:

What does the sun do that affects the goal?

- It evaporates water.

- It dries the soil.

Step 4. State the links of the components to the goal.

Team members now examine the relationship between each component and the goal statement, using the understanding gained from Step 3. They start with component #1 and ask how they can ensure that the component contributes to reaching the goal. Team members should start the question with "How can we ensure that . . . so that the plants in the flower and vegetable garden get enough water to flourish and grow?" These become problem statements from which the best statement will be picked.

Example

Using the picture shown in Figure 1-1, the team can examine the links or relationships between each component and the goal of ensuring that plants in the flower and vegetable garden get enough water to flourish and grow. The team begins with component #1, the plant stem, and asks, "How can we ensure that . . . the sun doesn't dry the soil before water is absorbed into the plant stem? Or, "How can we ensure that enough water is absorbed into the stem of the plant so that plants in the flower and vegetable garden get enough water to flourish and grow?"

The team works this question through all of the major components, which produces 10 problem statements relative to the goal. Figure 1-2 lists these statements.

Component	Problem Statement "How can we ensure that . . ."
1. plant stem	the plant absorbs sufficient amount of water?
2. rain	the amount of rain will always be sufficient?
3. sun	the plant is protected against the sun's heat?
4. leaves	the loss of water at the plant's surface will be reduced?
5. ground surface	the evaporation of water at the surface of the soil will be reduced?
6. topsoil	falling rain will be stored close to the roots?
7. roots	water in the soil is brought up to the roots?
8. ground slope (positive)	rain will be directed toward the roots?
9. ground slope (negative)	the runoff of rain is slowed or prevented?
10. plant adaptation	the plant stores water for dry periods? (camel effect)

Figure 1-2: Linking the Components to the Goal of Ensuring Plants Get Enough Water

"To raise new questions, new possibilities, to regard old problems from a new angle requires creative imagination and marks real advances in science."

Albert Einstein

Chapter 1

Step 5. Construct a matrix for rating problem statements against designated criteria.

The team builds a matrix, which includes the following criteria: the likelihood of reaching the goal; ease of implementation; and the expected impact on the goal.

The matrix has 5 columns and as many rows as there are problem statements. The team labels each column, from left to right, with the following:

- Problem statement
- Likelihood of reaching the goal
- Ease of implementation
- Expected impact on the goal
- Total

Step 6. Compare each problem statement against the criteria; assign ratings; figure totals.

The team uses the following rating scale:

- Good/High = 3 points
- Average/Medium = 2 points
- Poor/Low = 1 point

Example

Figure 1-3 shows the team's ratings for the problem statements.

Problem Statement "How can we ensure that . . ."	Likelihood of Reaching the Goal	Ease of Implementation	Expected Impact on the Goal	Total
1. the plant absorbs sufficient amount of water?	3	2	3	8
2. the amount of rain will always be sufficient?	1	1	3	5
3. the plant is protected against the sun's heat?	2	2	1	5
4. the loss of water at the plant's surface will be reduced?	1	1	1	3
5. the evaporation of water at the surface of the soil will be reduced?	3	2	2	7
6. falling rain will be stored close to the roots?	2	2	2	6
7. water in the soil is brought up to the roots?	1	1	3	5
8. rain will be directed toward the roots?	3	3	1	7
9. the runoff of rain is slowed or prevented?	2	2	2	6
10. the plant stores water for dry periods? (camel effect)	1	1	2	4

Good/High = 3
Average/Medium = 2
Poor/Low = 1

Figure 1-3: Problem Statement Prioritization Matrix

> *Step 7. Discuss and choose the one or two preferred problem statements, based on their potential for directing the team toward a successful solution.*

The totals provide the team with information they should discuss. For example, just because a problem statement scored high on this matrix does not mean that it fits into the company's strategy, that its risk isn't beyond the risk level of the company, or that it is otherwise worth pursuing. The positives and negatives of each statement need to be discussed and determined by the team.

Team members then choose one or two statements to explore further. They can move forward with another tool, such as Classic Brainstorming (Chapter 2) or Brainwriting 6-3-5 (Chapter 3), to help the team generate ideas for a solution.

Example

The team might immediately recognize that some statements are beyond its control. For example, regulating the amount of rainfall is most likely beyond the team's capacity. However, instead of just guessing about efficient and inefficient problem statements, the team evaluates them against the criteria.

The team concludes that statements 2, 3, 4, 7, and 10 are either too difficult or do not have a strong likelihood of leading to a successful solution. They are thus too risky to be pursued. Statements 1, 5, and 8 seem to promise the best success, but the team believes that the new solutions will require state-of-the-art changes.

The team decides to explore statements 6 and 9 since they could lead to interesting innovations. The team decides to use the Brainwriting 6-3-5 tool to generate ideas for developing specific solutions. So at this point, the team can begin working on two approaches to solving the initial goal.

Summary of the Tool

This tool will help a team avoid rushing into solving a problem with only fixed assumptions or long-held ways of looking at the problem or situation. It will force a team to take the time it needs to look at the problem from several different perspectives. Such additional perspectives will help the team feel confident that it is attempting to solve the right problem and that it can reach its goal.

Enhancing the Process

Helpful Hints

View the Problem from Many Directions. Every problem statement provides a different direction in which to look for ideas for solutions. Teams should carefully consider the difference between "directions" and "solutions." While redefining a problem, some team members may immediately propose solutions rather than alternative views for addressing the problem, i.e., finding new problem statements.

Don't Jump to Evaluating the Problem Statements. The various problem statements can be evaluated, but it's not essential. It can be beneficial to explore all the statements, but it is more reasonable to confine idea-generation efforts to the most promising, in order to limit problem-solving work or to concentrate only on new approaches.

Think Innovatively. Useful innovation may consist of supplying an answer for an unsatisfied, latent need, or providing a new and superior solution for a well-known need. Since new needs are often harder to define, the chances of making innovations are often better if a team tries to find new ways to reach old goals. This does not only mean trying to improve something that already exists, but also developing characteristically new "patterns."

"Genius, in truth, means little more than the faculty of perceiving in an unhabitual way."

William James

Chapter 1

Examples of such innovations are:

fine-liner pens	*replacing*	pencil sharpeners	*instead*	of improving sharpener quality
audiotapes	*replacing*	long-playing records	*instead*	of finding scratch-resistant records
self-service	*replacing*	sales personnel	*instead*	of improving skills of current staff
plastic pegs	*replacing*	plastered wooden pegs	*instead*	of making better wooden pegs

Heuristic Redefinition of problems gives a team or an individual a considerably higher chance of innovating in "traditional" fields.

Frequently Asked Questions

Q. **Do other visualization tools work, besides pictures and icons? For example, activity diagrams or network charts?**

A. Yes, although without special training it is easier for most people to work with drawings or sketches even if they are rough.

Q. **What if no one in the group can draw?**

A. Rough sketches will work. Also, there is now a wide variety of clip art that can be very useful in finding images.

Q. **What is the optimal number of team members to use this tool?**

A. If the tool is used by a team, 4–8 team members is a good number. This tool can also be used by an individual working alone.

Q. Are there times when this tool should not be used?

A. This tool would not be needed by a team when there is only one practical statement of the problem. Also, this tool requires an experienced facilitator. See Figures I-1 and I-2 in the Introduction for a comparison of the tools and the problems for which each tool is best suited.

Q. Is it necessary for the team to choose a subject that everyone is familiar with in redefining the problem?

A. It is important to have at least some members of the team who have expertise in the field. Novices may sometimes ask clarifying questions that could trigger some fresh approaches.

For Further Study

There are other tools that a team may want to explore when Heuristic Redefinition has been mastered. **The Idea Matrix** and the **House of Quality Matrix** are two separate matrices that can help a team focus on the best approach to reach the goal.

The Idea Matrix expands on the notion that creativity is the combination of two different items that have not been brought together before. For example, "How should a car be designed and equipped (Subject A) to be made road worthy for winter conditions (Subject B)?"

The matrix is constructed by experts in the field in which the various options of car design and equipment are placed across the top of the matrix and the various kinds of winter conditions are placed on the side of the matrix. The matrix is filled out by putting an asterisk (*) in each box where the two items are related.

Special emphasis and study is put on those columns and rows where there are a lot of asterisks. The categories identified are then pursued by using one or more of the creativity tools. The Idea Matrix is particularly helpful when the team has experts in the field who are looking to identify new opportunities.

The House of Quality Matrix is another tool to help a team focus on the right problem. With this tool, the needs and wants of the customer are placed on the side of the matrix and the quality characteristics are placed on the top of the matrix. Those quality characteristics that most strongly correlate with the voice of the customer are business opportunities to be considered if they match the company's business plan. For more information on this matrix and other types of matrices, consult the Recommended Resources list at the end of this book (Appendix C). The House of Quality Matrix is described in more detail in the book *Better Designs in Half the Time* by Bob King.

Additional Examples of Tool Usage

Situation: A team is analyzing the quality of one of its key products: concrete floors. One of the challenges in pouring a concrete floor is to end up with a smooth surface. A potential problem is when air bubbles rise and cause holes or bumps in the surface. The team decided to use Heuristic Redefinition to look at ways of improving the concrete-pouring process. Figure 1-4 is the team's drawing of the components of the process.

Figure 1-4: How can we pour a concrete floor so that air bubbles do not rise to the surface and create bumps and craters?

The Idea Edge

The next step for the team, after they had drawn and labeled the components, was to link the components back to the goal of pouring smooth concrete floors. Figure 1-5 shows how the team completed this step.

Component	Problem Statement "How can we ensure that . . ."
1. cement composition	the cement is well mixed?
2. base surface	the base surface does not create bubbles?
3. condition of cement at time of delivery	the moisture content is correct?
4. air temperature when concrete is poured	the cement does not dry too quickly?
5. smoothing techniques	any bubbles are removed in the final smoothing?

Figure 1-5: Linking the Components Back to the Goal of Pouring a Smooth Floor

Figure 1-6 shows how the team rated each problem statement against the three chosen criteria: 1) likelihood of reaching the goal; 2) ease of implementation; and 3) expected impact on the goal.

"Innovation is both conceptual and perceptual. Purposeful, systematic innovation begins with the analysis of potential opportunities."

Peter Drucker

Chapter 1

Problem Statement "How can we ensure that . . ."	Likliehood of Reaching the Goal	Ease of implementation	Expected Impact on the Goal	Total
1. the cement is well mixed?	3	3	1	7
2. the base surface does not create bubbles?	2	2	2	6
3. the moisture content is correct?	3	3	2	8
4. the cement does not dry too quickly?	1	1	2	4
5. any bubbles are removed in the final smoothing?	2	2	2	6

Best   = 3 points
Average = 2 points
Poor   = 1 points

Figure 1-6: Problem Statement Prioritization Matrix

Through discussion, team members came to an agreement that #5 was reactive and that it would be better to change the process to prevent the bubbles from occurring. The team had already experimented with #1, #3 and #4, but the problem persisted even when the cement composition and air termperature were consistently controlled. The team decided to look more closely at #2, which seemed to hold the most promise for a solution.

Outcome/Breakthrough: The team discovered that the way to prevent bubbles is to pour one layer of cement, spread a cheese cloth over it, and then pour a second layer of cement.

Situation: The manager of a movie theater posed the following challenge to a cross-functional team of employees: The only time customers make purchases at the concession stand is before or during a movie. What can we do to increase sales at the concession stand? The team discussed the challenge and drew the picture shown in Figure 1-7.

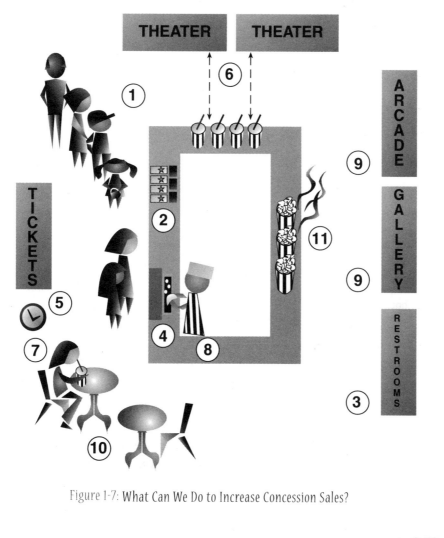

Figure 1-7: What Can We Do to Increase Concession Sales?

Chapter 1

The next step for the team, after they had drawn and labeled the components, was to link the components back to the goal of increasing sales at the concession stand. Figure 1-8 shows how the team completed this step.

Component	Problem Statement "How can we ensure that . . ."
1. customers waiting in line	waiting time is minimized?
2. items at the concession stand	there is a good selection and quantity of items?
3. customers using the restrooms	time in the restroom is minimal?
4. prices of items at the concession stand	prices are reasonable?
5. time for making purchases	customers have enough time to make purchases?
6. distance between concession stand and movie theater	distance is short?
7. intermission times	intermissions are available?
8. service at concession stand	service is prompt and friendly?
9. entertainment	arcade games/gallery draw customers closer to concession stand?
10. seating areas for dining	seating area for eating is available?
11. aromas from concession stand	aromas from concession stand attract people?

Figure 1-8: Linking the Components to the Goal of Increasing Sales at the Concession Stand

Figure 1-9 shows how the team rated each problem statement against the three chosen criteria: 1) likelihood of reaching the goal; 2) ease of implementation; and 3) expected impact on the goal.

The Idea Edge

Problem Statement "How can we ensure that . . ."	Likliehood of Reaching the Goal	Ease of Implementation	Expected Impact on the Goal	Total
1. waiting time is minimized?	2	2	2	6
2. there is a good selection and quantity of items?	3	3	3	9
3. time in the restroom is minimal?	2	1	2	5
4. prices of items are reasonable?	3	3	3	9
5. customers have enough time to make purchases?	2	2	3	7
6. there is a short distance between concession stand and movie theater?	2	1	2	5
7. intermissions are available?	2	2	2	6
8. service is prompt and friendly?	3	3	3	9
9. arcade games/gallery draw customers closer to concession stand?	2	1	3	6
10. seating area for eating is available?	2	2	3	7
11. aromas from concession stand attract people?	2	1	3	6

Best = 3 points
Average = 2 points
Poor = 1 point

Figure 1-9: Problem Statement Prioritization Matrix

"The most drastic and usually the most effective remedy for fear is direct action."

William Burnham

Chapter 1

The team discussed the results and agreed that #2, #4, and #8 could be easily addressed and were critical for continued sales. Although #9 and #10 would require additional expenses, the team thought they were innovative approaches that merited a closer look.

This example is based on work contributed by Janice Marconi, Innovation Specialist and President of Marconi Works International.

Classic Brainstorming

Introduction

More than 50 years ago, Alex Osborn, an outstanding contributor to the advertising field, observed that problem-solving meetings were often quite inefficient. He analyzed the causes and came up with a set of behavioral rules to minimize distractions and to maximize creative output. He called this improved thinking technique "brainstorming," but his behavioral rules apply well to all creative activity.

The success of Osborn's approach led to the widespread use of brainstorming around the world and it has become the most popular form of idea generation. Brainstorming's effectiveness depends on:

- using the knowledge of several people to solve a problem
- eliminating mental blocks
- restraining people from being critical
- disciplining oneself to follow the brainstorming rules
- expanding effective participation by all
- avoiding discussions that are not focused on the task at hand

"Every really new idea looks crazy, at first."
A. H. Maslow

Definition of the Tool

This tool allows team members to pool their knowledge and creativity in an open, non-critical environment. Brainstorming discourages "same-old-way" thinking by creating more and more ideas that team members can build upon. It gets all the team members enthusiastic and involved by putting an equal value on every idea. Finally, it allows each person to be creative while focusing on the team's common purpose.

Use of the Tool

Brainstorming is effective when a solution can likely be found with existing knowledge. It can also serve as a preface to using more advanced tools by first getting out ideas that are the most apparent and accessible.

Overview of the Tool Process

The application of this tool involves the following steps: 1) form a team consisting of people with a variety of knowledge and experience appropriate to the topic; 2) clarify and agree to the wording of the topic and review the rules for participation (also clarify the rules if they are not understood); 3) generate ideas until all ideas have been exhausted (this includes 3–5 dead points in the conversation while participants think about what else to add); and 4) rewrite the ideas so everyone understands them. The best ideas are then chosen, using one or more of the selection tools.

Applying the Tool

Outline of Steps

Step	Activity
1.	Identify the appropriate team to conduct the brainstorming session.
2.	Convene the team and clarify the topic and ground rules.
3.	Generate ideas.
4.	Clarify ideas and conclude the brainstorming session.

Step-by-Step Instructions

Step 1. Identify the appropriate team to conduct the brainstorming session.

For a brainstorming session to reach its full potential, the team leader or facilitator should prepare in advance of the session by doing the following:

- Clarify the topic of the session by using Heuristic Redefinition, as described in Chapter 1, or some other tool that helps clarify the best route to reach the goal.

- Assemble a team, based on the problem to be solved. Team members should have expertise in the disciplines that are most likely to be helpful for solving the problem, and should come from a range of backgrounds (even if they are not experts) to provide a variety of ideas.

- The facilitator should try to map out the various directions that could be explored in the brainstorming session, so that he or she can coach the participants if some key avenues are missed.

Example

The problem was defined as: "How can we expand the use of the World Wide Web (a.k.a. the Web or Internet) in the company to increase sales leads?" In assembling the team, the team leader decided to choose a mix of employees who easily learned how to use new software, as well as those who didn't. The facilitator thought one possible direction the brainstorm could take was the consideration of what new problems could arise from introducing a new technology in the company.

Step 2. Convene the team and clarify the topic and ground rules.

- When the team comes together, it is important for the leader or facilitator to clarify the topic selected and the meaning of each word.

- The leader or facilitator should review the ground rules for participating in a brainstorming session. These ground rules are described below.

Ground Rule 1. Don't criticize or judge the quality, good or bad, of any idea during the brainstorming session. The purpose of the session is to generate ideas, not to evaluate ideas. This distinction ensures that:

- the flow of ideas and the chain of associations will not be interrupted.

- long-winded discussions about the pros and cons of an idea are postponed for later sessions.

- the participants will not be frustrated or mentally blocked, especially by "killer phrases." Some examples of killer phrases are: "This might be theoretically true, but . . ." "Are you ready to take responsibility for that?" "We've tried that before . . ." "Much too costly!" or "But that's just wishful thinking!" It is important to note that criticism of ideas is not only expressed by words, but by non-verbal cues, such as gestures or facial expressions.

Ground Rule 2. Combine the ideas of other team members to create new ideas. Team members should not claim a "copyright" on their contributions. Instead, everybody should offer ideas as material for modifications and further development by the group.

Ground Rule 3. Give free rein to your imagination. Team members need to be willing to let their thoughts run free and to be encouraged to speculate and experiment with ideas. This freedom of thinking encourages all the members of the team to participate in the brainstorming session, and allows genuinely new solutions to be created.

The team should agree that it will encourage free association and short digressions from the subject at hand, since such a free flow can lead to surprising ideas. This process of "going astray" and then reconnecting remote thoughts to the problem can be a challenge for the facilitator. It is, however, representative of the "art of brainstorming."

Ground Rule 4. Produce as many ideas as possible in the time available. The team should concentrate on the quantity of ideas rather than the quality of ideas, since the more ideas the team generates, the better the chance of generating new and interesting ideas. An emphasis on quantity ensures that the flow of thoughts is more spontaneous and thus stimulates team members to think of more unusual ideas. Monologues and long explanations are avoided; team members must quickly get to the point!

Corollaries to the Ground Rules

1. Acknowledge each participant to be of the same rank and equal voice as yourself.

2. Engage yourself without reservation; offer all your knowledge to the team.

3. Don't present yourself as a leader or expert.

4. Avoid any judgment of proposed ideas.

5. Look for the positive attributes in the ideas of your teammates, and try to further develop these ideas.

6. Be courageous enough to express unusual ideas; give free rein to your imagination and intuition.

7. Dispel the notion that you should only share valuable, fully formed ideas. Let yourself get carried away with spontaneity.

8. Visualize (draw) your thoughts whenever it seems appropriate for clarification of an idea.

9. Keep your sense of humor.

10. Express yourself without using jargon.

11. When generating ideas, phrases or sentences that contain a verb are often more helpful than single words.

Step 3. Generate ideas.[1]

A typical brainstorming session tends to start off with a few ideas being offered and builds to a peak. Then it tapers off to a period of silence (the first dead point). Don't be uncomfortable with the silence. People need a little time to think.

After a short time, if the group does not "self-start" into the next phase, the facilitator can use a variety of techniques and questions to jump start the session. One technique includes reviewing the

---

1. The description in this step and the illustration of phases, shown in Figure 2-1, have been adapted from GOAL/QPC course materials that were developed by Helmut Schlicksupp and Janice Marconi.

"Someone once said, 'Ideas are a dime a dozen.' But now we know they are precious. In fact, ideas are not dimes but diamonds."

Alex Osborn

list of ideas and asking the group to play with some of the more interesting ones, going around the room for additional ideas (with an understanding that passing is allowed). Team members are encouraged to hitchhike or piggyback on one or more of the ideas already listed.

In the second phase, there will probably be a smaller quantity of ideas, but they will be newer and somewhat more creative. This period too will end in a dead point. It is generally useful to go to a third and perhaps fourth phase to get people thinking more deeply. It takes some experience, some judgment, some "feel" for when it is time to end the process. Generally, you want to continue long enough to let people think more deeply, but you don't want to brainstorm so long that people get tired or bored.

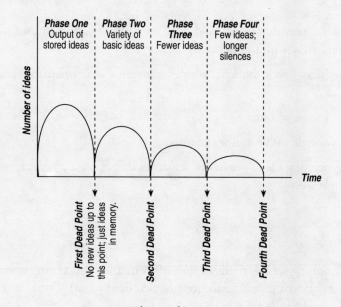

Figure 2-1: Phases of Brainstorming

Example

The team's problem statement is: "How can we expand the use of the Web (or Internet) in the company to increase sales leads?" The ideas that the team generated are listed on the following pages.

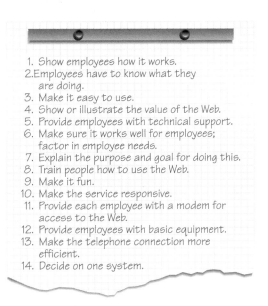

1. Show employees how it works.
2. Employees have to know what they are doing.
3. Make it easy to use.
4. Show or illustrate the value of the Web.
5. Provide employees with technical support.
6. Make sure it works well for employees; factor in employee needs.
7. Explain the purpose and goal for doing this.
8. Train people how to use the Web.
9. Make it fun.
10. Make the service responsive.
11. Provide each employee with a modem for access to the Web.
12. Provide employees with basic equipment.
13. Make the telephone connection more efficient.
14. Decide on one system.

Figure 2-2: Initial Ideas for Expanding the Use of the Web in the Company to Increase Sales Leads

First dead point. The facilitator asks the group, "How can you make the Internet easy to use (from comment #3)?" These were the team's ideas:

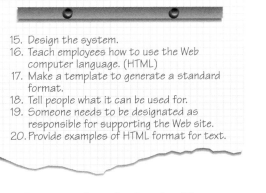

15. Design the system.
16. Teach employees how to use the Web computer language. (HTML)
17. Make a template to generate a standard format.
18. Tell people what it can be used for.
19. Someone needs to be designated as responsible for supporting the Web site.
20. Provide examples of HTML format for text.

Figure 2-3: Ideas After First Dead Point

Second dead point. The facilitator asks the group, "What other questions or concerns might you have about expanding the use of the Web in the company?" The team's response is:

21. Make a budget for Web application.
22. How much will it cost?
23. Update regularly.
24. Employees should have their own home page.
25. Why does everyone have to have a home page?
26. Sell books and materials on the Web.
27. Develop a systematic strategy on how to use the Web for our business.

Figure 2-4: Ideas After Second Dead Point

Third dead point. The facilitator asks the group, "How would you sell the employees on using the Web (a combination of comments #26 and #27)?" The team's ideas are on the next flipchart.

28. Make the purpose of the Web clear.
29. Define the benefits to internal customers and external customers.
30. Explain how customers and employees will benefit from the Web.
31. Draw up a schematic of a home page.
32. Need to know how to use the software.
33. Need a source for answers when I get stuck.
34. Have a contest for the best ideas from the Web.
35. Need good communication among business units and teams to make the company and the Web cohesive.
36. Provide access to resources on Web, such as newspapers and magazines.
37. Show that the Web's purpose is the same as our business purpose.

Figure 2-5: Ideas After Third Dead Point

Fourth dead point. The facilitator asks the group, "How can you ensure good communication among business units and teams to make the company and the Web more cohesive (comment #35)?" See the team's ideas on the next flipchart.

"You'll look up and down streets.
Look 'em over with care.
About some you will say,
'I don't choose to go there.'"

Theodore "Dr. Seuss" Geisel

Chapter 2

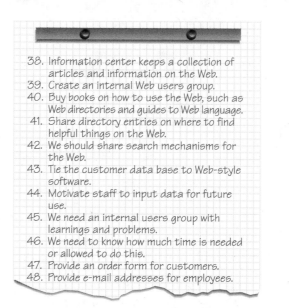

Figure 2-6: Ideas After Fourth Dead Point

It is clear that several good ideas came after several dead points. A review of the brainstormed ideas shows a number of more specific ideas in the later part of the session, e.g., #31, "Draw up a schematic of a home page" and #33, "Need a source for answers when I get stuck," and #39, "Create an internal Web users group." These results underscore the importance of continuing to work at brainstorming even after three or four dead points. A good facilitator will plan for the brainstorming session and think of questions or ideas to help restart the group after a dead point.

Step 4. Clarify ideas and conclude the brainstorming session.

There are several concluding activities:

- The list of brainstormed ideas should be reviewed to see that each one is clear. This review was not done during the session in order to keep the ideas free flowing. It must be done now because the person evaluating the ideas may be someone who was not at the session. Also, only the person who proposed an idea may be clear about its meaning.

- It should be clear who will evaluate the ideas, what follow-up actions are necessary, and how these decisions will be reported to team participants.

Example

The team agreed that the next step was for the technical specialist and the head of training to meet to set up an initial training session, with a plan for additional sessions. The first training session was scheduled to be held before the end of the month.

Summary of the Tool

Brainstorming is the most commonly used idea generation tool. It has almost become synonymous with the concept of idea generation. When a team uses this tool appropriately, it can generate many new and creative ideas. This tool is also the prototype for creative teamwork. The rules for a successful brainstorming session are just as valid for use during the application of any other creativity technique.

Enhancing the Process

Helpful Hints

Conducting a brainstorming session may appear to be easy but if team members ignore the basic ground rules of behavior, it will be difficult to maintain an open, non-judgmental atmosphere and this will affect the number and quality of ideas that are produced. Some tips for conducting a productive and successful session are listed below.

Choose an Experienced Facilitator. Sometimes, team members find that developing new insights to the problem is difficult. It is hard to abandon habitual paths or past solutions, and team members may have trouble moving into a free-wheeling, divergent way of thinking and relating new thoughts in a playful way. A facilitator who has experience and training will know some techniques firsthand that will unleash the group's imagination. (See Figure 2-7 for an example of how an experienced facilitator can affect a brainstorming session.)

Limit Team Size. A brainstorming session should be limited to 6–8 team members so that everyone can contribute ideas.

Stay Focused on the Question. Team members may misunderstand what it means to give free rein to the imagination. Team members should be encouraged to pursue imaginative, divergent thinking, but to stay focused on the issue being examined. The facilitator can help keep the team goal-oriented by asking a question such as "How does that idea link back to the problem statement?"

Don't Let Experts Rule. The facilitator and team members need to ensure that all participants feel their contributions are valued. No idea should be ignored. Nor should a few people, particularly those considered very knowledgeable in the subject area, be allowed to dominate the brainstorming process.

Don't Dig Too Deep. The team should avoid examining ideas too extensively. A subsequent session can be devoted to evaluating ideas.

Clarify, Don't Criticize. The recordkeeper should record every idea, even if it seems silly or inappropriate at the time, and should write exactly what is said. If a team member's statement isn't clear, the recordkeeper should ask the team member to restate the idea. The team should avoid using jargon, buzz words, and incomplete thoughts so that each idea is clear to everyone during the session and remains clear after the session is over.

Work Through the Quiet Times. The facilitator needs to take care that the brainstorming session is not cut off too soon, for example, at its first dead point. Up to this point, the team has usually explored only the more obvious ideas or has just pursued solutions that everybody already knew. The team needs to get through this dead point to advance into more creative phases.

Practice Creates Efficiency. If your team frequently holds brainstorming sessions on a more informal basis, team members can get through the preparation activities very quickly, particularly if they are familiar with the rules and the roles of all those involved.

Example of a Brainstorming Session with the Facilitator's Commentary

Practice in brainstorming will help team members learn how best to make contributions. The following example shows a sample of ideas and the facilitator's evaluation of each idea's quality and appropriateness to the problem. There are four participants (Jim, Bob, Lisa, and Lynn) and one facilitator in this brainstorming session. The example shows the participants' ideas on the left and the facilitator's comments in the balloons. The example follows the session up to the first dead point.

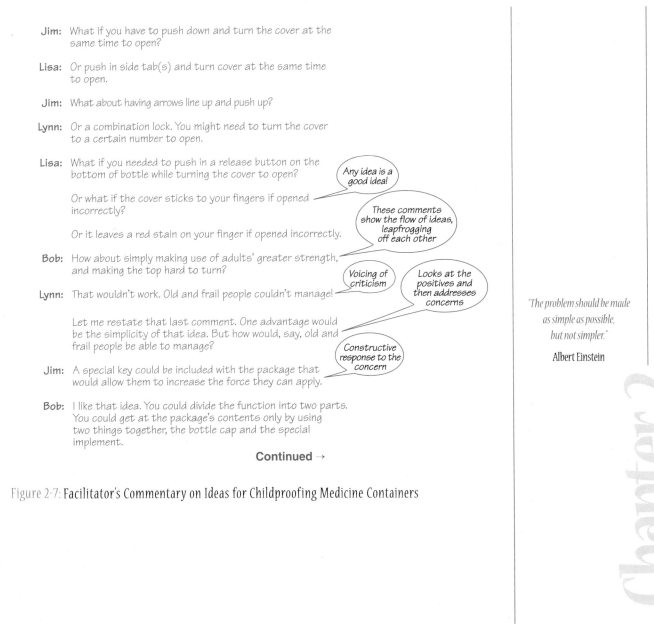

Jim: What if you have to push down and turn the cover at the same time to open?

Lisa: Or push in side tab(s) and turn cover at the same time to open.

Jim: What about having arrows line up and push up?

Lynn: Or a combination lock. You might need to turn the cover to a certain number to open.

Lisa: What if you needed to push in a release button on the bottom of bottle while turning the cover to open?

Any idea is a good idea!

Or what if the cover sticks to your fingers if opened incorrectly?

Or it leaves a red stain on your finger if opened incorrectly.

These comments show the flow of ideas, leapfrogging off each other

Bob: How about simply making use of adults' greater strength, and making the top hard to turn?

Voicing of criticism

Looks at the positives and then addresses concerns

Lynn: That wouldn't work. Old and frail people couldn't manage!

Let me restate that last comment. One advantage would be the simplicity of that idea. But how would, say, old and frail people be able to manage?

Constructive response to the concern

Jim: A special key could be included with the package that would allow them to increase the force they can apply.

Bob: I like that idea. You could divide the function into two parts. You could get at the package's contents only by using two things together, the bottle cap and the special implement.

Continued →

Figure 2-7: Facilitator's Commentary on Ideas for Childproofing Medicine Containers

"The problem should be made as simple as possible, but not simpler."

Albert Einstein

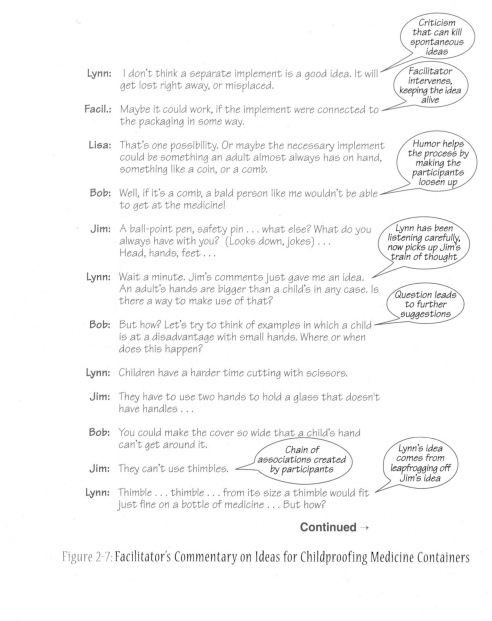

Lynn: I don't think a separate implement is a good idea. It will get lost right away, or misplaced.

Criticism that can kill spontaneous ideas

Facil.: Maybe it could work, if the implement were connected to the packaging in some way.

Facilitator intervenes, keeping the idea alive

Lisa: That's one possibility. Or maybe the necessary implement could be something an adult almost always has on hand, something like a coin, or a comb.

Humor helps the process by making the participants loosen up

Bob: Well, if it's a comb, a bald person like me wouldn't be able to get at the medicine!

Jim: A ball-point pen, safety pin . . . what else? What do you always have with you? (Looks down, jokes) . . . Head, hands, feet . . .

Lynn has been listening carefully, now picks up Jim's train of thought

Lynn: Wait a minute. Jim's comments just gave me an idea. An adult's hands are bigger than a child's in any case. Is there a way to make use of that?

Question leads to further suggestions

Bob: But how? Let's try to think of examples in which a child is at a disadvantage with small hands. Where or when does this happen?

Lynn: Children have a harder time cutting with scissors.

Jim: They have to use two hands to hold a glass that doesn't have handles . . .

Bob: You could make the cover so wide that a child's hand can't get around it.

Chain of associations created by participants

Lynn's idea comes from leapfrogging off Jim's idea

Jim: They can't use thimbles.

Lynn: Thimble . . . thimble . . . from its size a thimble would fit just fine on a bottle of medicine . . . But how?

Continued →

Figure 2-7: Facilitator's Commentary on Ideas for Childproofing Medicine Containers

Lisa: I've got it: the bottle gets an internal thread. The cap can then be shaped like a thimble. You just stick a finger in and can turn the cap by exerting pressure. (She goes to the flipchart and draws a sketch of her idea.) Something like this . . . And to make it even safer, the inside wall can be made perfectly smooth.

Lisa would not have hit on this solution alone!

It is good that she can visualize her idea!

Bob: I think that's great. But does it matter that adults don't all have fingers of the same size? I'm thinking of the difference between men and women, for one thing.

Constructive thought to develop the idea further

Facil.: I think that it could still work out all right. In an extreme case, a woman would have to use her thumb, and a man his little finger.

Facilitator and Jim provide positive feedback

Jim: Yes, I agree that this suggestion is usable.

Facil.: Good, let's note that suggestion down on the possibilities list. Now, how about caps with some trick for opening them?

Facilitator introduces a new line of thought

Lynn: Um . . . some kind of mechanism an adult is familiar with, but not a child . . .

Lisa: Could we work with some kind of layering?

You might have multiple layers of protection for each dosage.

Jim allows his imagination free rein

Jim: Or with a secret button, like in a mystery story?

This in turn suggests further ideas to Bob

Bob: Why not something totally inconspicuous? Something one would never think of as connected with the cap at all?

First Dead Point

Figure 2-7: Facilitator's Commentary on Ideas for Childproofing Medicine Containers

Frequently Asked Questions

Q. What if some team members are not participating?

A. The facilitator should ask if there are any analogies from his or her field of experience (while looking at a specific person). If this is a persistent problem, consider whether the right people were invited. If there are strong personalities, you may have to ask more questions to stimulate participation.

Q. What are some successful ways to break "dead points?"

A. The facilitator can review the list of ideas and ask the group to play with some of the more interesting ones. Encourage team members to hitchhike or piggyback on one or more of the ideas already listed. The facilitator should try to preserve the open, free-flowing climate of the brainstorming session, and so should avoid calling on a specific person.

Q. How should the facilitator end the session?

A. The facilitator should say something like, "Five more ideas and then we'll take a break."

Q. How should ideas be recorded?

A. The ideas can be written on a flipchart, overhead transparency, or Post-it™ Notes. The team also has the option of using a tape recorder during the session and later transcribing the ideas on paper, or using a computer with a projection screen and a printer.

Q. How does the facilitator ensure that team members follow the ground rules?

A. The facilitator should post the ground rules so they are visible to all the participants and when necessary, point out when a ground rule is not being followed.

Additional Examples of Tool Usage

Situation: A group concerned about the growth of the downtown business area met to come up with new ideas for fostering new business development. The problem, as they saw it, is: "How can we bring new business downtown?"

They decided to use the Classic Brainstorming tool because they had not worked together as a team before and needed practice in following the ground rules for brainstorming.

The group came up with the following ideas:

- lower crime
- more parking spaces/more affordable parking
- urban renewal mega-grant
- tax incentives
- community involvement
- better housing
- more affordable quality housing
- enclosed mall shopping
- clean up homeless situation

Figure 2-8: Initial Ideas for Bringing New Business Downtown

After a dead point of about a minute, the facilitator asked: "What is it about being in a downtown area that would be attractive to businesses?"

The group came up with these additional ideas:

- great restaurants
- mass transportation
- cultural events
- access to common space areas
- access to shopping
- more going on

Figure 2-9: Ideas After First Dead Point

"What lies behind us and what lies before us are tiny matters compared to what lies within us."

William Morrow

Chapter 2

The group continued to brainstorm additional ideas. After taking a break, they decided to try another creativity tool to generate more ideas. (See Chapters 4 and 5 for additional ideas that were generated from those sessions.)

Situation: The Federal Quality Consulting Group in Washington, D.C. had recently developed a Web site. A team was charged with coming up with ideas to solve the problem: "How can we get people to visit the Federal Quality Consulting Group's new Web site?"

The team decided to use the Classic Brainstorming tool to elicit the more obvious ideas.

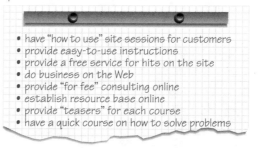

- have good-looking graphics
- have hot links to other popular sites
- link into *National Productivity Review* home pages
- publicize all written information we send out
- put "teasers" on coupons and business cards
- have good information
- keep information updated
- have a panel of experts online
- have chatrooms

Figure 2-10: Initial Ideas for Getting People to Visit FQCG's New Web Site

Idea generation slowed down and after two minutes of silence the facilitator asked, "What would 'good information' mean for customers?" That question resulted in the following additional ideas:

- have "how to use" site sessions for customers
- provide easy-to-use instructions
- provide a free service for hits on the site
- do business on the Web
- provide "for fee" consulting online
- establish resource base online
- provide "teasers" for each course
- have a quick course on how to solve problems

Figure 2-11: Ideas After First Dead Point

The team, while pleased with the outcome of this session, decided that they needed more innovative ideas. They decided to hold another session the following week, and to use another creativity tool for more idea generation. See Chapter 4 for the outcome of that session.

This example is based on work contributed by Tina Sung, Federal Quality Consulting Group.

'I had six honest serving men—they taught me all I knew.
Their names were Where and What and When—and Why and How and Who.'

Rudyard Kipling

Brainwriting 6-3-5

Introduction

In the last chapter, the highly verbal process of brainstorming was discussed. The brainstorming process allows group members to share their ideas by stating them verbally. Now suppose this idea sharing is done in silence; group members write down their ideas instead of saying them. This is the approach of brainwriting, which was developed in Europe in the 1970s as an alternative way of generating a large number of ideas. The most popular version of brainwriting is called Brainwriting 6-3-5. The numbers 6-3-5 refer to: 6 people in a group, 3 ideas for each "round," and 5 minutes of idea generating for each round.

When Brainwriting 6-3-5 is compared with brainstorming, one advantage is that brainwriting allows people the extra time to visualize and build on each other's ideas. But is something lost without the verbalization of brainstorming? There are advantages and disadvantages to both methods. The advantages and disadvantages of Brainwriting 6-3-5 are listed below.

"It should not be hard for you to stop sometimes and look into the stains of walls, or ashes of a fire, or clouds, or mud or like places, in which ... you may find really marvelous ideas."

Leonardo da Vinci

Advantages of Brainwriting 6-3-5

- Participation in brainwriting is unlimited; just add more groups of six. Brainstorming is realistically limited to six or eight people; a larger group makes it difficult for everyone to participate. Multiple brainstorming groups would mean multiple facilitators, whereas Brainwriting 6-3-5 is self-administered.

- Participants can think in more depth without the distraction of discussion.

- There is no criticism of ideas in brainwriting because there is no discussion.

- No one person can dominate the discussion and impose his or her own personal opinions.

- Participants who have a lower rank in the organization are able to share more freely.

Chapter 3

- The process does not require an experienced facilitator.

- Ideas are written by the participants, not a recordkeeper, which eliminates the possibility that someone could inadvertently distort the participants' ideas.

- Shy people feel more encouraged to contribute.

- Participants have some time to think about and build on each other's ideas, thus building synergy.

Disadvantages of Brainwriting 6-3-5

- Idea sharing is less spontaneous in brainwriting; a lively discussion in brainstorming can be more freewheeling and stimulate more diverse lines of thinking. However, if some silly or unusual ideas are written down, it sometimes frees the group to share more unusual ideas.

- In brainwriting there is no possibility for the facilitator to lead the discussion in promising directions that may otherwise have been considered.

- If an idea is not understood in brainwriting, there is no immediate opportunity to get it clarified as is possible in brainstorming.

Definition of the Tool

Brainwriting 6-3-5 provides teams with a method for generating and sharing ideas in writing, which differs from brainstorming where ideas are shared verbally. The silent nature of the brainwriting process increases the likelihood that everyone will participate and build on each other's ideas.

Use of the Tool

The Brainwriting 6-3-5 method is recommended if:

- there is significant disagreement on the topic and interpersonal debates and conflicts need to be avoided.

- certain individuals, because of their rank or expert status, are likely to dominate others in the group.

- the ideas to be generated will take longer to surface because the participants are thinking about the roots of the problem.

Brainwriting 6-3-5 can be adapted for use with a group larger than six people.

Overview of the Tool Process

The Brainwriting 6-3-5 tool follows this general process: Participants form into groups of six; each participant receives a 6-3-5 worksheet (illustrated in Figure 3-1); participants write down three ideas in the first row of the worksheet; each worksheet is passed to the person on the right; everyone reads the ideas in the previous row(s), then adds three more ideas; the worksheets are passed again and the process repeated until the worksheets return to their originators; and last, the team votes on the best ideas.

Problem:		Form #:
		Date:

Figure 3-1: Typical Worksheet for Brainwriting 6-3-5

Applying the Tool

Outline of Steps

Step	Activity
1.	Assemble the team.
2.	Distribute the worksheets.
3.	Provide instructions.
4.	Complete the worksheets.
5.	Analyze ideas and select the best ones.

Step-by-Step Instructions

Step 1. Assemble the team.

The team leader should select team members who will provide ideas related to the various aspects of the problem. It is also helpful to have people of diverse experience who, although they are unfamiliar with the problem, may expand the group's thinking.

The team leader should present the problem, have the group discuss it, and agree on the problem statement. It is important for the team to have a common definition of the problem since team members will be generating ideas in silence.

Example

The team works for a company that has recently decided it needs to speed up the time needed for developing new products. They have defined the problem as: "What can we do to reduce new product development time?"

Step 2. Distribute the worksheets.

A typical worksheet is shown in Figure 3-1.

The participants should sit in a circle. The optimum number of participants is six, but a larger group will also work. A group smaller than five is not effective for this tool.

Step 3. Provide instructions.

The facilitator or the team leader explains how the participants should use the worksheet and how the Brainwriting 6-3-5 process will work.

Based on the team's goal or problem statement, each participant writes three ideas in the top row of his or her worksheet. When everyone is finished, each participant passes the worksheet to the next person. For the purpose of illustration, these instructions describe passing the worksheets to the right.

In round two, each participant receives the sheet from the person on his or her left and takes time to read the ideas in the first row to stimulate his or her thinking. Each participant writes three more ideas in the second row. When participants are writing down ideas, they can:

- expand on an idea.
- write a variation of any previous idea.
- add a completely unrelated new idea.

When everyone is finished writing, each worksheet is passed to the next person, and round three begins. Ideally, each round should last approximately five minutes, however, some rounds may take less time, and others may take more time. The process continues until the worksheets are filled.

The facilitator or team leader should point out these tips:

- If participants cannot think of three ideas in a round, they should just leave a blank on the worksheet.

"The best cure for a sluggish mind is to disturb its routine."
William H. Danforth

Chapter 3

- Participants should remember to write clearly so that each word is legible. Sometimes participants find it helpful to add a little sketch or drawing to clarify an idea.

- Participants are free to write anything that comes to mind, but the idea should have some level of detail. Such detail will more likely lead the next person to new ideas. For example, if the team's goal is to design office space, the ideas "tear down the walls between offices" and "replace the cubicle walls with plants" will more likely generate novel ideas than "reconfigure the office space."

Step 4. Complete the worksheets.

Filling in each successive row on the worksheet tends to take team members a little longer for each round. This is because they need additional time to read the previous ideas and to think of ideas that have not been written on the worksheet yet.

The team continues filling in the rows and circulating the worksheets until each worksheet is full.

Example

Problem: Reducing new product development time		Form #: 1
		Date: June 1
	1	2	3
1	Hire experienced product developers	Work on various aspects of a new product concurrently	Work on several similar products at once

Figure 3-2: Reducing New Product Development Time, first row

As the worksheet circulates to the next person around the table, additional ideas are added.

Problem: Reducing new product development time		Form #: 1
		Date: June 1
	1	2	3

	1	2	3
1	Hire experienced product developers	Work on various aspects of a new product concurrently	Work on several similar products at once
2	Get more young and experienced people on the team	Split topic and compose results later	Compare with previous product designs

Figure 3-3: Reducing New Product Development Time, first and second rows

Step 5. Analyze ideas and select the best ones.

Once the worksheets are completed, (Figure 3-4 shows a completed worksheet), the team collects the ideas and decides how they will analyze them, i.e., which idea selection tool they will use. The team can use Nominal Group Technique or some criteria-based analysis tool to pick the best ideas. (See Chapters 8–11 for tools that help teams evaluate and select the best ideas.)

Another option is for each participant to choose three ideas on the worksheet that he or she likes the most and to draw a plus sign next to these ideas. Then the group passes the worksheets from one person to the next five more times. If there are six people in the group, there will be 18 plus signs on each worksheet, and a preferred idea will have a maximum of six plus signs.

To further develop the ideas that are most popular with the team, the facilitator can recommend that the team use the Affinity Diagram, Interrelationship Digraph, or Prioritization Matrix.

Example[1]

Once the worksheets are completed, the team collects the ideas and decides how they will analyze them, i.e., which idea selection tool they will use.

Problem: Reducing new product development time			**Form #:** 1 **Date:** June 1, 1997
	1	2	3
1	Hire experienced product developers	Work on various aspects of a new product concurrently	Work on several similar products at once
2	Get more young and more experienced people on the team	Split topic and compose results later	Compare with previous product designs
3	Share learning better. Figure out how to get the experience of 50 projects into the one team	Practice forward thinking, or how to think for the future. Create products for later stage	Develop a family of products around a core delivery system
4	Don't constrain team with **how** to do it; develop the **what**s	Use modular development with defined interfaces	Use/re-use modules and enhance for fast compromise in parallel with new generation
5	"Back up" to figure out what customers need	Create a high performance team	Eliminate unnecessary steps
6	Keep talking to users	Tie rewards to project goals and time frame	At regular meetings always review to see if focused on goals

Figure 3-4: Completed Worksheet

---

1. This example was developed in a workshop at the QFD Institute meeting in Novi, Michigan in June 1997.

Summary of the Tool

Brainwriting 6-3-5 is a powerful idea generation tool with several advantages over brainstorming. One advantage is that it allows a large number of participants to join in the creative group. In a Brainwriting 6-3-5 session there can be several six-member groups working simultaneously. Another advantage is that this tool provides time for personal concentration. Participants can think more deeply about the subject and since no one talks during the session, the ideas cannot be challenged verbally. The possibility of one person dominating the session and its outcome is eliminated. This tool encourages the contributions of individuals who may be shy about verbal participation in groups, and helps individuals at all levels in the organization feel freer about proposing their ideas since the possibility of their contributions being overlooked or discouraged is significantly reduced.

Enhancing the Process

Helpful Hints

Set a Generous Time Limit. In an ideal situation, a Brainwriting 6-3-5 process is finished in 30–45 minutes and results in 108 ideas (3 ideas x 6 rounds x 6 participants). In practice, however, both the time allotted and the number of ideas generated may vary because:

- similar ideas may be suggested by more than one participant.

- one or more participants have only one or two ideas, or no ideas, to complete the round.

- during the later rounds team members need additional time to read all of the ideas from preceding rounds.

Write Ideas Clearly. Team members need to be reminded to write clearly and legibly.

Use the Post-it™ Note Alternative for Speed. A popular option in constructing a Brainwriting 6-3-5 worksheet is to attach 18 Post-It™ Notes of suitable size on each worksheet. The addition of these notes helps speed up the sorting and classifying of ideas during the evaluation phase, especially if the group will be using an Affinity Diagram.

"There is strong evidence that the unconscious mind is a reservoir of information so vast and rich that it challenges the imagination."

George Prince

Chapter 3

Discourage Talking. The facilitator should discourage any discussion of ideas during the session or talking out loud to allow for maximum personal time to think.

Draw a Technical Idea If It's Too Hard to Describe. If the team is dealing with a technical problem, it may be a good idea, or a necessity, to illustrate ideas as drawings. To provide sufficient space on the worksheets, they may need to be enlarged to legal size paper or larger.

Virtual Team Option. An alternative to getting participants together for a Brainwriting 6-3-5 session is to ask people to contribute ideas as "virtual team members." For example, participants could fill in the 6-3-5 worksheets via their organization's internal computer network. When participants agree to complete the worksheets outside of a meeting, they need to follow through with a firm schedule and a specific plan for circulating the worksheets. It is very important to include the schedule, circulation plan, and the name of the person who should next receive the worksheet as the worksheets are passed from person to person.

Collective Notebook Method. An alternative to the Brainwriting 6-3-5 tool is the Collective Notebook Method. The team leader gives each team member or project participant a notebook. Each notebook has the following information: a description of the problem, goal, or situation; any requirements for solutions; and the problem statement, with any additional project objectives. Team members carry around the notebooks for a period of time, typically 2–4 weeks, and record or sketch out all their ideas, thoughts, and images that come to mind about the problem. Team members then return the notebooks to the team leader, who consolidates the ideas, gets clarification on any questions he or she may have on the notebooks, and schedules any appropriate follow up meetings. Such follow up could be a conference where the team members get together to jointly review the findings and engage in any additional problem solving.

The Collective Notebook Method has two advantages over Brainwriting 6-3-5. One, this method does not require an assembly of team members. Sometimes it isn't possible to bring together needed team members because they may work in geographically distant locations. Two, experience has shown that most people have breakthrough ideas when they are not at work; these ideas seem to pop up when a person is spending leisure time alone.

Frequently Asked Questions

Q. What if someone cannot think of three ideas for each round?

A. He or she should just leave the space blank or write down a wild or off-the-wall idea. It may prove later to be a good idea, you just never know!

Q. What if all team members don't finish completing a row in the time agreed on?

A. The team should take the time needed, but each team member should try to write quickly and spontaneously. That's the way to surface more creative ideas.

Q. How is this tool different from brainstorming?

A. It is more structured because a form is used, and the ideas are written instead of verbalized. Writing down ideas in silence allows participants to think without distractions, to review the ideas already written, and to think about how ideas can be combined. Also, the silence rule of Brainwriting 6-3-5 makes it more comfortable for quiet people and those at different levels in the organization to participate.

Q. What if there aren't six people, the group size that's recommended for this tool?

A. The Brainwriting 6-3-5 tool can work with a small group of people, but is designed for six or more. A smaller group might consider using one of the other idea generation tools such as Classical Brainstorming, Imaginary Brainstorming, or Word-Picture Associations and Analogies.

Additional Examples of Tool Usage

Situation: A team of employees from departments across the organization was formed to develop ideas to address the problem: "How can we increase employee satisfaction and commitment on the job?" Because the team members felt this was a sensitive subject and they wanted to get every-

The Idea Edge

one to contribute ideas, they decided to use Brainwriting 6-3-5. One of the completed forms is shown in Figure 3-5.

Problem: How to increase employee satisfaction and commitment on the job?		Form #: 1 Date: Jan. 20, 1998
	1	2	3
1	Give employees more responsibility	Have a "personal space" corner for every employee – even in cubicles	We should encourage and foster collaboration and cooperation
2	Provide flex-time and the possibilities of telecommuting	Give tasks to small teams	Foster more communication between upper management and all employees
3	Have more short-term and long-term job rotations	Consider personal interests when assigning jobs; don't have unreasonable expectations of the employee	Make the reasons for organizational changes more apparent
4	Install aquariums in the offices	Offer recreation rooms with mind machines	Managers should be honest with employees about their career chances
5	Provide music in the office	Take more personal interest in lives of colleagues	Show people how important their work is within the context of the whole company
6	Organize social events once a month after working hours	Allow choices in office-mate decisions	Open up sport clubs for employees' children

Figure 3-5: Ideas for Increasing Employees' Satisfaction and Commitment on the Job

When the team members analyzed the results of the session, they were pleased to see that a seemingly "off-the-wall" contribution from one team member—"Install aquariums in the offices"—had shifted the direction of the idea flow. From the more impersonal business environment, the ideas had moved to

The Idea Edge

a more personally focused view of the employee as a full individual. They realized that Brainwriting 6-3-5 provides people with an opportunity to reflect and allows their thinking to take a new route. They also realized that in a typical brainstorming session, the idea about installing aquariums in the offices might have been easily dismissed by the participants, or might not have even been mentioned by a more introverted team member.

Situation: A team of employees in a dentist's office was asked to come up with alternative ideas to address the problem of "How can we help patients be more relaxed during treatment?" The team gathered a group of patients who were willing to participate in the exercise and asked them to come up with ideas using the Brainwriting 6-3-5 forms. One of the completed forms is shown in Figure 3-6.

"The primary creativeness which comes out of the unconscious ... is very probably a heritage of every human being."

A.H. Maslow

Chapter 3

Problem: How can we help patients be more relaxed during treatment?		Form #: 1
		Date: Jan. 20, 1998
1	**2**	**3**
1 Teach the dentist active listening	Have the dentist read joke books	Get a vibrating chair
2 Dentist should watch for patient body language and take breaks when patient needs one	Put a TV in a position so patient can watch a favorite program	Have a variety of relaxation tapes for patient to use
3 Give the patient a panic button to push when it hurts	Provide earphones and tranquil music	Use aromatherapy—pleasant scents from the forest or beach
4 Connect the panic button to a vibrator in the chair	Teach the dentist not to ask questions when the suction device is in the patient's mouth	Find out ahead of time when and where the patient is happiest
5 Have pleasant smells and aromas in the office (cinnamon, lavender, etc.)	Have a "pain killer" patch that the patient can put on his/her arm	Have dentist chair look like a comfortable recliner
6 Using a VCR, show the patient a movie, cartoon or film clip	Offer the patient choices ("Shall I use a green or a blue drilling set?")	Dentist explains each step to the patient as dentist proceeds with treatment

Figure 3-6: Ideas for Relaxing Patients During a Dental Treatment

The team was quite pleased with the results and felt they had many good ideas to share with the dentist. (In real life, the dentist has implemented many of the ideas with great success.)

This example was contributed by Diane Ritter, GOAL/QPC.

Imaginary Brainstorming

Introduction

The name Imaginary Brainstorming might suggest that it is a slight variation on Classic Brainstorming, however, it has some significant differences. Imaginary Brainstorming uses a certain "trick" that will automatically shift a person's thinking. The "trick" consists in shifting one element of a problem by replacing it with a radically new element. For example, instead of getting employees to try the Web, you might try getting employees to wear cardboard noses or to try snowboarding.

With this "trick," the problem is made strange. It is different from the real problem. It becomes an imaginary problem but it is still strongly related to the real one. When group members solve this imaginary problem, their thoughts are shaped in new ways, and old conceptions that people may have about solutions to the problem are shattered.

Definition of the Tool

Imaginary Brainstorming is a tool that provides a team with the an opportunity to step out of the real problem, generate ideas for a radically different yet related imaginary problem, and apply the new ideas that are generated to the real problem. The greater number of ideas that a team can generate, the more opportunities the team will see in solving the problem. A team can have this "idea productivity" simply by combining the ideas generated in both an imaginary and classic brainstorming session. This tool is helpful if an "expert" is pushing a particular solution or if the team is polarized around more than one solution based on the team's function or a specific agenda.

"Method will teach you to win time."
Johann Wolfgang Von Goethe

Chapter 4

The Idea Edge

Use of the Tool

Imaginary Brainstorming helps a team break out of traditional, deeply ingrained patterns of thinking and is highly valuable for finding breakthrough ideas for problems that have a history of being solved in the same way all the time. This tool is particularly well suited for helping experts in the problem to question the core concepts that they have held for many years and have believed to be unchangeable.

Overview of the Tool Process

The team first defines the challenge or problem being investigated. Then a regular brainstorming session is held to generate and record initial ideas. The initial brainstorming session ends with a clarification of the essential elements of the problem. Once the team has listed the essential problem elements, it can then change an element to generate new ideas. The team then works with the ideas generated from the imaginary problem to apply them to the real problem.

For example, say that your team has defined the problem as "How can we improve communications with other departments?" The team defines the key elements of the problem statement as "improve," "communications," and "other departments." The team decides to change the element "other departments" to "Martians" and begins to explore the imaginary problem of "How can we improve communications with Martians?" This changes the team's perspective!

Applying the Tool

Outline of Steps

Step	Activity
1.	Define the goal or problem.
2.	Generate and record ideas using Classic Brainstorming.
3.	Define the essential elements of the problem or goal statement.
4.	Propose imaginary replacements for each essential element.
5.	Substitute a significantly different replacement for one of the essential elements to create an imaginary problem statement.
6.	Generate ideas for the imaginary problem.
7.	Transform these ideas for the imaginary problem into ideas suitable for solving the real problem.
8.	(Optional) Create a second imaginary problem statement and repeat Steps 6 and 7.
9.	Combine the list of ideas produced by Steps 2, 7, and 8. Explore these ideas further.

Step-by-Step Instructions

Step 1. Define the goal or problem.

The team should spend time analyzing the real problem and then defining it.

Example

The team defines the problem as: "How can a patient's fear of getting an injection be reduced?"

Step 2. Generate and record ideas using Classic Brainstorming.

The team should begin by brainstorming ideas around possible solutions to the real problem. Team members may find it helpful if the ground rules for brainstorming are posted on the wall, or the facilitator and team members review the rules together.

Example

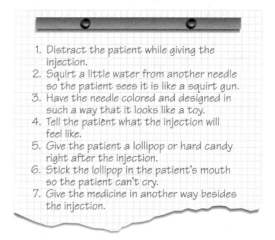

1. Distract the patient while giving the injection.
2. Squirt a little water from another needle so the patient sees it is like a squirt gun.
3. Have the needle colored and designed in such a way that it looks like a toy.
4. Tell the patient what the injection will feel like.
5. Give the patient a lollipop or hard candy right after the injection.
6. Stick the lollipop in the patient's mouth so the patient can't cry.
7. Give the medicine in another way besides the injection.

Figure 4-1: Initial Ideas for Reducing a Patient's Fear of Getting an Injection

Step 3. Define the essential elements of the problem or goal statement.

When the team defines the problem in detail, the essential elements will become clear. The essential elements are the who, what, when and where of the problem. These elements answer the following questions:

- Who or what is performing an action?
- Who or what is the recipient of the action?
- What is the action being performed?
- Where is the action being performed?
- Are there other elements directly involved in the dynamics of the problem?

The recordkeeper should list the essential elements on a flipchart.

Example

The team asked: "What are the essential elements of the problem?" Team members decided on three concepts that they thought would lead them to the best solutions for reducing a patient's fear of getting an injection.

1. A shift is required in the patients' perspective.
2. The team's goal is to reduce fear.
3. A patient's fear is triggered by the expectation of pain.

Figure 4-2: Essential Elements of the Problem/Goal

"You can't wait for inspiration. You have to go after it with a club."

Jack London

Chapter 4

The team then simplified the essential elements of the problem:

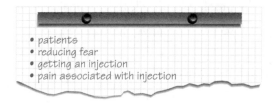

- patients
- reducing fear
- getting an injection
- pain associated with injection

Figure 4-3: Essential Elements Simplified

Step 4. Propose imaginary replacements for each essential element.

The team should propose *imaginary* replacements that are radically different from the essential elements of the real problem. For example, a doctor's drill is a poor replacement for "injection" because they are too similar. Every replacement will in effect define a different imaginary problem, as the team replaces one essential problem element with another. In doing this, it is important to keep in mind the basic intention of the method: **to break fixed patterns of thinking in creating ideas for solving a given problem.**

Example

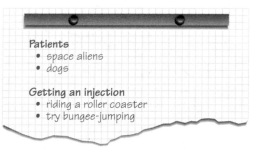

Patients
- space aliens
- dogs

Getting an injection
- riding a roller coaster
- try bungee-jumping

Figure 4-4: Possible Replacements for "Patients" and "Getting an Injection"

Step 5. Substitute a significantly different replacement for one of the essential elements to create an imaginary problem statement.

The choice of which element to replace should be guided by the questions:

- What would make the team see the problem quite differently?
- What would produce different ideas to solve the problem?

The team may want to explore other imaginary problem statements as well. Most likely it will be up to the facilitator to judge whether this process will produce new ideas.

Example

The team decided to use "riding a roller coaster" as a replacement for "getting an injection." The imaginary problem statement is: "What can be done to reduce a patient's fear of riding a roller coaster?"

Step 6. Generate ideas for the imaginary problem.

The team should spend about 15 to 20 minutes to generate ideas around possible solutions to the imaginary problem. All these ideas should be recorded verbatim.

Example

- Offer to have girls and boys accompany the people on the roller coaster ride to show that not much courage is required for a ride.
- Show a video of people who are having fun as they are riding a roller coaster.
- Interview people who have already completed the ride.
- Hand out "courage" pills.
- Equip riders with helmets that have visors which can be closed to "block out" horrible visions.
- Ask people to close their eyes during the ride.

Figure 4-5: Ideas for Reducing a Patient's Fear of Riding a Roller Coaster

Step 7. Transform these ideas for the imaginary problem into ideas suitable for solving the real problem.

The team reviews the ideas from the imaginary brainstorming session and starts to connect the solutions back to the real problem. To do this, three questions are helpful:

1. Can an imaginary idea also serve as an idea for the real problem, just like it is, without changing anything?

2. Can the imaginary idea be transformed, adjusted, or modified in an appropriate way?

3. Does the imaginary idea contain any element—a shape, function, material—that has never been used as a part of former solutions to the problem? Is this element something the creative mind can toy with to generate a new solution, or can it trigger a new insight into approaching the problem?

Experience shows that the first two questions offer fewer possibilities for the creation of new ideas, and that the third question offers more possibilities for new ideas. The following example shows how the third question offers more possibilities.

Example

The team connected the ideas for the imaginary problem to the real problem. Using the list of ideas from Step 6, where the team thought of ways to reduce the fear in people riding a roller coaster, the team applied some of these ideas to reducing the fear in patients getting an injection.

- Give patients the feeling that they are not at the mercy of the situation but can control it. For example: give patients a switch and explain that as soon as they push "the red button," all treatment will be stopped immediately.
- Get the patient to talk about an activity he or she enjoys doing.
- Put a local anesthetic on the skin so the injection doesn't hurt.
- Don't give the injection while the patient is alone, but in the company of another person he or she trusts, or in the company of another patient.
- Turn the attention of the patient away from the injection procedure by giving the patient earphones or setting up a video display.

Figure 4-6: Ideas for Solving the Imaginary Problem (Step 6) Applied to the Real Problem/Goal

The use of a local skin anesthetic and earphones are two examples of how treatment can be made more palatable.

Step 8. (Optional) Create a second imaginary problem statement and repeat Steps 6 and 7.

If time permits, and if the problem warrants the effort, the team can select another imaginary problem to generate additional ideas. The team should repeat Steps 6 and 7.

Example

The team repeated Steps 6 and 7 for the imaginary problem: "How can a space alien's fear of getting an injection be reduced?"

"What concerns everyone can only be resolved by everyone."
Friedrich Dürrenmatt

Chapter 4

> *Step 9. Combine the list of ideas produced by Steps 2, 7, and 8. Explore these ideas further.*
>
> The team takes the ideas produced by the initial brainstorming around the real problem and adds them to the list of ideas generated by Steps 7 and 8, so that any of these ideas can be further explored.
>
> The application of Imaginary Brainstorming is completed when all the ideas produced for the imaginary problem have been worked into practical ideas for the real problem. As the example indicates, this process takes more time than Classic Brainstorming to create ideas for the imaginary problem, however, it can result in more breakthrough ideas.

Summary of the Tool

The Imaginary Brainstorming tool can help a team break out of traditional, deeply ingrained patterns of thinking. It is of high value in approaching problems for which a traditional solution is not acceptable. This tool is particularly well suited for questioning long-held ideas that can constrain creative thinking.

Enhancing the Process

Helpful Hints

Practice for Better Results. The successful application of Imaginary Brainstorming may require some practice and experience. If no one in the group has ever used this tool, it is normal to have disappointing results with the first attempt. The key is for the team to be patient and get more practice!

Know the Two Critical Steps. There are two critical steps: defining the essential problem elements (Step 3), and transforming the imaginary brainstorming ideas into real problem ideas (Step 7).

Expand the Imaginary Problem Statement. Sometimes the imaginary problem is stated in "shorthand" because team members assume everyone else understands this shorthand. The team should avoid shorthand expressions and instead expand the problem statement to include all the essential elements of the problem. For example, "How can we design a better lawn mower?" should be expanded to "How can we design a better cutting device for grass?" The expanded statement gives the team a broader view of the problem, which will help the team produce a greater number of ideas. Instead of the team generating ideas related only to the lawn mower, it can look for ideas that include the lawn mower, the grass, and the combination of the two. The more ideas the team generates means that team members are flexing their mental muscles, and the more likely the team will generate new ideas and unusual connections.

Take Time to Explore Imaginary Ideas. The team should be careful about putting aside an imaginary idea too quickly if it doesn't immediately succeed in building a solution for the real problem. The team needs to explore each imaginary idea for at least a few minutes.

Each imaginary problem will stimulate a variety of ideas, but the team can never predict which imaginary problem will lead to the most valuable results. So if the team has the time, it can select a second or third imaginary problem to explore in the same brainstorming session, which will help the team generate an even greater diversity of ideas.

Have Fun in Exploring Imaginary Ideas. When exploring imaginary ideas, the team should avoid being too practical and looking only at what will actually work. It is very important to be able to play with imaginary ideas and look at them not only as possible solutions, but as having unusual influences, features, and attributes that can stimulate additional ideas. At this time the team should not try to connect the ideas generated for the imaginary problem back to the real problem; this will be done later.

Imaginary problems may be unusual, fun or crazy, and this exploration is to be encouraged. If this is not clearly understood, some team members might think the real problem is not being taken seriously. However, using this tool will free team members' thinking and allow them to come up with an unrestricted, fresh, and humorous flow of ideas. That's exactly what the team wants to do—to produce ideas that have not yet been connected to the real problem.

"Take a Break" Advisory: A 15-minute break between the initial brainstorming around the real problem and the exploration of the imaginary problem is recommended. This time gives team members a chance to mentally separate the real problem from the imaginary problem.

Chapter 4

Frequently Asked Questions

Q. Why does the team first do Classic Brainstorming before doing Imaginary Brainstorming?

A. Classic Brainstorming is a quick and easy way to "pluck" the most common, obvious, or spontaneous ideas from the team members' thoughts. It's possible that a team may find an acceptable solution right away in Classic Brainstorming.

Q. Why is it suggested that only one problem element at a time be substituted?

A. When more than one element is substituted, the problem is shifted even further away from the real problem. It can then take too much time or prove too difficult for the team to find the connections back to the real problem.

Q. How does the facilitator keep the team members from focusing on the real problem?

A. One way is to cover the flipchart sheet with the real problem statement and the ideas generated for it so that the team is not reminded of it. Other techniques are to take a break or do a short relaxation exercise.

Q. Can the element substitutions be crazy and playful or should team members stay realistic and not too wild in their thinking?

A. Team members should be encouraged think wildly if this helps them to disconnect from the real problem. It's also fun and empowering to say whatever comes to mind! Encourage it.

Q. How can the team take the ideas that were generated for the imaginary problem and apply them to the real problem?

A. Take each idea, one by one, and put it into the context of the real problem. Some ideas may apply very easily. Some ideas may require the team to spend several minutes to make connections between ideas. And some ideas may not help no mattter how long the team works with them.

Additional Examples of Tool Usage

Situation: A team has been wrestling with the problem of "How can we bring new business downtown?" (This is the same team that was introduced in the Additional Examples of Tool Usage in Chapter 2.) The team has decided to use Imaginary Brainstorming as a next step for generating additional ideas. First the team identified the essential elements of the problem as "new business" and "downtown." Next, the team thought of a few possible replacements for these elements, as shown in Figure 4-7.

Essential Elements	Possible Replacements
New business	Capistrano swallows
	tigers
Downtown	theme park
	desert

Figure 4-7: Essential Elements of the Problem of How to Bring New Business Downtown

The team agreed on the replacement "Capistrano swallows" and defined the imaginary problem as: "How can we bring the swallows of Capistrano to downtown?" The team's ideas and how they were related back to the real problem are shown in Figure 4-8.

"Two roads diverged in a wood, and I—I took the one less traveled by, and that has made all the difference."

Robert Frost

Chapter 4

Ideas for Imaginary Problem	Relating Back to the Real Problem
Install church bells of the same pitch as Capistrano bells	• study other cities that have attracted businesses and go one step further in providing amenities • create a climate where the government and press take an interest in and foster business
Build more Spanish missions	• fix up abandoned and dilapidated buildings • provide the infrastructure of good roads and signs so it is easy to do business • install parks and fountains • build convention space and attract top-line hotels • create an enterprise zone for reducing business expenses
Bring some birds inside and feed them; treat them so well they want to come back	• provide a good variety of restaurants • provide tax relief, low-cost loans, and low-cost rental space

Figure 4-8: Applying Ideas for the Imaginary Problem (Capistrano swallows) Back to the Real Problem

Using this tool, the team was able to find more innovative ideas than they had in the Classic Brainstorming session. Team members were excited about these ideas and felt encouraged to move forward in addressing their challenge.

This example was contributed by Diane Ritter, GOAL/QPC.

Situation: The team from the Federal Quality Consulting Group was working on the problem: "How can we get people to visit the Federal Quality Consulting Group's new Web site?" (This is the same team that was introduced in the Additional Examples of Tool Usage in Chapter 2.)

After the team used Classic Brainstorming, they moved on to using Imaginary Brainstorming. The team identified the essential elements of the problem as "people" and "Web site." The team's ideas for possible replacements for these elements are shown in Figure 4-9.

Essential Elements	Possible Replacements
People	penguins
	hummingbirds
Web site	garden
	zoo

Figure 4-9: Essential Elements of the Problem of How to Get People to Visit the FQCG's New Web Site

The team agreed on the replacement "penguins" and defined the imaginary problem as: "How can we get penguins to visit our new Web site?" The team's ideas and how they were related back to the real problem are shown in Figure 4-10.

Ideas for Imaginary Problem	Relating Back to the Real Problem
Write in "penguinese"	• write briefs of what specific people are doing on the job
Pack the computer in snow	• keep it fresh with up-to-date information • get endorsements from key government officials
Flash images of fish on screen	• create animated graphics
Offer them free fish	• provide a list of free resources
Get newborn penguins to imprint on computers instead of mother penguin	• create identity screen savers • create hot links from one part of the site to another • link the site to related sites
Create penguin post	• provide active, moderated chat function • provide easy-to-send e-mail function
Build giant igloo computer station	• reference the site on all business cards and organization literature
Make computer release penguin pheromones	• address the most frequently asked questions • provide anytime, anywhere education

Figure 4-10: Applying Ideas for the Imaginary Problem (Penguins) Back to the Real Problem

While the idea for this example originated in a training session, a team in the real world that is addressing this same issue could use some of the ideas that are illustrated in the flipchart above. For example, the idea of having screen savers with special messages may be a worthwhile consideration.

This example is based on work contributed by Tina Sung, Federal Quality Consulting Group.

Word-Picture Associations and Analogies

Introduction

The knowledge explosion over the last 30 years has led to increasing specialization. For example, college students have increasingly specialized in electrical, mechanical or chemical engineering. Major companies often hire students from a select set of schools and focus their work within a narrow specialization.

Without a doubt, our efficiency justifies this departmentalization. Our time is limited. But as a person develops his or her own thought patterns, he or she may lose sight of the multiple sources of ideas spawned by our world's knowledge explosion. There is a comfort in staying in our areas of expertise, but there is also a real opportunity to expand the richness of our idea generation when we draw ideas from other disciplines. Word and picture associations, as well as analogies, bring a wellspring of ideas into our creative process.

When dealing with a complex problem, team members should try to think outside the borders of a narrow problem definition; to reach beyond the problem itself into a larger field of similar problems. These mental excursions should be as far-reaching and diverse as possible. Team members should look around in all technical fields and all disciplines; stroll imaginatively through cities, countries and continents; visit history or mythology, or explore the future, always keeping their eyes open for situations close to the problem at hand and the answers given there. And if a team member finds a truly analogous experience, he or she should not just regard its obvious meaning but should try to examine it thoroughly to understand the fundamental structure and inner workings of it—to let the creative mind produce the most valuable insights for the problem at hand.

"Knowledge doesn't pay—it is what you do with it."
Arnold Glasow

Associations and Analogies Defined

Associations and analogies are often used synonymously, however, there is a key distinction. *Associations* are mental *connections* that are triggered by an idea, a memory, a picture, or an event. For example, a piece of apple pie, for some, might stimulate a memory of a grandmother's home, a sense of family, or a recollection of some very special dinner.

Analogies, on the other hand, are *comparisons* of a principal characteristic, action, or behavior between two objects or objects and people. For example, "He is as quiet as a mouse," or "She stands straight as an arrow" are analogies because of the comparison being presented.

An example of the use of analogy follows. Swiss inventor George de Mestral was trying to develop a new kind of fastener. During a walk through a field one day, he was struck by how cockleburs stuck to his pants and his dog's coat. His curiosity led him to examine the reasons why the burs stuck so well. Under a microscope, he observed their natural hook-like shape. The hooks latched onto the soft loops in the wool fabric. The sticking bur made him think of his fastener problem. His application of the hook and loop structure of the cocklebur led him to develop a new type of fastener, called Velcro™, which has revolutionized the fastener business. This illustrates how analogies are used to solve problems.

While there are many ways to generate associations and analogies, this chapter considers three variations: words, pictures, and biotechniques. The next few pages describe these variations in more depth.

Random Words

To generate associations and analogies, a team can apply a random word to the problem at hand. The team examines the unique characteristics of the object, activity, or idea or problem conveyed by the word to see if they will help with the problem. What associations do they bring to mind? What connections and/or comparisons do they stimulate in the minds of the team members?

Pictures

The technique of using picture associations also helps teams to generate ideas and solutions for the problem at hand. Team members look at a picture, photograph, postcard, or other visual image, examine the components and composition of the image, and try to apply these elements to the problem under investigation.

The use of pictures or other visuals for drawing associations and analogies allows team members to replace insufficient or incomplete information in their imaginations with an image of a real object or place.

For example, if someone is trying to draw the face of his or her wristwatch without looking at it, it would be difficult to reproduce it exactly, even though the person probably looks at the watch several times every day. The image of an object in a person's mind is normally only a skeletal version of its real completeness. A photograph of the watch, however, will help a person to include more details in the drawing than if the person relied solely on the image in his or her mind. Because pictures usually present a sharper image than the mind can, Picture Association is often a more powerful tool than Word Association.[1]

Biotechniques

Using Biotechniques (also known as biomechanics or bionics) is another approach for generating analogies. Biotechniques apply the principles associated with some living thing, an animal or plant, for example, to the problem at hand. Team members examine the living thing to see how it moves, processes food, and performs other functions to see if reproducing that activity will help with the problem.

This technique makes use of the prodigious number of solutions nature has developed for all its beings—from the structure of an atom, the shape of crystals, the photosynthesis of plants, the social systems of ants, and the complexity of our brains. Nature, the unequaled master of creativity, can be a teacher in all fields, in individual or social behavior, health care, technology, or any other endeavor. Looking at "how nature solves it" can always produce ideas, especially when technical problems have to be solved.

Mobile robots, for example, were judged for a long time in Europe to be costly and unnecessary. This estimation changed rapidly with the catastrophe at the nuclear energy plant in Chernobyl. Startled by this accident, the European community funded a research program for the development of "walking machines," which could be brought into action in nuclear-contaminated areas.

As part of that effort, researchers at the Technical University in Munich are developing a mobile robot that is modeled after the body of a species of grasshoppers. Its six legs are of similar length, have only three joints, and can be moved separately. Furthermore, the grasshopper has a highly efficient system of sensors in its front legs to feel and to prod, which allow it to explore its environment without using its eyes. The researchers have studied these natural capabilities and can now apply the same biomechanics to the development of the robot.

---

1. The Picture Association technique is based on the work of William J. Gordon, who used the term "synectics" to describe his special methodical approach to creative problem solving. The word synectics derives from the Greek verb "synechein," which means to "bring together," or to "connect with each other." A synectical method is anything that includes a search for elements of knowledge or experience that are remote from, but later connected to the problem, in order to create ideas for solutions.

Another team of researchers using biotechniques is trying to understand the body shapes of Adelie penguins. These penguins have extraordinary hydrodynamics that are 10 times superior to modern cars and three times superior to submarines. These very streamlined penguins are being imitated and optimized with a computer program which, much like nature, improves the concepts from one generation to the next. The penguins' streamlined bodies are serving as the model for new jet and submarine designs.

Figure 5-1: Study of penguins as an example of biotechnical research

Definition of the Tool

Word-Picture Associations and Analogies expand idea generation through the use of random and seemingly unrelated pictures, words, and biotechnical information to stimulate thinking about new dimensions and solutions for the team's problem or challenge. By identifying the inner workings of objects, events, pictures, or animals and applying those principles to the problem, a team can access an almost unlimited supply of sources of inspiration to promote breakthrough thinking and new solutions.

Use of the Tool

One of the key operations of the creative mind is the ability to combine heretofore unrelated elements to yield new patterns or structures, representing the creative result. This operation in most cases involves the ability to take a problem and let the creative mind search through personal stores of experience and knowledge. The mind then feeds these new bits of information into a process of combining and pattern-forming, for the purpose of generating new solutions for the problem. This tool will help team members widen the range of resources available to them to feed a greater amount of material into the creative process.

A team should consider using this tool when there is a distinct need for breakthroughs or when the problem calls for going one step beyond the ordinary. When the idea flow is fading in a brainstorming session, the team leader or the facilitator can restart the flow by encouraging team members to search for analogies or associations to the problem or to explore fields where such analogies and associations can be found. To support this diversity of thinking "outside" the problem, the majority of team members should have a broad spectrum of experiences so that the associations and analogies that are triggered are also diverse.

Random associations and analogies, triggered by words, pictures and biotechniques, can be used in a team or by individual team members to generate ideas.

Overview of the Tool Process

The team defines the problem and gets initial ideas and solutions out on the table by using either Classic Brainstorming or Brainwriting 6-3-5. The team next decides if it wants to use words, pictures, or biotechniques, or some combination of these techniques. With the help of a facilitator, team members generate new ideas and solutions from associations and analogies that are triggered by random words, pictures, and biotechniques, which the team can then link back to solving the problem.

"I used to think that anyone doing anything weird was weird. I suddenly realized that anyone weird wasn't weird at all and that it was the people saying they were weird that were weird."

Paul McCartney

Chapter 5

Applying the Tool

Outline of Steps

Step	Activity
1.	Present, discuss, and define the problem. Use Classic Brainstorming or Brainwriting 6-3-5 to get initial ideas for solutions on paper.
2.	Determine which techniques to use: Word Associations and Analogies, Picture Associations, or Biotechniques.
3.	Choose one word, picture, or living thing at a time to stimulate team members' associations with it. Record these ideas or images on a flipchart.
4.	Take the ideas or images identified in Step 3 and apply them to the problem. Write down the ideas on a flipchart.
5.	Go back to Step 2, if desired.
6.	Combine the lists of ideas (from Steps 1 and 4) for possible solutions. Review the list to clarify ideas, then select the best ideas.

Step-by-Step Instructions

Step 1. Present, discuss, and define the problem. Use Classic Brainstorming or Brainwriting 6-3-5 to get initial ideas for solutions on paper.

The team leader determines who will work on the problem to ensure appropriate diversity of experiences, perspectives, and expertise on the team. The team first discusses and defines the problem, then generates initial ideas for solutions using Classic Brainstorming or Brainwriting 6-3-5.

Example

A team has been assembled to explore solutions to the problem "How can we bring new business downtown?" These are the initial ideas they brainstormed:

- lower crime
- increase affordable parking
- get urban renewal mega grant
- create tax incentives for businesses
- get community involvement
- provide better housing that's affordable
- put in enclosed malls
- get homeless people off the streets

Figure 5-2: Initial Ideas for Bringing New Business Downtown

Step 2. Determine which techniques to use: Word Associations and Analogies, Picture Associations, or Biotechniques.

Word Associations and Analogies: The facilitator needs to have available lists or collections of words that are completely independent from the problem. Possibilities for finding random words, in addition to the lists at the end of this chapter, include:

- Using the thesaurus, dictionary, newspaper, magazine, or book

- Opening up a mail-order catalogue at random

- Asking a colleague for a list of words

The choice of words to be explored should be random. To randomize the search in a dictionary or a catalogue, the team can select a page number and a location on the page. Then a team member opens the book, magazine, etc. to the correct page number and locates a word. Another alternative is to have a team member close his or her eyes and open the book, randomly select a page and point to a spot on the page, choosing the word that is under his or her finger.

The most effective category for words depends on the type of problem. For technical problems, usually design problems such as "how to design a new toaster," the random words must relate to material objects. Words that relate to buildings, animals, or pieces of furniture are all appropriate. What associations or comparisons would you make in response to questions like: How does the design of a new toaster relate to a barn? A lion? A couch?

If the problem that the team is examining concerns social issues, behavior, strategies or similar non-tangible challenges, then stimulating words should refer to events or activities in present society, like "marriage," "political election," "school," "Olympic Games," or themes out of history, fairy tales, or mythology. For example: How does implementing a change in the department's customer response procedure relate to a wedding? An election primary? The tale of Hansel and Gretel?

Picture Associations: The team will need a variety of different pictures or images. A randomly chosen set of pictures can be shown to the team, preferably with a slide or overhead projector and a screen. The facilitator randomly selects pictures or slides and projects them onto the screen. Pictures should be clear, portray a variety of situations and activities, and be different from the problem. Good sources for pictures include magazines, books on nature, travel, or industry. There are also many images now available by the thousands on compact disks. The facilitator should review the pictures beforehand to ensure they are upbeat and positive, and are likely to stimulate many types of associations.

Biotechniques: The team will need access to models, actual specimens, books or research material, and/or subject matter experts. In addition, if using Biotechniques, the team would first want to look at the actual problem and define what essential principles or processes are at work in the problem. While this task in a way diminishes the randomness of the activity, such a review, and any required preliminary research, will help in the next step.

Example
The team that is exploring solutions to "How can we bring new business downtown?" has decided to use pictures to generate ideas.

Step 3. Choose one word, picture, or living thing at a time to stimulate team members' associations with it. Record these ideas or images on a flipchart.

The facilitator helps team members make connections and comparisons with a word, picture, or living thing. The facilitator should instruct team members to think about the word, picture, animal, or object in terms of its fundamental structures, functions, or principles of operation, the images it brings up, or the meanings it might have for team members. A team member or the facilitator should record the team's comments on one side of a flipchart or white board. Some questions that the facilitator can ask to help team members make appropriate associations and comparisons are listed in the table below.

Technique	Some Questions to Ask
Word Associations and Analogies	What does the word mean? What images does it call forth? What connections or comparisons can be made? How is the object structured? How does it function? How is the object shaped? Any special or unique attributes? How is the object used? What effects does it have on people? Nature?
Picture Associations	In addition to the questions listed above: What is going on in the picture? Who is doing what? How? Where? When? Why?
Biotechniques	With what feelings or motivations? How does the living thing function? How does it breathe? Perform other daily functions? What special problems does it solve? What special or unique features does the thing possess? How does it use these features?

Figure 5-3: Questions that Prod Team Members to Make Associations and Comparisons

"You can't build a reputation on what you're going to do."

Henry Ford

An alternative approach is for team members to take more time by themselves to examine the pictures, words, or living things. They draw their own logical conclusions and take their own notes of all the ideas that were triggered. Three to five minutes may be taken for this step. Then team members share their ideas with each other to create a master list, which should be recorded on a flipchart or white board. Whether a facilitator decides to use this approach depends on the size of the group and the team's preferences.

Example

The team chose a photograph of two astronauts in space. These are some of the associations they made:

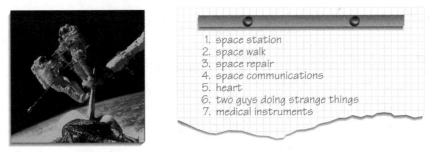

1. space station
2. space walk
3. space repair
4. space communications
5. heart
6. two guys doing strange things
7. medical instruments

Figure 5-4: Associations Stimulated by a Photograph of Astronauts in Space

Step 4. Take the ideas or images identified in Step 3 and apply them to the problem. Write down the ideas on a flipchart.

The team generates possible ideas for solving the problem by looking at the associations generated in Step 3 for a particular word, image, or picture. By examining the attributes or features of an association, the team tries to further develop connections, impressions, or thoughts to spin off ideas or solutions to the problem at hand. The recordkeeper lists these ideas in a second column on the flipchart or white board. When the team is done making connections back to the problem for the word, image, or picture, the facilitator moves the team on to the next trigger. This process continues until a sufficient number of ideas have been generated.

Example

The team looked at the associations (stimulated by the astronaut photograph) and applied them to the problem of how to bring new business downtown.

Associations	Application to the Problem
1. space station	• hi-tech center for businesses • hi-tech communications available
2. space walk	• build walking trails through downtown
3. space repair	• make sure the highways are in good repair
4. space communications	• hi-tech communications available • network new businesses with the old
5. heart	• develop heart and soul for the city
6. two guys doing strange things	• provide some new sources of entertainment
7. medical instruments	• do an "Organization Rx" • check to see what businesses in downtown area need

Figure 5-5: Associations from Astronaut Picture Applied to the Problem

Step 5. Go back to Step 2, if desired.

If the team is satisfied with the ideas generated in the initial round, move on to Step 6. If team members wish to explore additional techniques, they should return to Step 2.

Example

The team decided to examine another picture, one with two men canoeing down a stream. They generated the following associations:

1. peaceful and cool
2. danger
3. healthy
4. clean air
5. lack of caution
6. adventure
7. wet
8. took wrong turn

Photo: Courtesy of Old Town Canoes, Old Town, Maine.

Figure 5-6: Associations Stimulated by a Picture of People Canoeing Downstream

Next the team connected the associations back to the problem of how to bring new business downtown.

Associations	Application to the Problem
1. peaceful and cool	• provide more parks and places to relax
2. danger	• address the crime issues
3. healthy	• advertise the clean air and smoke-free policies • advertise the quality of the hospitals in the area
4. clean air	• advertise the clean air and smoke-free policies
5. lack of caution	• look at the risks new businesses might face in moving downtown • figure out how to help businesses manage the risks
6. adventure	• provide more fun places for families
7. wet	• advertise the proximity to water
8. took wrong turn	• provide maps of the downtown and surrounding areas

Figure 5-7: Associations from Canoeing Picture Applied to the Problem

> *Step 6. Combine the lists of ideas (from Steps 1 and 5) for possible solutions.*
> *Review the list to clarify ideas, then select the best ideas.*
>
> The team can use any of the idea selection tools discussed in Chapters 8–11. The team should also define the next action steps for proceeding toward problem solution.

Example

The team reviewed the ideas generated in Steps 1 and 5, combined them, and then decided to use Nominal Group Technique (Chapter 8) to select the best idea.

Summary of the Tool

This chapter has shown how randomly selected words, pictures, and biotechniques can expand the sources of input into the creative process. The world beyond the confines of the team's immediate environment is rich with ideas. Nature, life, history, and a wide variety of experiences and knowledge can be copied, imitated, or otherwise used to generate new, fascinating solutions.

Enhancing the Process

Helpful Hints

Make Use of Specialized Word Sources. For a random word search, there are several sources: dictionary, pre-established lists, such as those at the end of this chapter, catalogues, newspapers, magazines, or books. The facilitator should be sure the words selected are commonly understood.

When solving a technical problem, the team should confine a random word search to material objects. Catalogues are often better sources for such material objects than a dictionary. For behavioral or strategic problems, on the other hand, the team should choose events, organizations, and institutions.

If the team is using a randomized process, such as a number or set of numbers to select the word to be used to generate ideas, the team will need to agree on how it will deal with a randomized process that cannot discriminate between words that are objects, places, people, or events. For example, if the

"One of the virtues of being very young is that you don't let the facts get in the way of your imagination."

Sam Levenson

team is looking for random objects, should the team agree to choose the next numbered word that is an object or agree on a different method?

Use a Wide Variety of Uplifting Pictures. If the team will be using Picture Associations often, the facilitator should have available a large collection of pictures or slides that include a variety of motifs. These pictures should be positive, even inspirational. They should not embarrass people or make them feel uncomfortable. The message of the picture should be clear and simple. These pictures should also have more than one object in them and be different from the problem at hand. Color photographs seem to be more stimulating than black and white.

Seek Expert Knowledge to Benefit from Biotechniques. When using biotechniques to generate associations and analogies, a team may need some additional knowledge to ensure this approach is successful. Unfortunately, many people have an understanding of nature that they acquired in grade school or high school, and their knowledge has faded considerably. A person may know that a hedgehog defends itself with spines and the skunk with an awful smell. A person may know that snails draw themselves back into their shells, that bats have a sort of a radar-orientation system, and that rattlesnakes have a deadly poison. Yet, most people don't have much in-depth knowledge about exactly how the tentacles of jellyfish are built, or why a woodpecker can hit a branch with such force without blacking out.

If the team wants to further explore the associations and analogies provided by nature, this knowledge is indispensable. One way for the team to learn about biotechniques is to invite a biologist to the creativity tool session. A biologist will be able to contribute interesting facts that will stimulate the team's thinking in exploring how nature solves problems. Another way to learn about biotechniques is to gather information from books, videos, or the Internet.

Do Your Own Research to Benefit from Biotechniques. A team can usually only make superficial use of the associations and analogies created with biotechniques, unless team members have an extensive knowledge of biotechniques in the natural world. A biotechnical or biomechanical textbook with pictures or other pertinent material can help support the team's ability to generate new ideas. Another alternative, if certain analogies or associations seem interesting, is to have the team dig up some information by visiting a museum or library, or logging on to the Internet. The development of ideas and solutions may often require doing some thorough research, which can be a prerequisite for the team's success.

Practice Patience. With all of these techniques, team members should not expect to generate ideas for each trigger (random word, picture, or living thing). It may be that the team tries several combinations without success. Team members should not get discouraged because their patience will be rewarded, several creative minds working together are capable of generating many thoughtful combinations and transformations after a short period of time. If only one out of 20 trials produces an idea for the problem, the process is still very powerful. Team members will notice that their rate of "hits" will increase with practice because creative thinking expands with use.

Frequently Asked Questions

Q. Are there any special guidelines for pictures?

A. Yes, the team should have a wide variety of pictures. The pictures should be positive and uplifting, and should not make people uncomfortable or embarrassed (pictures of war, poverty, or nudity for example). If advertisements will be used, be sure the message is clear and doesn't include specific advertising symbols. Cartoons are not a good idea because, like abstract pictures, they are already intended to be symbolic. There's already a "message" there that the team will have to "fight through." Specific guidelines are listed below.

1. The people or children in the pictures should be doing something significant and interesting. They should be captured in some identifiable activity so that the viewer can tell what they are doing. Photographs of people sitting or standing do not necessarily bring forth associations but pictures of people doing something interesting will.

2. Events are great sources of new ideas. Pictures of events, such as a parade, a wedding, a graduation, are terrific.

3. Pictures of places and buildings can also be good sources of ideas. A carnival site, a cathedral, or a picture of a local hardware store are good examples.

4. Pictures of insects or animals, (e.g., bees swarming, termites building nests, birds feeding their young), can be helpful.

5. Pictures of nature need to be detailed, identifiable, and interesting. A picture of an interesting tree might work, or a child picking a flower, or a bee buzzing around a flower.

6. Pictures of operating machines need to be identifiable, with a commonly understood purpose and involving some commonly understood activity. Examples are a lawnmower, a sewing machine, a buzz saw, an electric drill.

7. One guiding principle—when there are questions about the appropriateness of a picture—is that the picture should quickly evoke many different associations. Does the picture make a person stop and ponder what is going on and does it bring forth a number of memories, associations, or questions?

Q. What if the word, picture, or biotechnique doesn't trigger an association or analogy immediately?

A. Not all words, pictures, or biotechniques will help generate ideas for a problem. The team needs to try to find a connection before discarding the trigger (random word, picture, or biotechnique) too quickly. At the same time, the purpose of Word-Picture Associations and Analogies is to be quick and generative. Therefore, if after a short period of time no ideas have been generated, the team should try another trigger. Team members should go through the pile of pictures or the list of words, and play with elements that interest them.

Q. Does there have to be action in the picture?

A. Shapes, textures, actions, and colors will all work well. All the pictures need to be in focus and fairly simple in composition. The facilitator or team leader should keep in mind that abstract pictures are already symbols. Literal pictures seem to create more possibilities for original interpretations.

Additional Examples of Tool Usage

Situation: A team has been formed to address ways to improve company-wide communications. To begin addressing this issue, the team used Brainwriting 6-3-5 to get initial ideas out on the table. Team members were not entirely satisfied with the results, however, and agreed that, to really stretch their thinking for generating really different ideas, they would use Word-Picture Associations and Analogies.

As a first step, the team agreed on the problem definition, "How can we improve communications between departments in the organization?" Then team members discussed whether they would use words, pictures, or objects in nature, and after five minutes, decided the best method would be biotechniques. The team chose a picture of a tree to use as a trigger for new ideas. Some of the ideas are shown in Figure 5-8.

What is Happening to the Tree?	Application to the Problem
tree is growing	• need continued training to improve communication
tree is budding	• encourage new ideas • take all suggestions seriously • listen to all ideas
striving to be bigger	• refreshments at meetings will make us as all "bigger" • provide all employees with access to product information • takes a bigger person to encourage and foster communication
providing a home	• agree on one standard means of communication, e.g., e-mail, voice mail
absorbing the sun	• give positive reinforcement to people who make an effort to improve their work communications with other

Figure 5-8: Associations from Tree Picture Applied to the Problem of How to Improve Communications in the Company

The team shared these ideas at an organizational meeting. As a result of the discussion that ensued, the president of the company agreed to support more training for employees. The team also decided to hold more frequent team meetings to foster internal communications and ensure that they were all pursuing activities that fit in with their goals.

"The significant problems we face cannot be solved by the same level of thinking which created them."

Albert Einstein

Situation: In a training session on the use of this tool, participants were given the following information: *XYZ Company has decided to locate its new facility in the Tennessee Valley. The new facility will employ approximately 750 people, with about 200 people coming in from other locations across the country. Part of the negotiations in getting XYZ to relocate its new facility to the Tennessee Valley was the offer to help the 200 employees and their families reduce the stress of relocating to a new community.*

The training participants were asked to look at methods of reducing the stress of moving and welcoming these newcomers to the area. The training participants, who were now a team, defined the goal as, "How can we reduce the stress of relocating for these employees and their families?"

Team members brainstormed several ideas, but they weren't satisfied that they had really explored all the innovative approaches that could be used. They decided to use a list of random words to help them come up with more innovative ideas. The team chose a list of words that referred to events and themes out of history, fairy tales, and mythology. The team randomly selected the term "jury duty," then generated ideas and applied them back to the goal of reducing employees' stress. Some of these ideas and their applications to the problem are shown in Figure 5-9.

Term: Jury duty	Application to the Problem
sequestered	• give employees time to prepare for the move
involves time away from work	• provide house hunting services
formality	• keep it simple, casual • have someone handle the closing for the employee; get a power of attorney
public duty	• screen schools, malls, parks
something to avoid	• arrange utilities, letters of reference, video snippets of area
scary	• have a welcoming party for the children
evokes self-analysis, questioning	• provide therapists
imprisonment/ freedom	• offer to have professional movers pack and move emplo...

Figure 5-9: Associations with the Term "Jury Duty" Applied to the Goal of Reducing the
Stress of Moving to a New Community

A team working on this goal could use many of these ideas to provide a much more caring transition for families moving into the area. Having someone else handle the closing on a new home, arranging for all the utilities to be turned on, and having a welcoming party for the children are all ideas that could fairly easily be implemented and that could have a great impact on whether the move is a smooth one, or one loaded with disaster.

Random Word List for Non-Technical Problems

This list includes actions and events only; no objects. The reason is that actions and events tend to trigger many, many connections and a wide range of solutions. This is ideal for solving non-technical problems. One option for randomly choosing words from the list is to ask a team member to look at a wristwatch or stopwatch and call out the number that he or she sees in the digital display. Also, a team member can use the second hand of a watch or clock to randomly choose a number.

1. presidential election	16. speeding	31. beauty contest	46. first day at school
2. olympic games	17. World Series	32. evening news	47. sending a valentine
3. high school graduation	18. poker game	33. baking cookies	48. Halloween
4. senior prom	19. April 15 (taxes due)	34. camping	49. rollercoaster ride
5. spelling bee	20. aerobics	35. New Year's Eve	50. meeting future in-laws
6. getting a driver's license	21. Thanksgiving	36. losing weight	51. moving day
7. Watergate	22. Boston marathon	37. wine tasting	52. eating lobster
8. wedding	23. bingo	38. jumping rope	53. first day of spring
9. tennis match	24. finger painting	39. karaoke singing	54. snow storms
10. bootcamp	25. fishing	40. solar eclipse	55. high tide
11. family vacation	26. house painting	41. corporate retreat	56. end-of-season sales
12. state fairs	27. jury duty	42. conference call	57. garage sales
13. Earth Day	28. debates	43. car buying	58. spring cleaning
14. Fourth of July	29. Christmas	44. going to the zoo	59. wall papering
15. dental exam	30. barbecue	45. learning to swim	60. birthdays

Figure 5-10: Random Word List—Actions and Events Only

Random Word List for Technical Problems

This list includes objects only; no actions and events. The reason is that actions and events tend to trigger too many connections that can lead a team to stray off target. Objects, however, provide a focus that a technical problem needs. One option for randomly choosing words from the list is to ask a team member to look at a wristwatch or stopwatch and call out the number that he or she sees in the digital display. Also, a team member can use the second hand of a watch or clock to randomly choose a number.

1. toothbrush	16. lightbulb	31. eye	46. watch
2. wine	17. rabbit	32. dragon	47. unicorn
3. elephant	18. soap	33. cheese	48. tailor
4. baseball bat	19. violin	34. bayonet	49. silver
5. bird	20. diamond	35. moose	50. sombrero
6. book	21. clothes hanger	36. motorcycle	51. river
7. cup	22. butter	37. pickle	52. pretzel
8. pipe	23. monk	38. hammer	53. orange
9. whale	24. rainbow	39. barrel	54. mirror
10. seashell	25. sand	40. garlic	55. letter
11. rose	26. steam	41. oasis	56. flea
12. window	27. leaf	42. mayonnaise	57. umbrella
13. fork	28. helicopter	43. bubble gum	58. dice
14. bell	29. giraffe	44. toga	59. ant
15. chair	30. fountain	45. frog	60. coffee

Figure 5-11: Random Word List—Objects Only

"One clear idea is too precious a treasure to lose."

Caroline Gilman

Chapter 5

"All worthwhile men have good thoughts, good ideas and good intentions
—but precious few of them ever translate those into action."

John Hancock Field

TILMAG

Introduction

Word-Picture Associations and Analogies described in the previous chapter are useful in generating a large number of ideas for many problems. For the really tough and stubborn problems, those for which there is a scarcity of solution ideas, the structured TILMAG approach is the most helpful.

TILMAG is an acronym for the German words that, loosely translated, mean "the transformation of ideal solution elements in an association matrix." This technique, developed by Dr. Helmut Schlicksupp during the 1970s, is a systematic and structured approach for generating ideas. Team members first define the characteristics or elements of an ideal solution to the problem or challenge. Then they use the associations that were generated by a matrix of the ideal solution elements to identify objects and events that share the same characteristics as the solution to the problem. Team members are more likely to produce good ideas with TILMAG than by choosing objects or events at random. The guiding principle is rather simple and convincing: the team uses two ideal solution elements at a time as "launching platforms" for identifying analogous objects and events and then come up with new ideas to solve the problem or challenge.

Definition of the Tool

Through its structured and systematic approach, TILMAG helps a team to define ideal solutions for the problem at hand, create and explore associations based on paired combinations of ideal solution elements, and use these associations to inspire unusual and breakthrough ideas to solve the problem.

"We have a hunger of the mind which asks for knowledge of all around us, and the more we gain, the more is our desire; the more we see, the more are we capable of seeing."

Maria Mitchell

Chapter 6

Use of the Tool

The TILMAG tool helps teams discover material to add to the creative process that is outside the experts' fields of experience. TILMAG can steer team members to infrequently accessed regions of their individual and collective knowledge, where they can find breakthrough ideas and solutions to a given problem or opportunity. The tool uses an approach that is best described as "guided association." Through this guided association, TILMAG can provide very stimulating triggers, which can then lead to optimal solutions. TILMAG is extremely useful when a team wants to bring in rich, creative material from many different sources.

Overview of the Tool Process

As a team uses TILMAG, it will go through three "phases." In the first phase, the team discusses the problem to make sure everyone understands the problem correctly, and then defines the required elements of a successful solution. In the second phase, the team constructs a matrix with these critical elements. The matrix provides the structure for the team to identify associations from pairs of solution characteristics. In the last phase, the team uses the associations generated by the matrix to create solutions to the real problem.

Applying the Tool

Outline of Steps

Step	Activity
1.	Present, discuss and define the problem. Use Classic Brainstorming or Brainwriting 6-3-5 to generate ideas.
2.	Define Ideal Solution Elements (ISEs).
3.	Construct a TILMAG matrix with the ISEs.
4.	Make associations for the paired ISEs and write them in the cells of the matrix. Move randomly from cell to cell until each cell has at least one association.
5.	One at a time, choose an association from the TILMAG matrix, identify its features, generate ideas for solutions based on these features, and apply the ideas back to the problem.
6.	Combine the ideas brainstormed for solutions (from Step 1) with the ideas generated using TILMAG (Step 5).

Step-by-Step Instructions

Step 1. Present, discuss, and define the problem. Use Classic Brainstorming or Brainwriting 6-3-5 to generate ideas.

A team first needs to discuss and define the problem. With some problems, particularly complex ones, the team should consider using the Heuristic Redefinition tool so it can better analyze the various approaches, and then select the most promising one.

The team generates possible solutions to the problem using Classic Brainstorming or Brainwriting 6-3-5. The brainstorming should continue until at least the first dead point; all the "easy" and spontaneous ideas will surface in this time.

Example

A team in a dentist's office is trying to come up with innovative solutions to the problem "How can we reduce the fear that children have about coming to the dentist's office?" Some of the team's ideas are listed below.

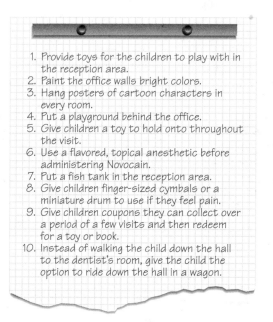

1. Provide toys for the children to play with in the reception area.
2. Paint the office walls bright colors.
3. Hang posters of cartoon characters in every room.
4. Put a playground behind the office.
5. Give children a toy to hold onto throughout the visit.
6. Use a flavored, topical anesthetic before administering Novocain.
7. Put a fish tank in the reception area.
8. Give children finger-sized cymbals or a miniature drum to use if they feel pain.
9. Give children coupons they can collect over a period of a few visits and then redeem for a toy or book.
10. Instead of walking the child down the hall to the dentist's room, give the child the option to ride down the hall in a wagon.

Figure 6-1: Initial Ideas for Reducing Children's Fear of the Dentist

The Idea Edge

Step 2. Define Ideal Solution Elements (ISEs).

The team generates ideas for the elements it thinks would make up an ideal solution to the problem or challenge. ISEs are the functions, attributes, qualities, or properties that any potential solution *must have*. TILMAG requires that the ISEs are formulated as concisely as possible. To find and define the ISEs, the team may first produce a draft list of proposed elements. When the final ISEs are chosen from that list, the team must make sure that:

- The ISE is specific for the given problem. An ISE must not be stated in general or generic terms. Examples of general functions or qualities of solutions would be "reliable," "recyclable," or "cheap." For TILMAG to work properly, the team needs to identify specific characteristics of the solution.

- The ISE is described in a positive way. The description must focus on what is to be included, not what must be excluded. For example, "environmentally safe" is a proper definition, while "non-toxic" is not.

- The ISE is clear and free of jargon. For example, "Be environmentally safe" is preferable to "Be green."

- The ISE is brief (six words or less), but precise. For example, "small" is not precise but "densely packed" is. If an ISE is more than six words, this could mean the team has not yet determined the ideal solution element.

- The number is limited to no more than six ideal solution elements.

- In the case of new product development, the ISEs are, as much as possible, tied to customer demands.[1]

The team then checks the possible ISEs against these criteria and selects the best ones. Then the team defines the abbreviated version of each ISE.

"If one cares about ideas, one wants to gather them from every available source and test them in every way possible."
Mary I. Bunting

Chapter 6

---

1. Customer demands are discussed in Chapters 2 and 3 of *Better Designs in Half the Time*, Bob King (Methuen, MA: GOAL/QPC, 1987).

Example

The team at the dentist's office selects the following ideal solution elements, or ISEs, that any potential solution must have:

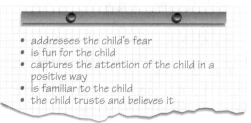

- addresses the child's fear
- is fun for the child
- captures the attention of the child in a positive way
- is familiar to the child
- the child trusts and believes it

Figure 6-2: Ideal Solution Elements for Reducing Children's Fear of the Dentist

The shorthand ISEs are:

- addresses fear
- is fun
- captures attention
- is familiar
- is believable

Figure 6-3: Ideal Solution Elements in Shorthand

If the team has taken more than an hour to get to this point, team members may need to take a break.

Step 3. Construct a TILMAG matrix with the ISEs.

To generate rich, new ideas, the team constructs a TILMAG matrix to aid in the systematic listing and paired comparison of all possible combinations of the ISEs. The matrix will have a header row and a header column, and then additional rows and columns equal in number to one less than the number of ISEs. For example, if 5 ISEs are defined, there will be 4 rows and 4 columns in addition to the header column and row.

All the ISEs are listed across the top of the matrix, except for the last one. The same ISEs are also listed down the side of the matrix, except they are listed in reverse order from the ISEs listed across the top of the matrix, and the first ISE is omitted. This arrangement puts duplicate ISE pairs into the lower right-hand corner.

Using the example of 5 ISEs, ISE 1 through 4 would be listed in that order across the top of the matrix, and ISE 5 through 2 would be listed in that order down the side. A generic example is shown in Figure 6-4.

	ISE 1	ISE 2	ISE 3	ISE 4
ISE 5				
ISE 4				
ISE 3				
ISE 2				

Figure 6-4: Generic Form for a TILMAG Matrix

The team then crosses out the cells in the matrix where there is a combination of one ISE with itself, e.g., the pairing of ISE 2 down and ISE 2 across, AND where there is a repeat pairing of two ISEs, e.g., the pairing of ISE 2 down and ISE 3 across is repeated in the pairing ISE 3 down and

ISE 2 across. The resulting matrix should have the lower right-hand corner cells crossed out or blocked out. See Figure 6-5.

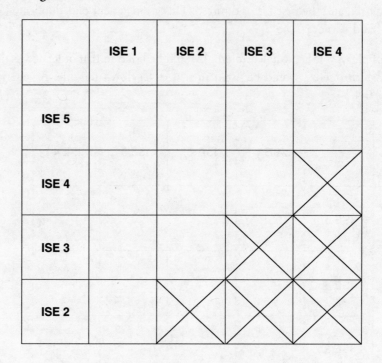

Figure 6-5: Generic Form for a TILMAG Matrix—Invalid Pairings of ISEs Crossed Out

Chapter 6

Example

The dentist office team began constructing a TILMAG matrix for their problem using the five ISEs from Step 2.

	ISE 1 Addresses Fear	ISE 2 Is Fun	ISE 3 Captures Attention	ISE 4 Is Familiar
ISE 5 Is Believable				
ISE 4 Is Familiar				
ISE 3 Captures Attention				
ISE 2 Is Fun				

Figure 6-6: Blank TILMAG Matrix for Reducing Children's Fear of the Dentist

Step 4. Make associations for the paired ISEs and write them in the cells of the matrix. Move randomly from cell to cell until each cell has at least one association.

In this step, the facilitator asks the team for cell-by-cell associations from the paired combination of any two ISEs. Associations can be people, animals, objects, places, events, or activities. The ideas are written in the cells of the matrix. There should be at least one association per cell, if possible. Not every combination will always trigger an association, but it's quite rare when an association is not triggered.

"Human history is, in essence, a history of ideas."

H. G. Wells

This process is continued until all the cells in the matrix have been filled or until the allotted time has been met. If team members are tired, this is a good time to take a break.

Example

The team generated several associations from the different combinations of ISEs. The completed matrix is shown in Figure 6-7.

	ISE 1 Addresses Fear	ISE 2 Is Fun	ISE 3 Captures Attention	ISE 4 Is Familiar
ISE 5 Is Believable	– therapist – fireman	– photograph – Mr. Rogers – cartoon characters	– police officer – clock	– Volkswagen – money – tooth fairy
ISE 4 Is Familiar	– home – cartoon characters	– toys – ice cream	– story books – sunset – thunderstorm	
ISE 3 Captures Attention	– nursery rhymes – highway signs	– funhouse mirrors – parades		
ISE 2 Is Fun	– petting zoo – outdoor adventure program			

Figure 6-7: Completed TILMAG Matrix for Reducing Children's Fear of the Dentist

Step 5. One at a time, choose an association from a cell in the TILMAG matrix, identify its features, generate ideas for solutions based on these features, and apply the ideas back to the problem.

The proposed associations now serve as stimulating triggers for further idea generation on the actual problem. The associations should represent concrete objects that possess functions and properties that are well-suited for producing practical solutions.

The team then takes the first association as a trigger to stimulate ideas that connect the association back to the problem. The recordkeeper carefully records all ideas, using the following format on a flipchart:

Association	Principle or Feature	Connection

Figure 6-8: Format for Recording Ideas

In making connections back to the problem, the team should focus on asking why the combination of the two ISEs resulted in the association. What principle or feature was behind the association? The team develops possible solutions in much the same way as with Word-Picture Associations and Analogies. The difference here is that the team is working with guided associations that are triggered by the combination of two ISEs. The process is thus less random than with the other idea generation tools.

Example

In the dentist office example, the team spent time connecting the associations to the problem. For example, the team chose "petting zoo," and explored the principles behind this concept. What is it about a petting zoo that is "fun" and "addresses fear"? In a petting zoo, children get a chance, in a very safe environment, to touch and pet animals that they might have feared otherwise. The animals are usually babies and are therefore smaller than those that children fear. A petting zoo is a fun environment where fear has been reduced or eliminated.

Then the team analyzed how it could apply the petting zoo principle to the problem: In the dentist's office, children could play with child-size, toy dental equipment and chairs. The dental chair could be brightly colored and the toy dental equipment could be soft and fun to touch. The point is, everything could be smaller and touchable. This is analogous to the "petting zoo," where the baby animals are smaller and can be petted without fear.

Choosing another cell, the team explored the principles behind "cartoon characters." What is it about cartoon characters that is "familiar" and "addresses fear"? The cartoon characters at theme parks are larger than life. Why aren't children afraid of them? As a matter of fact, children usually run up and hug them. They already know these larger-than-life cartoon characters. As large as they are, they are still perceived by small children as familiar, warm, and friendly.

In applying the cartoon principle back to the problem, the team suggested that the dentist, office receptionist, dental hygienist and other staff could be in "character." They could be dressed in costumes that are warm, friendly, and familiar to small children. See Figure 6-9.

Association	Principle or Feature	Connection
petting zoo	– safe environment – smaller sizes	– brightly colored dental chair – toy dental equipment
cartoon characters	– familiar – warm – friendly	– dress up in costumes

Figure 6-9: Associations Applied Back to the Problem of Reducing Children's Fear of the Dentist

Step 6. Combine the ideas brainstormed for solutions (from Step 1) with the ideas generated using TILMAG (Step 5).

The team combines the possible alternative solutions generated by brainstorming with those generated by using TILMAG to produce one complete list. The team reviews the ideas on the list for any points that team members need to clarify or want to eliminate. The team can use any of the idea selection tools discussed in Chapters 8–11 to select the best ideas from the list. The team also defines the next action steps for proceeding toward problem solution.

Example

The team decided to combine the ideas from Steps 1 and 5 to create a single list. As a next step, they used the Affinity Diagram and Interrelationship Digraph to narrow down the number of ideas.

Summary of the Tool

The TILMAG tool offers teams a structured method to tap the unexplored knowledge of their members. In principle, the development of ideas is done in the same way as with word and picture associations. The

"Creativity comes from trust. Trust your instincts. And never hope more than you work."

Rita Mae Brown

Chapter 6

difference here is that a team does not consider just any function or structure, but *only* those that were triggered by the combination of two ISEs. Through guided associations between paired ideal solution elements, this tool triggers ideas from team members and from others who are involved in the idea generation process. It is in these unexplored regions of knowledge where the team can find breakthrough ideas and solutions to a problem.

Enhancing the Process

Helpful Hints

Keep ISE Definitions Conceptual. In using TILMAG, the most critical step is the correct definition of the Ideal Solution Elements (ISEs). Mistakes at that step can lead a team in completely wrong directions. Experience has shown that team members may tend to confuse ISEs with features of ideas that they already have in mind. For example, in the problem of how to reduce a child's fear of going to the dentist's office, team members might propose "must provide toys in the office," as a concrete possibility to meet the objective instead of the more conceptual "must address the child's fear," which is the correct ideal solution element. The more specific definition is too solution-oriented and will limit the possibilities to be explored.

Freely Explore Associations and Avoid Quick Solutions. Sometimes team members become impatient if they can't immediately shape an association into a suitable idea for a solution to the problem. As a result, they jump from one association to the other, picking up on some easily suggested ideas. They don't take the time to really play with the associations—to create variations of an idea or to shape, restructure, or combine ideas. This impatience can restrict team members to making associations that lead to solutions that already exist.

The team should be reminded that impatience will undermine the effectiveness of this tool. When they are completing the TILMAG matrix, team members need to keep their minds open, and let their thoughts roam to come up with possible associations. For example, in Figure 6-9, the association of cartoon characters may lead to the quick idea of dressing up in costumes. However, some consideration of how cartoon characters create "magic" may lead to a much richer consideration of the whole environment of the dentist's office.

Do Advance Work to Shorten Team Sessions: Three Different Approaches. *The first approach* to saving time in the team session is to ask team members, or others who are familiar with and knowledgeable in the problem, to prepare the ISEs in advance. This preparatory work is a good idea because properly-defined ISEs are the most critical step in using this tool. Team members who are new to the TILMAG process can easily get frustrated with the process. A shorter session may help prevent this frustration.

The second approach to saving time is to circulate a TILMAG matrix with the ISEs already completed by those knowledgeable in the problem. Other team members, who know less about the problem, can be asked to complete the TILMAG matrix before the problem-solving session. The associations that team members make can be more free flowing without a context. This activity can be done in a separate meeting, or online. The TILMAG session would then consist of three steps:

1. Presenting, discussing, and defining the problem

2. Spontaneous ideas (Brainstorming or Brainwriting 6-3-5)

3. Linking the attributes or features of the associations (or the associations themselves) that were produced before the session, back to the problem.

The third approach is to have the three different phases of the process completed by separate teams or subsets of team members. This approach allows a team to be more flexible with time constraints and the special skills of team members who need to be involved. The approach can also help in maximizing the variety of ideas from the individuals who are contributing. With this alternative, individuals who are well acquainted and knowledgeable in the problem generate the ISEs, while a second team works on generating associations from the ISEs, and a third team links the associations back to the problem.

A variation on the approach described above, which would incorporate remote teams linked by e-mail, is to have the ISEs completed by a team that meets face to face to define the ISEs. Then the matrix can be put on an Internet/Intranet bulletin board, allowing individuals who work in different geographic locations to generate associations. Another team, most likely one that meets face to face, would link the associations to the problem.

Frequently Asked Questions

Q. How large can the team be?

A. The size of the team working on a TILMAG exercise can vary depending upon the phase of the exercise. A smaller team, e.g., three or four people, can be involved in generating the ISEs. A larger team can take the ideas, construct a TILMAG matrix, and generate associations. A smaller team can then focus on linking the associations back to the problem.

Q. How much time should be allocated to a session using TILMAG?

A. If the team has already been trained and is familiar with the tool, then 2–4 hours is a good amount of time to work with the problem. The complexity of the problem might also have an impact on the amount of time allocated to the session.

If the team requires training in the tool, the facilitator should plan on an additional 45–60 minutes for instruction and practice time.

Q. What are some ways to help guide the team in defining the appropriate ISEs?

A. To create and/or validate the ISEs for a problem, the team can review specific customer demands established through customer studies, the results of the use of other tools such as the Tree or Affinity Diagrams, or best-in-class qualities of similar products and services.

Additional Examples of Tool Usage

Situation: A team has been assigned the challenge of figuring out how to get workers to accept reduced office space. They decide to use the TILMAG tool because this is a particularly thorny problem that requires a lot of focus. They define the Ideal Solutions Elements as:

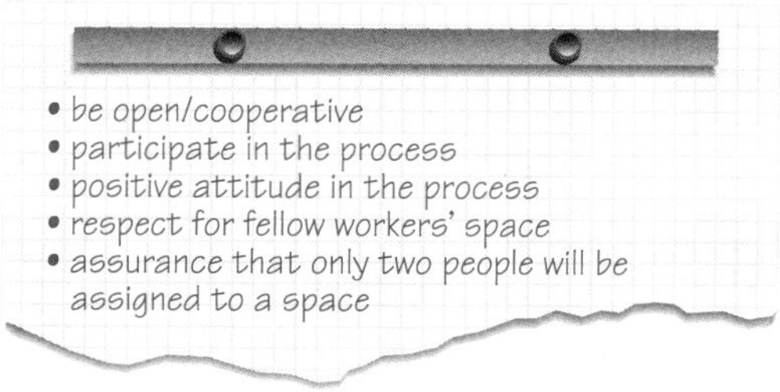

- be open/cooperative
- participate in the process
- positive attitude in the process
- respect for fellow workers' space
- assurance that only two people will be assigned to a space

Figure 6-10: Ideal Solution Elements of Getting Workers to Accept Reduced Office Space

The TILMAG matrix that the team developed and the associations that were generated are shown in Figure 6-11.

"There is a time when what you're creating and the environment you're creating it in come together."

Grace Hartigan

Chapter 6

	ISE 1 Be open	ISE 2 Participate	ISE 3 Positive Attitude	ISE 4 Respect for Space

ISE 5
Two People
Max
Per Space
	– college dorm
	– summer
	  camp
	– compromise
		– marriage
		– dating
			– parents
			– police
			  partners
				– beavers
				– jail

ISE 4
Respect for
Space
	– park ranger
	– museum
	  guide
		–team members
		–championship
		  baseball team
		– team
		  teaching
			– coaches
			– parent and
			  child	

ISE 3
Positive
Attitude
	– public
	  figure
	– teachers
		– ants
		– animal
		  kingdom/
		  herds		

ISE 2 Participate	– this group – children's honesty			

Figure 6-11: Completed TILMAG Matrix for Getting Workers to Accept Reduced Office Space

As a result of creating the TILMAG matrix, the team came up with some ideas that could be applied back to the problem, as shown in Figure 6-12.

Association	Principle or Feature	Connection
summer camp (1st day)	– orientation, unpack and set up cabin or tent together	– "getting to know you" ice breaker meetings between people sharing office space
marriage	– love is a decision for "better or for worse"	– trust in the commitment and relationship
counselor	– helps the patient stand back and look at what is happening	– taking care of those who are having adjustment problems
animal kingdom/herds	– animals know and respect safe space	– not being "piggish" in establishing turf
parent and child	– love leads to caring, acceptance, honest feedback	– open communication means no retribution for problems, non-threatening work environment
championship baseball team	– everyone plays a specific position on the team, but all the players help each other out with yells and signals	– clear roles, everyone knows personal responsibility to team
coaches	– teach game and continually reinforce appropriate behavior	– coach provides guidance and encouragement when needed

Figure 6-12: Associations Applied Back to the Problem of Getting Workers to Accept Reduced Office Space

The team found several of the ideas interesting enough to explore further. In preparing a report for management, the team proposed recommendations for carrying out three of the ideas generated with TILMAG: 1) set up "ice-breakers," 2) take care of the people who were having adjustment problems, and 3) get coaches to provide guidance and encouragement to those who need it.

Situation: A team at the Federal Quality Consulting Group was trying to figure out how to get their current and future clients to see them as a required or "got to have" resource. The team decided to use the TILMAG tool because they had exhausted the ideas that were generated by the other creativity tools. They developed a list of possible Ideal Solution Elements, as shown in Figure 6-13.

Figure 6-13: Possible Ideal Solution Elements for Making FQCG the #1 Source for Clients

The team reviewed the list and decided that only five ISEs were critical. These are shown in Figure 6-14.

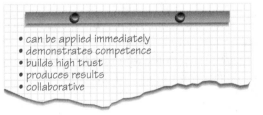

Figure 6-14: Critical Ideal Solution Elements for Making FQCG the #1 Source for Clients

The TILMAG matrix that the team developed and the associations that were generated are shown in Figure 6-15.

	ISE 1 Can Be Applied Immediately	ISE 2 Demonstrates Competence	ISE 3 Produces Results	ISE 4 Builds High Trust
ISE 5 Collaborative	– pot luck dinner – barn raising	– America Cup – team sport – bank – parents raising a child	– championship – child – military campaign – search and rescue	– church activities – counseling & therapy – sky diving – water skiing
ISE 4 Builds High Trust	– visit doctor – counseling – rescue operation	– surgery – trapeze – mountain climbing – acrobats – tightrope	– blood drive – visit to the doctor – good nanny – coaching – auto repair	
ISE 3 Produces Results	– laxative – mow lawn – video game	– acupuncture – hair cut – teaching – appraisal		
ISE 2 Demonstrates Competence	– play a sport – dance ballet – play musical instrument – write a book			

Figure 6-15: Completed TILMAG Matrix for Making FQCG the #1 Source for Clients

As a result of creating the TILMAG matrix, the team came up with some ideas that could be applied back to the problem, a few of which are shown in Figure 6-16.

"It is the mark of a good action that it appears inevitable in retrospect."

Robert Louis Stevenson

Association	Principle or Feature	Connection
search and rescue	– objective is short term – stakes are high – need to train rescuers fast – need highly skilled leaders – need to assess situation	– use the diagnosis to quickly solve the problem – develop a powerful diagnosis tool for evaluating the problem and getting stakeholders to change – use several different tools to assess and solve the challenge
acupuncture	– training must be precise – must have understanding of circumstances – global interrelationship of systems – can provide immediate relief from pain	– develop a systems-wide view of the problem – find critical points that will relieve the pain and then focus in on them
parents raising a child	– deep commitment – good communication needed – provide guidance and expertise	– provide guidance and experience, not dependence
barn raising	– have equipment and materials ready – many people are needed – everyone has a role – comes together fast – fun and spirited	– have a detailed plan that can be adapted to fit any assignment so that the team can be highly responsive – develop a winning and fun team spirit

Figure 6-16: Associations Applied Back to the Goal of Making FQCG the #1 Source for Clients

This example is based on work contributed by Tina Sung, Federal Quality Consulting Group.

Chapter 6

Morphological Box

Introduction

Although the word "morphology" is not a common household term, it has been around for a couple of centuries. Johann Wolfgang von Goethe used the term in reference to his study of plants and animals in the late 1700s. He used morphology to map the essential structure and formation of things material and immaterial. To sum this up, what this morphology describes are the essential features of each plant and animal species and where they fit in the evolution of living things.

When morphology is applied to creativity, morphology helps people look at the fundamental structure of a problem in such a way as to identify the full spectrum of possible solutions. It is a structured method for systematically looking at each *key characteristic* or *parameter* of a solution and the realistic *options* for each parameter. The structure of morphology places it in stark contrast to creativity tools such as brainstorming and random associations, which are free-wheeling, spontaneous ways to stimulate people's ideas.

Because of the structure of morphology, some may ask "Where is the creativity?" or "Are morphological boxes really so creative?" The answer rests in one of the most basic definitions of creativity, i.e., creativity is the bringing together of two previously unrelated items in a productive and useful way. The Morphological Box, through the use of a table, provides the team with a systematic method for choosing one or more options for each parameter and combining the options to produce different alternative scenarios, designs, or strategies.

The creative power of morphology can be demonstrated in a simple exercise. In a simple 10 x 10 Morphological Box, there are 10 parameters of the problem down the left side and 10 options across each row. The total number of combinations of items is 10 billion. A brainstorming session that is generating five ideas per minute would have to continue around the clock for over 3,800 years to match this productivity!

"So you see the imagination needs moodling—long, inefficient, happy idling, dawdling and puttering."
Brenda Ueland

Chapter 7

Parameters	Options									
	1	2	3	4	5	6	7	8	9	10
A										
B										
C										
D										
E										
F										
G										
H										
I										
J										

Figure 7-1: A 10 x 10 Morphological Box

Definition of the Tool

The Morphological Box helps teams to identify all practical solutions to a problem. This process is accomplished by first defining the essential characteristics or parameters of possible solutions. For each parameter, multiple options are then defined. Combinations of options for each parameter yield a multitude of unique solutions, from which teams can choose the best possibilities. Using a table that connects all of the possible solutions to the entire problem, the Morphological Box presents an exhaustive picture of all the potential solutions to every essential part of the problem.

Use of the Tool

Like Brainstorming and Brainwriting 6-3-5, the Morphological Box is suited for a wide variety of applications. Teams are at an advantage in using this tool with complex problems because the parameters of a problem can describe either small details or numerous, large sub-systems.

Because this tool can cover such a wide range of problem solutions, it almost always takes a team into new areas of possibility. This breaks down old stereotypes and stretches the team members' thinking.

Using this tool requires analytical and clear thinking and the ability to define things precisely. In addition, using this tool requires knowledge in the field. In a brainstorming session, anyone can contribute by stimulating new ideas, but for this tool **expert knowledge is required**. Often a single expert or a small group works with this tool. When this tool is applied to complex problems, it is normally conducted over the span of several days, with a number of breaks included.

Overview of the Tool Process

The purpose of this process is to help people generate all the possible solutions to a given problem. The first step in the process is to identify and define what characteristics are essential to a solution. These essential characteristics, the "parameters," are those which all possible solutions have in common.

For example, alternative solutions to developing a murder mystery plot need to include these parameters: the victim, the cause of death, the scene of the crime, the murderer, the motive, the hero, and the method for solving the murder mystery.

Each parameter by itself represents only part of a solution. For a solution to work, all the parameters must be present. To test whether the parameters for a given solution are correct, the murder mystery team, for example may ask, "In developing a story plot, we must include the victim and the cause of death, the scene of the crime, the murderer, the motive, the hero, and the method for solving the murder mystery." If the team agrees that there are no other parameters to a solution and that there are no overlaps in the chosen parameters, then the list of parameters is complete and essential.

Each parameter can have many options. The options are the specific choices. For example, in trying to create alternative solutions to the problem of developing a murder mystery plot, each parameter should have several options. A Morphological Box for developing a murder mystery plot is shown in Figure 7-2.

Parameters	Options				
Victim	butler	Wall Street broker	parrot	doctor	lawyer
Cause of death	suffocation	poisoning	gun shot	bomb	fire
Scene of the crime	restaurant	home	conference	pool	mall
Murderer	chamber maid	investor	game hunter	patient	prince
Motive	greed	revenge	jealousy	insanity	love
Hero	senator	computer technician	gardener	detective	psychic
Solving method	laboratory results	logical reasoning	photograph	confession	vote

Figure 7-2: Morphological Box of Murder Mystery Plots

A Morphological Box is not three-dimensional. It is more like a list or a table. As Figure 7-2 shows, the parameters are listed in the first column, and all the specific options for each parameter are written in the columns to the right of the parameter.

To build one of many potential scenarios, the team selects at least one option for each parameter, marks each one with a dot, and connects the options. The various combinations can have a straight, diagonal, or even a zigzag line connecting them to distinguish among the various alternative solutions. In Figure 7-2, the team could choose as a story plot the murder of a doctor who is poisoned at a conference by a jealous investor. A computer technician then solves the mystery by way of laboratory results.

Applying the Tool

Outline of Steps

Step	Activity
1.	Assemble the team and the experts.
2.	Define the parameters for all possible solutions.
3.	List all the possible options for each parameter.
4.	Build alternative solutions.
5.	Analyze the solutions and select the best one.

"Creation is a better means of self-expression than possession; it is through creating, not possessing, that life is revealed."

Vida D. Scudder

Step-by-Step Instructions

Step 1. Assemble the team and the experts.

The leader calls together the team, including the expert or experts for the area being studied. The experts in this case are the people who have technical knowledge of the problem. The team, after being instructed on how to proceed with the process, begins by agreeing on the problem statement.

Example

A team has been assembled to come up with alternative solutions to the problem: "How can we use Quality Function Deployment (QFD) in our new product development process?"[1] The team

---

1. This example of a Morphological Box was generated during a workshop on the GOAL/QPC Creativity Tools, during the QFD Novi, Michigan Symposium in June 1997. This tool allowed the group to consider various approaches and options in the QFD system. A company group may wish to pursue new product development, in general.

Chapter 7

is composed of representatives from marketing, product development, and training, as well as two individuals who are very knowledgeable about the QFD process.

Step 2. Define the parameters for all possible solutions.

The parameters of the solution are established, through analysis of the essential characteristics of possible solutions. For the Morphological Box to be effective, the parameters must meet the following criteria:

- The parameters are independent from each other.
- The parameters are valid for all potential solutions.
- All the parameters together must describe the solution. (Each parameter by itself represents only part of a solution. For a solution to work, all the parameters must be present.)
- The parameters should represent only essential characteristics. If a problem can be solved without including a certain characteristic, then that characteristic is not an appropriate parameter.

Arrange the parameters in the Morphological Box in order of importance, i.e., the parameters that are most likely to influence the success of the solution are listed at the top of the parameters column. If there is no order of importance, arrange the parameters in a way that is logical and useful to the team.

Example

The team first defined the parameters of a program to integrate Quality Function Deployment in the company's new product development process. Then the team added these parameters to a template. The result is shown in Figure 7-3.

Parameters	Options					
Means for gathering customer data						
Means for selecting the priority focus						
Means for generating new concepts						
Means for selecting new concepts						
Means for taking costs out of the product or service design						
Means for improving reliability of the product or service						
Means for reducing design time						

Figure 7-3: Parameters for Using QFD in the New Product Development Process

Step 3. List all the possible options for each parameter.

The team generates as many options as possible for each parameter through a Classic Brainstorming session. All the options for a parameter should be independent of each other and should not overlap. See Figure 7-2 for an example.

Example

The team generated a list of possible options for each parameter. The options are shown in Figure 7-4 below.

Parameters	Options					
Means for gathering customer data	in-depth interview	questionnaires	jointly with suppliers	historical data	going to the customer workplace	focus group
Means for selecting the priority focus	weighted voting (spreading 100 points)	analytical hierarchy process	customer rating	house of quality		
Means for generating new concepts	creativity tools	patent research (TRIZ)	research	competitor analysis	reverse engineering	benchmarking
Means for selecting new concepts	boss decides	Pugh New Concept Selection Tool	dart board	single criterion	matrix ideas against the strategic plan	apply minimum customer satis-faction criteria
Means for taking costs out of the product or service design	dropping features	value engineering ("trimming")	activity-based costing	customer input	concurrent engineering	
Means for improving reliability of the product or service	forced failure (TRIZ)	Fault Tree Analysis (FTA)	Failure Mode Effect Analysis (FMEA)	apply Taguchi methods for Robust Design	component failure analysis	reliability network diagram
Means for reducing design time	map the design process and optimize	identify priority breakthroughs up front	design priority breakthroughs up front	key decision makers regularly updated on design process	database of best solutions readily available	use TRIZ pat-terns of evolution to identify a string of breakthroughs

Figure 7-4: Options of Parameters for Using QFD in the New Product Development Process

Step 4. Build alternative solutions.

The team selects at least one option from each row and draws a line to connect the options. This line represents one possible solution to the problem. The team defines additional solutions by connecting alternative options for each parameter until all the possibilities are identified. The lines should be drawn in various coded versions (e.g., straight, wavy, dotted, color-coded, etc.) to distinguish them from each other.

Example

From the various alternative solutions, the team selected two to explore in more detail. The first solution (see Figure 7-5), is marked with alternating circles and dotted lines. The team chose this alternative by combining the least structured option for each parameter. It involved using questionnaires to gather data, using customer ratings to select the priority focus, analyzing competitor data to generate concepts, and establishing the minimum customer satisfaction criteria to select the new concept to be implemented. To take costs out, features could be dropped, and FMEA (Failure Mode Effect Analysis) would define the means for improving reliability. (FMEA is a process for identifying the most serious reliability problems so they can be worked on first.) To reduce design time, priority breakthroughs could be identified up front.

The second alternative solution was selected by combining the most rigorous option for each parameter. It is marked with alternating black triangles and solid lines. In this case, the team chose this alternative by gathering data through in-depth interviews, selecting the focus via "house of quality" method, and using the creativity tools to generate ideas. This alternative made use of Pugh's New Concept Selection Tool to choose the option "value engineering" for taking costs out, Taguchi methods for robust design for a more systematic, comprehensive approach, and a database of the best solutions readily available as a means for reducing design time.

"Few minds wear out; more rust out."

Christian Bovee

Parameters	Options					
Means for gathering customer data	in-depth interview	questionnaires	jointly with suppliers	historical data	going to the customer workplace	focus group
Means for selecting the priority focus	weighted voting (spreading 100 points)	analytical hierarchy process	customer rating	house of quality		
Means for generating new concepts	creativity tools	patent research (TRIZ)	research	competitor analysis	reverse engineering	benchmarking
Means for selecting new concepts	boss decides	Pugh New Concept Selection Tool	dart board	single criterion	matrix ideas against the strategic plan	apply minimum customer satisfaction criteria
Means for taking costs out of the product or service design	dropping features	value engineering ("trimming")	activity-based costing	customer input	concurrent engineering	
Means for improving reliability of the product or service	forced failure (TRIZ)	Fault Tree Analysis (FTA)	Failure Mode Effect Analysis (FMEA)	apply Taguchi methods for Robust Design	component failure analysis	reliability network diagram
Means for reducing design time	map the design process and optimize	identify priority breakthroughs up front	design priority breakthroughs up front	key decision makers regularly updated on design process	database of best solutions readily available	use TRIZ patterns of evolution to identify a string of breakthroughs

●----- Alternative #1

▲——— Alternative #2

Figure 7-5: Using QFD in the New Product Development Process: Two Alternative Solutions

Step 5. Analyze the solutions and select the best one.

The Morphological Box can generate a very large number of alternative solutions but it does not provide suggestions on which one is best to solve the problem. This evaluation must be made against criteria that relate back to the goals and circumstances of the problem. Determining what promises to be the best solution requires an additional step of evaluation. This evaluation can be done in at least three different ways, which are described below.

Intuitive Evaluation

Team members select from the options of the parameters, based on their intuition or gut instincts, and record interesting partial or complete solutions. In the process of doing this, new ideas for details may be stimulated. The best size Morphological Box for this approach is 5–6 parameters and the same number of options for each parameter. Intuitive evaluation has not been found to be very effective for more than six parameters.

Optimization

In this approach, the best options for each parameter are combined to provide the overall solution. This is a fairly workable procedure for approaching the best solution in the Morphological Box. This approach, however, overlooks an important consideration: even if the team finds a solution based on the best option for each parameter, it may be less than ideal overall if the combined options don't work well together. As a result, it may be necessary for the team to use a combination of less-than-best options to find a workable solution. For example: What is the optimum means for gathering customer data? Probably focus groups or in-depth interviews, if thoroughness is important. The team should continue in a similar way for each parameter.

Sequential Evaluation

In this approach, the parameters are listed top-down in order of their importance to finding a solution. For example, if a team is designing a car, the type of engine is more important than the color of its steering wheel. The team first considers the two, three, or four most important parameters and their options. At this point, the number of resulting combinations is still fairly limited. The most promising combinations can be determined simply by looking at the Morphological Box. For each of the remaining parameters, the team selects the options that look like the best combination with the options chosen for the most important parameters. This process is completed sequentially for all the parameters until the optimal solution is found. For example: Agree on the means for gathering customer data before moving on to the means for selecting the priority focus.

In addition to these three evaluation methods, the team leader can also choose to use any of the idea selection tools described in Chapters 8–11.

Example

The team decided that the second alternative (shown in Figure 7-5) provided the most promise as an optimal approach to using QFD at the company. They decided to use FMEA as a means for improving the reliability of the company's products and services. The product design team was already trained in the FMEA method. Since the team's recommended approach involved several new tools, the team felt that keeping one tool with which the company was already familiar would minimize any possible resistance to the recommendation.

Summary of the Tool

The Morphological Box is a highly flexible tool that can be used with a wide variety of problems. This tool can produce a large number of possibilities for solutions and designs, e.g., house designs, training strategies. Using the parameters, i.e., the fundamental distinguishing characteristics of any solution, the Morphological Box builds multiple scenarios from the options within these parameters. It can provide an extensive array of solutions. The Morphological Box goes beyond one-dimensional thinking, breaks habitual patterns, widens horizons, and reassures team members that they did not inadvertently overlook possible solutions. A subject matter expert is required as part of the team or as an advisor to the team.

Enhancing the Process

Helpful Hints

Work in Intervals Over Time and Take Breaks. Working in intervals over a longer period with several breaks is highly recommended because of the effort involved.

Evaluate the Quality of Solutions. The goal of generating the maximum number of solutions with a Morphological Box can be misleading if a team defines obviously nonsensical options. For example, if a team is developing a new telephone handset, one parameter might be "material for telephone housing." Theoretically, "ground and reshaped nutshells," "compressed cotton swabs," or "Norwegian amber," are all possible materials, yet no team member would realistically consider them for manufacturing a telephone handset. If such options were included in the Morphological Box, they would not add any value to the creative thinking process.

On the other hand, a team doesn't want to miss out on opportunities for creativity and innovation. Therefore, team members must be very careful not to confine themselves to only self-evident options or to those options they have "always used." In the first step, perhaps a brainstorming session is best for proposing options that are different from each other. Then a Morphological Box can be built with only those options that have a reasonable chance of becoming part of a solution. The combination of options will provide enough information to allow the team's creativity to flourish.

Frequently Asked Questions

Q. The Morphological Box is quite structured. Is it really a creativity tool?

A. Although it is more structured in approach than some of the other tools, it can generate a wide spectrum of solutions, some of which would rarely emerge from other creative processes.

Q. Can the Morphological Box yield all possible solutions?

A. That depends on the nature of the parameters that have been defined. Some parameters have a limited number of possibilities. For example, the parameter "gender" has only a few options: female, male, and neither. If all the parameters have a limited number of potential options, then the Morphological Box is considered to be "close-ended." A close-ended Morphological Box will indeed represent all possible solutions.

If, on the other hand, the box is "open-ended," i.e., the parameters have a large number of options, then the Morphological Box will not represent all possible solutions. It will, however, represent an incredibly large number of solutions—more than most teams can imagine! Most innovation problems involve a very large number of options, which require the use of an open-ended Morphological Box. An open-ended Morphological Box will generate new and different approaches, strategies, or designs for the problem, where a close-ended Morphological Box will not.

"The truly fearless think of themselves as normal."

Margaret Atwood

Chapter 7

For Further Study

An alternative to the Morphological Box is the Morphological Matrix. Like the Morphological Box, the Morphological Matrix is a systematic problem-solving tool that is suited for a wide variety of problems. Like the Morphological Box, the Morphological Matrix requires a solid knowledge of the subject matter area, however, the Morphological Matrix takes the analysis to an even deeper level by comparing the set of options from one parameter with the set of options from another parameter. The intersection of two options can represent new business opportunities, such as new products, new market niches, new processes and services, as well as many possible future scenarios.

The Morphological Matrix has one set of parameters across the top and one set of parameters down the side. Such a matrix can be very effective for suggesting areas to look into for new business opportunities. For example, in developing ideas or strategies for finding market niches for new books, a team defined the parameters of the problem as:

- Field or subject of the book

- Format (e.g., entertainment, historical, educational, etc.)

- Audience

- Volume number

- Quality and price of the book

The team constructed a Morphological Box to define strategies for finding market niches, by providing several options for each one of the parameters listed above. When this effort was completed, they decided to use some of the information to define opportunities for new books. They took the first two parameters defined above and constructed a Morphological Matrix with the columns being the options for the first parameter, and the rows representing the options for the second parameter. By comparing a pair of options from each column and row, the team could identify possible opportunities for new books. For the sake of expediency, the team coded the cells. This example is shown in Figure 7-6.

	Parameter 1: Subject	Option 1: Women's literature	Option 2: History of animals	Option 3: Ancient religious buildings
Option 1: Pop entertainment		2	1	2
Option 2: Historical fiction		1	2	1
Option 3: Personal diaries		2	3	3

1 = Market already saturated
2 = Needs further research
3 = A real possibility

Figure 7-6: Looking for Market Niches for New Books

Additional Examples of Tool Usage

Situation: Over the past several years, relations between East and West in Europe have changed; the threat of communism has almost disappeared. Along with this reduced threat has come a reduction in the need for military equipment and weapons production. One company recognized the need to deal with this situation and charged an internal team to develop alternatives for new business where its highly sophisticated technology could be put to new uses. The team defined the parameters of the problem and listed them on a flipchart, as shown in Figure 7-7.

1. planned growth in sales
2. planned profit rate
3. structure of product lines
4. targeted product mix
5. technological level
6. targeted market position
7. future markets
8. product strategy
9. market delivery strategy
10. status within holding company

Figure 7-7: Parameters for Developing an Alternative Type of Business that Makes Use of Company's Current Technology

For each of the parameters, the team identified options and wrote them in the cells of a Morphological Box. The team looked at several alternative solutions by combining different options. Two of the team's possible solutions are shown in the Morphological Box in Figure 7-8.

Parameters	Options				
Planned growth in sales	same as last five periods	consolidation	average of branch	similar to GNP growth	about 5% a year	more than 5% a year
Planned profit rate	same as last year	same as other divisions	between 4–5%	more than 5% a year		
Structure of product lines	emphasis on goods	goods and related services	mix of goods and services	emphasis on services		
Targeted product mix	components	groups of components	subsystems	complex systems	balanced mix	
Technological level	low-tech	middle-tech	high-tech	demand oriented		
Targeted market position	price leadership	technological leadership	market share leadership			
Future markets	today's markets	environmental management companies (air and soil)	environmental management companies (water)			
Product strategy	based on production costs	value added	synergy with other business units in the company	based on current equipment	balanced loading of capacity	
Market delivery strategy	stand-alone operation	alliances within holding company	alliances beyond holding company			
Status within holding company	division as today	expansion to own business unit	spin-off to new organization			

★----- Alternative #1

▲——— Alternative #2

Figure 7-8: Developing an Alternative Type of Business: Two Possible Solutions

"Great inventors and discoverers seem to have made their discoveries and inventions as it were by the way, in the course of their everyday life."

Elizabeth Rundle Charles

The team began discussing specific strategies of the two possible solutions that were drawn on the Morphological Box. Here's a summary of the team's conversation:

Alternative #1 (Selected options marked with stars)

The company could develop a fairly aggressive strategy to help grow its product sales by about 5% a year, with a planned profit rate of more than 5% a year. To do so, the company would need to provide a mix of goods and services that reflected a balanced mix of components, subsystems, and complex systems focusing on the high-tech market where it would aim for market share leadership. In addition to its current markets, the team wanted to address the needs of environmental management companies that specialized in water management. The team recommended a product strategy that relied on a balanced loading of capacity and a market delivery strategy that involved making alliances with companies outside of its own organization. The team agreed that such expansion would be possible only if it were its own business unit.

Alternative #2 (Selected options marked with triangles)

This alternative solution represents a more conservative strategy. The strategy would involve a growth in product sales that would be equal to the growth in GNP for the country, with a planned profit rate equal to the average within the holding company. The company would focus on providing goods and related services, with a product line composed of component groups within the mid-tech level. This strategy would involve working within current markets, but striving for leadership within the mid-tech field. The team would focus on adding value to the component groups, in alliances with other groups within the holding company, maintaining its current structure as a division within the company.

Situation: A TVA partnership has decided to communicate "best practices" as a new service for its members. A team was selected to develop the best alternatives for collecting and distributing this best practice information. The team's objective was to "Develop several alternatives for collecting and communicating best practice information to partnership members."

The parameters of the problem, as the team defined them, are shown on the flipchart in Figure 7-9.

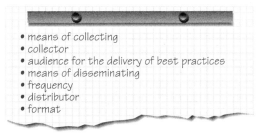

- means of collecting
- collector
- audience for the delivery of best practices
- means of disseminating
- frequency
- distributor
- format

Figure 7-9: Parameters for Developing Alternatives for Collecting and Communicating
Best Practice Information to Partnership Members

The team brainstormed options for each parameter, then constructed a Morphological Box. The completed Morphological Box in Figure 7-10 shows two possible solutions chosen by the team for further development.

Parameters	Options					
Means of collecting	literature review	industry association	benchmarking	survey	Web search	focus groups
Collector	contractor	industry group	university	TVA staff	distributors	mixed group committee
Audience for the delivery of best practices	senior distributor management	process owners	industry groups	TVA (selective)	survey audience	
Means of disseminating	seminar/ workshop	presentation meeting	report	online	consulting	news organization
Frequency	one time	monthly	quarterly	semi-annually	annually	as needed
Distributor	TVA	industry group	distributor	distributor association	mixed	
Format	written	presentation	computer or Web-based	audio-visual		

● ——— Alternative #1

■ - - - - - Alternative #2

Figure 7-10: Developing Alternatives for Collecting and Communicating Best Practice Information: Two Possible Solutions

The team began discussing specific strategies of the two possible solutions that were drawn on the Morphological Box. Here's a summary of the team's conclusions:

Alternative #1 (Selected options marked with circles)

Picking one option for each of the parameters, the team developed a strategy which they termed "middle of the road." In it, a university selected by the partnership would use a survey to collect best practices. The university would then produce a quarterly report that the TVA partnership would distribute to industry groups through computer/Web-based channels.

Alternative #2 (Selected options marked with squares)

Team members also considered a second approach, marked by squares and dotted lines, that they thought would be more innovative. They would form a committee, representing a variety of constituencies, to collect the best practice information via a web search. The committee would then produce an online version of the report or the update, to be distributed by the committee to senior management on a monthly basis via computer or Web-based channels.

In reviewing the application of this tool, all the team members were quite pleased with the process and the immediate results. Since they found the tool had covered many, if not all of the bases, had stimulated their thinking for other possibilities, and had produced some very useful approaches, they decided to work with the tool for another hour to see what additional combinations of options they could develop.

This example was contributed by Tracy Schmidt, Tennessee Valley Authority.

"I could never tell where inspiration begins and impulse leaves off. I suppose the answer is in the outcome. If your hunch proves a good one, you were inspired; if it proves bad, you are guilty of yielding to thoughtless impulse."

Beryl Markham

Morphological Box

Chapter 7

"The more an idea is developed, the more concise becomes its expression;
the more a tree is pruned, the better is the fruit."

Alfred Bougeart

Section II:
The Idea Selection Tools

Idea generation is not the whole story. Equally important are tools that help teams select the best alternative to explore, build on, and then implement. The tools in this section can help a team select the best alternative and to plan and implement the chosen solution.

Several of the tools were chosen from *The Memory Jogger Plus+*®, an in-depth handbook on the tools for management and planning activities. Two other tools, Nominal Group Technique and Pugh New Concept Selection, are included because of their special applicability for idea selection. Information on the use of these tools and their application is provided in Chapters 8–11(named in the list below). Chapter 12 describes three tools that can help a team plan and manage the implementation of the selected idea or solution.

8. Nominal Group Technique
9. Interrelationship Digraph with the Affinity Diagram
10. Prioritization Matrices
11. Pugh New Concept Selection Tool
12. Implementing Ideas: Project Management Tools at Work

Teams can use the idea selection tools in any sequence, however, a team may find it helpful to set up a progression for screening out ideas. This is especially true when a team is dealing with a large number of ideas or alternative solutions, and/or when a team is trying to solve a particularly difficult or complex problem.

A team may want to consider using Nominal Group Technique and/or the Interrelationship Digraph to reduce a large number of ideas down to a more manageable set. Then, when the ideas have been culled, the team can use the Prioritization Matrix or the Pugh New Concept Selection tool to establish the best ideas and possible solutions.

"When you get to a fork in the road—take it."

Yogi Berra

Nominal Group Technique[1]

Introduction

Once a team has generated innovative ideas to address challenges and solve problems, it needs tools to select the best from among the new ideas. The Nominal Group Technique is a tool for ranking choices. It is called "nominal" because it requires minimal or "nominal" interaction compared to the usual amount of interaction that occurs in group sessions. It is an easy and useful tool for a team to use to reduce the number of alternatives from a very large number to a few, more select choices where the team can then apply the more rigorous data-based tools, such as the Prioritization Matrix (Chapter 10).

Definition of the Tool

Nominal Group Technique (NGT) provides teams with a method for narrowing down a list of ideas and reaching consensus around a more manageable number of ideas; finding the major causes of disagreement among team members; ranking issues without pressure from other team members. NGT provides a technique for integrating individual rankings into a team's final set of priorities among ideas or solutions. Once team members become familiar with its steps, they can easily use this tool as a way to assess the team's position and priorities in a variety of settings.

Use of the Tool

This tool builds commitment to a team's choice since all team members equally participate in the process. Because it allows every team member to rank issues without being pressured by others, it puts quiet team

"Creations, whether they are children, poems, or organizations, take on a life of their own."

Starhawk

Chapter 8

1. Material in this chapter has been adapted from the following sources: Michael Brassard and Diane Ritter, *The Memory Jogger™ II: A Pocket Guide of Tools for Continuous Improvement and Effective Planning* (Methuen, MA: GOAL/QPC, 1994), 91–94; Michael Brassard et al., *Coach's Guide to The Memory Jogger™II: The Easy-to-Use, Complete Reference for Working with Improvement and Planning Tools in Teams* (Methuen, MA: GOAL/QPC, 1995), 123–128; and Michael Brassard, *The Memory Jogger Plus+®* (Methuen, MA: GOAL/QPC, 1989), 298.

members on an equal footing with more dominant members. It also makes visible the team's consensus, or lack of it. With this information, team members can discuss the major causes of their disagreement.

The Nominal Group Technique is used when a team is faced with prioritizing a large number of ideas that it produced using one of the creativity tools (Chapters 1–7). If a team wants to use a structured method for selecting which idea or solution to explore further, this idea selection tool can help with prioritization of the ideas and/or solutions. This tool also allows a team to quickly come to a consensus on the relative importance of issues, problems, or solutions. It can depersonalize the process of working through an issue and provide team members with breathing room when they are dealing with controversial or difficult issues.

If a team needs to decide among issues that are based on data that can be compared, the team should explore the use of data-gathering tools such as the Pareto Chart.[2] After a team has used the Nominal Group Technique to narrow down its options, it should consider using the Prioritization Matrix (Chapter 10) to make its final selection.

Overview of the Tool Process

After a team has generated a list of ideas or possible solutions with any one of the creativity tools, it can use the Nominal Group Technique to assign priority to the list of ideas. To do this, the team writes the idea or solution statements on a flipchart or whiteboard so that all team members can see them. Team members address questions, make clarifications, and remove any duplicates from the list.

The recordkeeper puts the final list on a flipchart or whiteboard with a letter to identify each statement. Each team member records the letters on a sheet of paper, then ranks the list of ideas in order of importance or preference. The rankings of all team members are combined, and then the team analyzes and discusses the results. The team can then select the idea with the highest rank for further investigation. If the team is not comfortable with selecting just one idea, or if there are too many ideas to choose from, the team can choose the top 2–5 ideas for further analysis.

---

2. See *The Memory Jogger™ II*, pages 95–104, for more information.

The Idea Edge

Applying the Tool

Outline of Steps

Step	Activity
1.	Generate the list of issues, problems, or solutions to be prioritized.
2.	Write ideas on a flipchart or whiteboard.
3.	Eliminate duplicates and/or clarify meanings of any of the ideas.
4.	Record the final list of statements and assign a letter to each.
5.	Rank the ideas.
6.	Combine the rankings of all team members.
7.	Select the idea or ideas with the highest rankings for further investigation.

Step-by-Step Instructions

Step 1. Generate the list of issues, problems, or solutions to be prioritized.

The team should generate ideas with one or more of the creativity tools. Before the team begins using this tool, members should review the list to see if there are any items to add. Some of the ideas may have been generated by another group, or generated without discussion in a Brainwriting 6-3-5 session. It is important to make sure team members understand all the ideas in the same way.

Example

A team of five members—Jack, Laurie, Marc, Dana and Carla—were charged with coming up with a team recommendation for the best new product development strategy for their department. They first used the Brainwriting 6-3-5 tool (Chapter 3) to generate ideas. When they reviewed the list, it seemed very comprehensive, so no one had any items to add.

Step 2. Write ideas on a flipchart or whiteboard.

The recordkeeper should record verbatim the list of ideas and any additions on a flipchart or whiteboard so that they are visible to all team members. If the team decides to shorten the ideas into more manageable form, the recordkeeper or facilitator should check with the originator of the idea to be sure nothing has been lost in the abbreviation process.

Example

The team wrote all 18 ideas generated in the Brainwriting 6-3-5 session onto a flipchart.

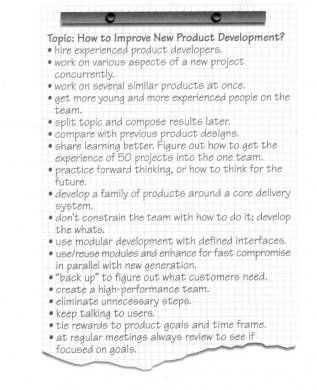

Figure 8-1: Ideas Generated for a New Product Development Strategy

Step 3. Eliminate duplicates and/or clarify meanings of any of the ideas.

In this step the team reviews the list of ideas to determine if there are any duplicates and to be sure that all team members understand the meaning of the statements. The team should ask for the permission and guidance of the team member who generated the idea before it changes statements or eliminates any that appear to be duplicates.

As the team reviews the list, it may want to consider the size of the list. If the list is long, team members may want to consider shortening it. One way to do this is to ask each team member to pick the two or three most important items from the list.

Example

The team reviewed the list of 18 items. They came to quick consensus to eliminate two items as duplicates. They decided that the following items had the most promise for more exploration.

- work on various aspects of a new project concurrently.
- get more young and more experienced people on the team.
- share learning better. Figure out how to get the experience of 50 projects into the one team.
- practice forward thinking, or how to think for the future.
- develop a family of products around a core delivery system.
- use modular development with defined interfaces.
- keep talking to users.
- "back up" to figure out what customers need.

Figure 8-2: Best Ideas for a New Product Development Strategy

The team also spent some time exploring the meanings of three of the ideas to be sure everyone understood them the same way.

Step 4. Record the final list of ideas and assign a letter to each.

Once the team has reviewed the list and narrowed it down as appropriate, the recordkeeper should record the items on a large and widely visible surface (a flipchart or whiteboard). Each item needs to be identified with a letter so it can be differentiated from the numbers used to rank order the items in the next steps.

Example

The team's recordkeeper listed the items on a flipchart and identified each item with a letter.

A. work on various aspects of a new project concurrently.
B. get more young and more experienced people on the team.
C. share learning better. Figure out how to get the experience of 50 projects into the one team.
D. practice forward thinking, or how to think for the future.
E. develop a family of products around a core delivery system.
F. use modular development with defined interfaces.
G. keep talking to users.
H. "back up" to figure out what customers need.

Figure 8-3: Team's Final List of Ideas

Step 5. Rank the ideas.

Each team member records the letters (for all the ideas on the list) on a piece of paper and rank orders the ideas according to the ranking method and criteria the team has agreed to use. The ranking should be from highest to lowest. The criteria could be based on the importance of the option in reaching the goal, the most fun to implement, or some other criteria that the team has agreed on. Team members should rank all the items this way. For example, if there are eight items, the most important is marked with an "8" and the least important receives a "1."

Example

Each team member prepared a list of the ideas, then ranked the ideas. Two of the individual sheets are shown below.

Jack's sheet looked like this:

```
A.  8
B.  5
C.  1
D.  7
E.  4
F.  6
G.  2
H.  3
```

Carla's sheet looked list this:

```
A.  3
B.  4
C.  8
D.  2
E.  5
F.  6
G.  1
H.  7
```

Step 6. Combine the rankings of all team members.

The facilitator should combine the rankings of all team members. The recordkeeper might then construct a table to record the rankings. The team reviews the results.

Example

The team's final table for the "Best New Product Development Strategy for Department N" is shown below.

	Jack	Laurie	Marc	Dana	Carla	Total
A.	8	7	6	6	3	30*
B.	5	4	2	1	4	16
C.	1	5	3	3	8	20
D.	7	1	1	4	2	15
E.	4	3	4	8	5	24
F.	6	2	7	5	6	26
G.	2	6	5	2	1	16
H.	3	7	8	7	7	32*

Figure 8-4: Table for Compiling Rankings of All Team Members

Step 7. Select the idea or ideas with the highest rankings for further investigation.

In reviewing the results, team members should discuss any surprises or new pieces of information that were revealed in the process. If all team members agree with the results, they can select the top-ranked option for further exploration. When agreeing on the results, the team should consider both the highest numbers and also the diversity of rankings among team members. If there are dramatic differences or if the team is uncomfortable with the results, the team should work to address this lack of agreement. Team members can decide to take another vote, select the top two or three options for further investigation, or choose what other action steps (use another tool, collect more data) they feel is appropriate.

Example

As a result of the ranking process, the team selected ideas A and H to work on next. The issue was how to reduce product development time. The group had decided to work on this problem but they needed to agree on where to start. Using Nominal Group Technique was a simple way to do that. The team initially agreed to explore the following areas to reduce development time:

A. Work on various aspects of a new project concurrently

H. Back up to figure out what customers need

Summary of the Tool

When a team needs to have a consensus for one choice from a list of ideas or options, the Nominal Group Technique is a useful tool. This idea selection tool can also help surface unspoken assumptions and concerns that a team needs to address. Once ideas have been generated, it is necessary to pick the solution to be used. Nominal Group Technique provides buy-in by letting those involved vote.

Enhancing the Process

Helpful Hints

Selecting a Ranking Method. While there are several methods that a team can use, a team should try to adopt one that does not allow for distortion because of blanks. For example, a scale of "5" as the most important ranking and "1" as the least important will correct for distortion. Since individual rankings will later be combined, this "reverse order" minimizes the effect of team members leaving some statements blank. A blank with a value equal to zero will not, in effect, increase the importance of that statement.

Another Ranking Tool. NGT is an excellent tool to use when a team needs to find out the range of team members' opinions. If exploring the nature of the opinions is also important and/or if there are data that the team should consider, then the team should consider using a different ranking tool such as the Prioritization Matrix in Chapter 10.

"If you have one good idea, people will lend you twenty."
Marie von Ebner-Eschenbach

When Time is Tight. If a team doesn't have time for a full cycle of Nominal Group Technique, it can take a verbal vote to get a quick sense of the team's opinions. This is not a good option, however, if the team is newly formed or the ideas being considered are complex or controversial.

Dealing with the "Wrong Answer." Occasionally a team may not be satisfied with the results of this tool. Team members may not like the idea or option that received the most points or votes. At this point a team has two choices. The facilitator and the team can openly discuss the reasons for the conflict and/or concerns. Alternatively, the team can use more criteria-based tools such as the Prioritization Matrix, determine the results from that tool, and then compare those results with the results from the use of Nominal Group Technique. Team members can then decide which set of results they prefer.

Pre-screening Ideas. If a team is working with a lot of ideas, it may want to consider pre-ranking or pre-selecting items for the first round of using the Nominal Group Technique. If each team member picks the most important two or three items from the original list, the final list could be more manageable. The general rule for the team to follow in this process is that the larger the team, the fewer the number of items each team member can select. Another technique for narrowing down a large list is the "One Half Plus One" method. In this method, each team member ranks only a portion of the total list of ideas. For example, if 20 ideas have been generated, team members rank only the top 11 choices. For more information, refer to page 93 in *The Memory Jogger*™ *II*.

Other Ranking Methods. There are several alternatives for the team to use in ranking items. If team members are comfortable with each other, they can take turns calling out their rankings to the recordkeeper. Another way is for team members to use stickers that they can place next to the items they rank the highest. In this case the items with the highest number of stickers would receive the highest ranking.

Frequently Asked Questions

Q. How large can the team be?

A. Nominal Group Technique can be used in groups of 10–15 people. However, to facilitate any meaningful discussions around interpretations, assumptions, or issues, a maximum number of 8 people is recommended.

Q. Are there alternatives to using Nominal Group Technique?

A. An alternative is to use Weighted Multivoting. In this technique, each team member rates, not ranks, the relative importance of choices by distributing a value among the choices. For example, each team member can distribute 100 points across the options. The 100 points can be distributed between as many or as few choices as desired.

The following is an example of the use of Weighted Multivoting to illustrate its difference with NGT. A team is trying to determine why a department has inconsistent output. The possibilities are as follows:

A.	Lack of Training
B.	No documented process
C.	Unclear quality standards
D.	Lack of cooperation with other departments
E.	High turnover

Figure 8-5: Ideas for Why the Department Has Inconsistent Output

Instead of ranking these alternatives from 5 to 1, individual team members could distribute 100 points across the five possibilities:

	Larry	Nina	Norm	Paige	Si	Total
A.	20	0	10	0	0	30
B.	40	80	50	100	45	315
C.	30	5	10	0	25	70
D.	0	5	10	0	20	35
E.	10	10	20	0	10	50

Figure 8-6: 100 Points Distributed Across Five Options

"No documented process" would be the highest priority. The team would work on this first and then move through the rest of the list as needed.

With a large number of choices, or when the voting for the top choice is very close, the team can repeat this process for an agreed upon number of items. The team would stop when the choice is clear.

For Further Study

Consult the following GOAL/QPC publications for more information:

- *The Memory Jogger™ II: A Pocket Guide of Tools for Continuous Improvement and Effective Planning*, pages 91–94

- *Coach's Guide to The Memory Jogger™ II: The Easy-to-Use, Complete Reference for Working with Improvement and Planning Tools in Teams*, pages 123–128

- *The Memory Jogger Plus+®*, page 298

Interrelationship Digraph with the Affinity Diagram[1]

Introduction

During idea generation, a team will often experience an explosion of great, new ideas. To move forward in solving the problem, or developing a new product or service, or improving a process, the team needs to take those ideas and logically organize them. However, most conditions or events do not lend themselves to orderly logic and are not caused by a straight line cause and effect "stream" that is neat and tidy. In fact, the "stream" of causes looks more like a spider web than a predictable path.

The Affinity Diagram provides a team with a way to group together related ideas. The Interrelationship Digraph (ID) helps the team to organize the major ideas in the Affinity Diagram and to map the links between related items. Constructing an ID is a process that shows how every idea can be logically linked with more than one idea at a time. It allows for "multidirectional" rather than "linear" thinking.

For many teams, the process of constructing an Interrelationship Digraph will be uncomfortable because it can appear messy. It is not easy (nor is it recommended) for team members to follow each and every connection among the issues. Building an ID requires sitting back and reserving judgment while the patterns in an ID emerge. If a team can adjust to dealing with this ambiguity, it will be rewarded since the ID process produces unanticipated findings that are worth the wait.

"The process of writing, any form of creativity, is a power intensifying life."

Rita Mae Brown

---

1. Material in this chapter has been adapted from the following sources: Michael Brassard and Diane Ritter, *The Memory Jogger™ II: A Pocket Guide of Tools for Continuous Improvement and Effective Planning* (Methuen, MA: GOAL/QPC, 1994), 76–84; Michael Brassard et al., *Coach's Guide to The Memory Jogger™II: The Easy-to-Use, Complete Reference for Working with Improvement and Planning Tools in Teams* (Methuen, MA: GOAL/QPC, 1995), 99–110; and Michael Brassard, *The Memory Jogger Plus+®* (Methuen, MA: GOAL/QPC, 1989), 41–71.

Definition of the Tool

The Interrelationship Digraph (ID) provides teams with a method for thinking in multiple directions; finding relationships between and among ideas; and identifying issues that drive each other. It helps a team to systematically identify, analyze, and classify the cause and effect relationships that exist among critical issues so that key drivers or outcomes can become the heart of an effective solution.

Use of the Tool

The ID encourages team members to think in multiple directions rather than in a linear direction. It also helps them explore the cause and effect relationships between all the issues, including the most controversial. It allows the key issues, values, and priorities to emerge naturally rather than letting the issues be raised by a dominant or powerful team member. In a similar way, the ID prevents a dominant or powerful team member from covering up key issues, values, and priorities. The ID allows the basic assumptions and reasons for disagreements among team members to surface and helps a team to identify root causes even when credible data doesn't exist.

This tool is valuable for a team to use when an issue is complex enough that it's difficult to determine the interrelationships between and among ideas. A team should consider using this tool after it has generated a number of ideas and sorted them using an organizing method such as the Affinity Diagram. The ID can be used with both operational and organizational issues and questions, particularly when team members feel that the problem under discussion is really only a symptom of a deeper problem.

This tool also helps teams determine the correct sequencing of management actions. It is especially helpful when a team has limited resources and needs to establish one or two priorities where it should focus its efforts. Because this tool takes a bit of dedication and time, especially on the first try, there should be ample time allowed to complete the process, review the ID, and then modify it as necessary.

Overview of the Tool Process

After a team has generated a sufficient number of ideas (using any one of the creativity tools) and categorized them (using either an Affinity Diagram or another method) team members need to review and agree on one statement that clearly defines the key issue under discussion. The next step is to lay out all of the ideas or issue cards that identify the components or elements of the key issue. Then the team looks for the cause or influence relationships between the ideas and draws relationship arrows. After reviewing this first round ID, team members tally the number of outgoing and incoming arrows to determine key drivers and outcomes.

Construction of an Affinity Diagram for Use with the ID

The Affinity Diagram allows a team to organize a large number of ideas and issues and then summarize natural groupings among them to understand the essence of the problem and its breakthrough solutions. A "typical" Affinity has 40–60 items, however, it is not unusual to have 100–200 ideas in an Affinity Diagram.

When the team has finished generating ideas using any one or more of the creativity tools, similar ideas get grouped together. The number of these "groupings" should be limited to between 6 and 10, and if the issue is complex, to no more than 17 groupings. Each grouping is summarized with a header card that captures all the ideas in the grouping. All or some of these header cards can be used as issues for the Interrelationship Digraph.

Instructions for Constructing an Affinity Diagram

1. **Review the ideas that were produced with one of the idea generation tools described in Chapters 1–7.** One of the team members or the recordkeeper makes sure that each idea is recorded on a Post-it™ Note in bold, large print so that it is visible from 4–6 feet away. A team member or the recordkeeper makes sure that each of the ideas is stated, using at a minimum, a noun and a verb, with a guideline of four to seven words per Post-it™ Note. If any of the ideas generated in the creativity tool session do not include a noun and a verb, these ideas should be rewritten to include both noun and verb, and all the team members should agree on the meaning of a new phrasing of an idea.

Example

In the problem-solving session described in Chapter 2, a team is dealing with the problem: "How can we expand the use of the Web (or Internet) in the company to increase sales leads?"

Figure 9–1 shows some of the team's ideas for expanding the use of the Web in the company.

1. show employees how it works.
2. employees have to know what they are doing.
3. make it easy to use.
4. show or illustrate the value of the Web.
5. provide employees with technical support.
6. make sure it works well for employees; factor in employee needs.
7. explain the purpose and goal for doing this.
8. train people how to use the Web.
9. make it fun.
10. make the service responsive.
11. provide each employee with a modem for access to the Web.
12. provide employees with basic equipment.
13. make the telephone connection more efficient.
14. decide on one system.

Figure 9-1: Some Ideas for Expanding the Use of the Web in the Company to Increase Sales Leads

2. **Without talking, sort ideas simultaneously into 5–10 related groupings.** Team members should sort ideas in silence to focus on the connections between ideas, instead of emotions and "history" that often arise in discussions. As they sort the ideas, team members can place the Post-it™ Notes where they fit best. If a team member doesn't think an idea belongs in the grouping, he or she can simply move it without asking anyone. When an idea is moved back and forth, team members should try to see the logical connection the other person is making. If this movement continues beyond a reasonable point, team members can agree to create a duplicate Post-it™ Note.

Sorting will slow down or stop when each team member feels sufficiently comfortable with the groupings. When sorting has stopped, there may be some notes that have not been put into any groupings. These "loners" can be just as important as the other ideas that fit into groupings naturally.

Example

The Affinity Diagram below shows how the team began grouping related ideas.

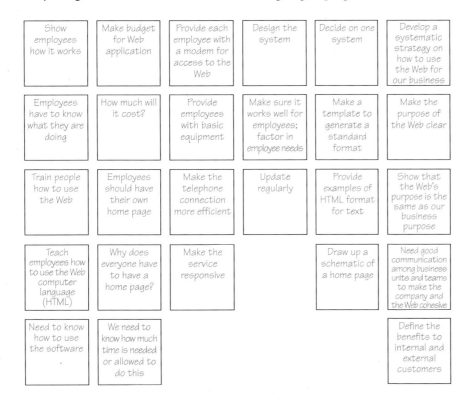

Figure 9-2: Groupings of Related Ideas

"To develop imaginative powers, we must specialize in our own fields but be alert to new ideas from any source and continually seize and set down our inspirational flashes when they come to us. The longer our imagination retains the idea, the clearer and more attainable it becomes."

Carl Holmes

3. **For each grouping, create summary or header cards using consensus.** Team members should develop a quick team consensus on a word or phrase that captures the central idea or theme of each grouping. This is the draft "header card." It is possible to use a note within a grouping as a header card, however, the team should be careful not to choose the "closest one" because it's convenient. The hard work of creating new header cards often leads to breakthrough ideas.

For each grouping, the team agrees on a concise sentence that combines the grouping's central idea with the specific Post-it™ Notes in that grouping. The team needs to spend the extra time required to do header cards that capture the essence of all of the ideas in each grouping. Shortcuts here can greatly reduce the effectiveness of the final Affinity Diagram. The recordkeeper and/or a team member records the new sentence and replaces the draft version. This is the final header card for the grouping.

If needed, the team can divide large groupings into subgroups and create appropriate subheaders.

The team then draws the final Affinity Diagram connecting all finalized header cards with their groupings.

Example

Part of the team's Affinity Diagram with header cards is shown below.

Provide Training to Employees for Best Use of the Web	Develop a Plan to Ensure the Correct Level of Resources	Provide Right Hardware/ Software for Best Use	Design an Efficient System to Maximize Use	Standardize the System for Best and Easiest Use	Create a Strong Business Case for Integration of Web Use into Business
Show employees how it works	Make budget for Web application	Provide each employee with a modem for access to the Web	Design the system	Decide on one system	Develop a systematic strategy on how to use the Web for our business
Employees have to know what they are doing	How much will it cost?	Provide employees with basic equipment	Make sure it works well for employees; factor in employee needs	Make a template to generate a standard format	Make the purpose of the Web clear
Train people how to use the Web	Employees should have their own home page	Make the telephone connection more efficient	Update regularly	Provide examples of HTML format for text	Show that the Web's purpose is the same as our business purpose
Teach employees how to use the Web computer language (HTML)	Why does everyone have to have own home page?	Make the service responsive		Draw up a schematic of a home page	Need good communication among business units and teams to make the company and the Web cohesive
Need to know how to use the software	We need to know how much time is needed or allowed to do this				Define the benefits to internal and external customers

Figure 9-3: Groupings of Related Ideas with Header Cards

The team continued to explore the issue of expanding the use of the Web in the company by next using an Interrelationship Digraph (ID). The ID helps a team see which issues are drivers and which are outcomes.

Applying the Tool (ID)

Outline of Steps

Step	Activity
1.	Review and agree on the issue/problem statement.
2.	Assemble the right team.
3.	Lay out all of the ideas/issue cards.
4.	Look for cause/influence relationships between all of the ideas and draw relationship arrows.
5.	Review and revise the first round ID.
6.	Tally the number of outgoing and incoming arrows and select key items for further planning.
7.	Draw the final ID.

Step-by-Step Instructions

Step 1. Review and agree on the issue/problem statement.

The team needs to clearly define one statement that summarizes the key issue under discussion. This statement should be a complete sentence that is clearly understood and agreed on by team members. The statement should have a single focus. To test the statement, team members can ask "If we achieve this, what will things/our situation/the world look like?" If the answer is clear, then the problem statement passes the test.

If the team is using input from other tools, such as an Affinity Diagram,[2] team members need to verify that the goal under discussion is still the same and clearly understood by all. It is a good idea to keep the problem statement visible during the construction of the ID.

Example

The team reviewed the original problem statement and agreed that it was still appropriate. ("How can we expand the use of the Web in the company to increase sales leads?")

Step 2. Assemble the right team.

The team leader should review the diversity of the team to be sure that all necessary expertise is included. The ID requires intimate knowledge of the subject under discussion if the final cause and effect patterns are to be credible. As with most of the idea generation and selection tools, the ideal team size is generally 4–6 people. However, this number can be increased as long as the issues are still visible and the meeting is well facilitated to encourage participation and maintain focus.

Example

The team leader considered the team members on the Internet project and decided that the company's technical specialist on Internet/Intranet usage would be a useful addition to the team for the purpose of constructing the ID.

Step 3. Lay out all of the ideas/issue cards.

Team members should agree on the key idea/issue cards that will be used for the ID. The cards are then set out in a large circular pattern, leaving as much space as possible (at least 2" between them for drawing arrows. Use large, bold printing, including a large number or letter on each idea for quick reference later in the process.

---

2. See *The Memory Jogger Plus+®*, pages 45–47 for further examples of the issue or problem statement.

"All the really good ideas I ever had came to me while I was milking a cow."

Grant Wood

Example

The team took the header cards from the Affinity Diagram it had generated and laid them out to begin creating an ID.

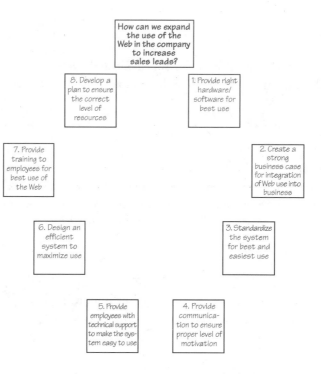

Figure 9-4: Idea/Issue Cards for ID

Step 4. Look for cause/influence relationships between all of the ideas and draw relationship arrows.

The team can choose any of the ideas as a starting point. If all of the ideas are numbered or lettered, the team should work through them in sequence.

Team members now look for cause/influence relationships between the idea they have chosen and every other card, asking:

- Is there a cause/influence relationship between these two ideas?

- If yes, which direction of cause/influence is stronger?

An outgoing arrow from one idea to another idea indicates that the former has the stronger cause or influence. The team should draw only one-way relationship arrows in the direction of the stronger cause or influence. Team members need to make a decision on the stronger direction, and not resort to drawing two-headed arrows. The discussion around the directions for the arrows is often revealing because it can surface unstated assumptions and push the team to address some tough questions.

To keep track of where the team is at any given point, the facilitator can place a Post-it™ Note with an anchor drawn on it at the point under discussion. He or she should check off items that have been considered.

Example

The team drew the following arrows:

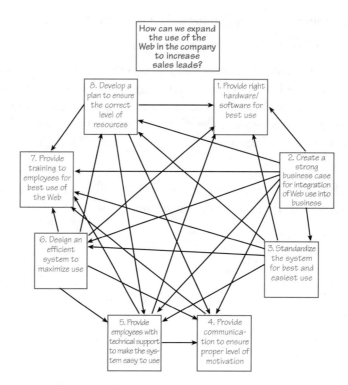

Figure 9-5: Cause/Influence Relationships of Ideas Shown with Arrows

Step 5. Review and revise the first round ID.

When the initial ID is completed, the team should get additional input from people who are not on the team to confirm or modify the team's work. Team members can either take the paper version to others or reproduce it using available software. Changes should be noted with a different size print or a color marker.

Example

The team took its first round ID to the Director of Training and Development for a sanity check. She suggested one change; she thought that the outgoing arrow from #4 into #7 should be turned so that it would be an outgoing arrow from #7 into #4. This arrow is marked in bold.

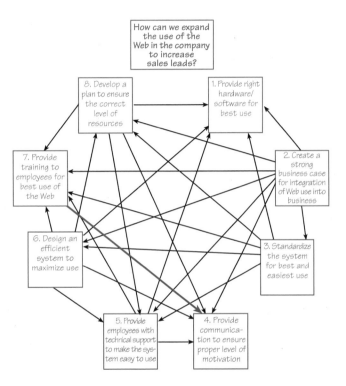

Figure 9-6: First Round ID with Revision

"Imagination and fiction make up more than three quarters of our real life."

Simone Weil

Chapter 9

Step 6. Tally the number of outgoing and incoming arrows and select key items for further planning.

This step reveals the answer to the question: "What does this all mean?" To get to the answer, team members should count up and clearly record next to each issue the number of arrows going in and out of it. Then team members find the item(s) with the highest number of outgoing arrows and the item(s) with the highest number of incoming arrows.

A high number of outgoing arrows indicates that an item is a *root cause* or *driver*. This item is generally, although not necessarily, the issue that the team will want to tackle first. A high number of incoming arrows indicates that an item is a *key outcome*. This item can become a focus for planning as a meaningful measure of overall success or as a redefinition of the original issue under discussion. The issues with a *high number of both incoming and outgoing arrows* are often referred to as "bottlenecks." The team will want to take these issues into consideration when developing implementation plans to address the driver and achieve the key outcome.

The team should use common sense when it selects the most critical issues to focus on. Team members should carefully review issues with very close tallies. In the end, it is a judgment call, not a science.

Example

The team reviewed the ID and the number of incoming and outgoing arrows. They identified the driver with a double box and the outcomes with a thick, bold box.

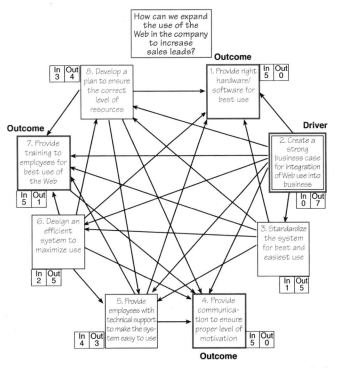

Figure 9-7: Completed ID with Driver and Outcomes Identified

Step 7. Draw the final ID.

The team completes the ID and visually identifies both the key drivers and key outcomes. A typical method is to draw a double box around the drivers and a thick bold box around the outcomes. Boxes that have the highest number of arrows pointing out are drivers and those with the highest number of arrows pointing in are outcomes.

The session ends with an action plan for addressing next steps.

Summary of the Tool

The Interrelationship Digraph (ID) can be seen as a systematic identification of targets and means. While it may appear chaotic at times, it is more reflective of reality than "neater" models. Teams that trust in the process will often be rewarded with surprising results. While teams should not ignore the need to faithfully gather and use data to guide them, it's important to remember that the collective experience and intuition resident in most working teams can be as powerful and reliable as much of the data they generate.

Enhancing the Process

Helpful Hints

Provide a Large Work Surface. The team needs an appropriately sized work surface to properly display an ID. The best work surface is flipchart paper, with two sheets taped together. These sheets can be taped to the wall or a table. Rolled "butcher" paper is an alternative to flipchart paper.

Recordkeeper Not Needed. A recordkeeper is not needed for the use of this tool. Usually the facilitator is responsible for drawing the arrows. A team member can also take on this responsibility.

Use Post-it™ Notes. Writing ideas on Post-it™ Notes is practical because the notes can be easily moved and will stick in place.

Keep the Issue Statement Visible. It is a good idea to keep the problem statement visible at all times. If the team gets bogged down in defining the direction of relationships, the facilitator can keep referring back to the problem statement and asking, "Is there a relationship between these two ideas?" and "Which drives which?"

Flag Deep Disagreements and Keep Moving. When team members are having trouble deciding which way the arrow should go, they need to keep in mind that the strongest direction is the one that matters most. If the team seems stuck, using a different color arrow or some other marker to help them remember to turn to that item before they finish the ID.

Value the Discussions. Since one of the major benefits of constructing an ID is the discussion that surrounds the direction of the arrows, team members need to listen carefully to others as they state their opinions and reasons. The direction of an arrow should represent the opinions of all the team members, not just those who are the loudest or most persistent.

What to Do with Unexpected Results. When reviewing the final ID, team members may be surprised or discomforted by the results. The facilitator needs to encourage team members to discuss the surprise or discomfort to explore whether the ID reflects the team members' view of the situation. The team should continue to discuss any issues that arise to increase team members' comfort levels with the results.

Pace the Team. If the construction of the ID takes more than an hour, a short break should be scheduled.

Tool Variation. Further details on constructing an ID, including a variation using a matrix format, are available in *The Memory Jogger Plus+*® and the *Coach's Guide to The Memory Jogger™ II.*

Frequently Asked Questions

Q. What is the ideal number of issues/cards?

A. While there are instances of diagrams with more than 100 interrelated items, an ID is most effective with between 5 and 15 items. Less than 5 items indicates that the problem is too simple for an ID. More than 15 items will generate a very complicated digraph.

Q. Can the team add a card after the initial ID has been built?

A. Unless the team finds an unacceptable hole or glaring omission among the cards, it should try not to add any additional cards to avoid the tendency for the ID to explode into an unmanageable mess of issues.

Q. Should the cards be arranged logically or randomly?

A. Since an ID is an exercise in multidirectional thinking as opposed to linear thinking, random placement will help the team think more multidimensionally, without any predetermined patterns to fall into. While the resulting ID may appear chaotic, the random method will be more productive and produce more creative insights.

"When we are writing, or painting, or composing, we are, during the time of creativity, freed from normal restrictions, and are opened to a wider world, where colors are brighter, sounds clearer, and people more wondrously complex than we normally realize."

Madeleine L'Engle

Q. How much discussion should accompany the construction of an ID?

A. An ID requires discussion about the direction of the arrows and the placement of the cards. However, these discussions should be as brief as possible to avoid letting the process bog down into hair-splitting. Team members will have additional chances to review and revise once the initial ID has been constructed. If the discussion continues (especially if it turns into a one-on-one discussion), the team should flag that connection and come back to it. It may turn out to be much less important or controversial by the end of the process.

Q. What is the ideal team size for working on an ID?

A. In the construction of an ID, larger teams can sometimes be very beneficial. More people means more ideas and information. However, the facilitator will need to manage the reluctance of some people to speak up and will also need to determine how consensus will be assessed.

Q. Is there software to support this tool?

A. Yes, *The Memory Jogger Plus+® Software* supports the use of this tool and six other management and planning tools and is available from GOAL/QPC.

For Further Study

Consult the following GOAL/QPC publications for more information on the Interrelationship Digraph and the Affinity Diagram:

- *The Memory Jogger™ II: A Pocket Guide of Tools for Continuous Improvement and Effective Planning*, 12–18 (Affinity) and 76–84 (ID)

- *Coach's Guide to The Memory Jogger™ II: The Easy-to-Use, Complete Reference for Working with Improvement and Planning Tools in Teams*, 11–20 (Affinity) and 99–110 (ID)

- *The Memory Jogger Plus+®*, 17–39 (Affinity) and 41–71 (ID)

Prioritization Matrices[1]

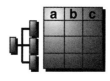

Introduction

The idea selection tools described in Chapters 8 and 9 can help a team reach consensus around issues and identify bottlenecks, root causes, and dominant themes. A team may also want to use criteria-based decision-making tools to choose the best actions and options to pursue. One category of decision-making tools is the Prioritization Matrix. The Prioritization Matrix is used for testing assumptions and judgments. It is most useful in strategic planning choices and in finding common ground between people with differing opinions.

There are several ways to construct a Prioritization Matrix, but two will be described in this chapter.[2] The first one is the basic Prioritization Matrix, which was introduced in Chapter 1. The second way is the more detailed Full Analytical Criteria Method.

Both constructions will help the team define criteria for selecting an idea to pursue and will support the selection process. However, the team may want to use the basic Prioritization Matrix to narrow down alternatives that have been generated by the creativity tools and/or screened out by the Nominal Group Technique or the Interrelationship Digraph.

"All good things which exist are the fruits of originality."

John Stuart Mill

---

1. Material for this chapter has been adapted from the following sources: Michael Brassard and Diane Ritter, *The Memory Jogger™ II: A Pocket Guide of Tools for Continuous Improvement and Effective Planning* (Methuen, MA: GOAL/QPC, 1994), 105–114; Michael Brassard et al., *Coach's Guide to The Memory Jogger™II: The Easy-to-Use, Complete Reference for Working with Improvement and Planning Tools in Teams* (Methuen, MA: GOAL/QPC, 1995), 141–158; and Michael Brassard, *The Memory Jogger Plus+®* (Methuen, MA: GOAL/QPC, 1989), 99–134.

2. Two other methods, the Consensus Criteria Method and the Combination ID/Matrix Method, are explained in *The Memory Jogger Plus+®*.

Chapter 10

Because it is easy to use, the basic Prioritization Matrix can help a team look at a large number of ideas and select the best five or six ideas. The team can then use the Full Analytical Criteria Method to examine these five or six ideas in more detail.

Basic Prioritization Matrix

Chapter 1, Heuristic Redefinition, presented an approach for better defining a problem. This creativity tool includes the basic Prioritization Matrix. This matrix can also be used with any number of ideas generated from the other creativity tools.

Definition of the Tool

The basic Prioritization Matrix is an easy-to-use method for selecting an idea by using criteria based on data.

Use of the Tool

The basic Prioritization Matrix provides a simple method for idea selection. It is particularly useful when a team needs to decide on where to focus its activities among many ideas and wants to base that decision on specific data or criteria. Since it requires fewer criteria than the Full Analytical Method, it is an easier option for narrowing down a large list of ideas.

Overview of the Tool Process

A team must first determine the criteria for rating ideas. Once the team has established the criteria, a team member can construct a matrix that will allow the team to easily rate and choose the best alternatives.

Applying the Tool: Basic Prioritization Matrix

Outline of Steps

Step	Activity
1.	Determine the criteria to be used in rating the ideas.
2.	Construct a matrix for rating ideas against the designated criteria.
3.	Rate each idea against the criteria; assign ratings; figure totals.
4.	Discuss and choose the idea(s) based on the total rating.

Step-by-Step Instructions

Step 1. Determine the criteria to be used in rating the ideas.

The team should discuss the criteria for rating the ideas. One option is to use the criteria listed in Chapter 1:

- Likelihood that the idea will help the team successfully achieve the goal
- Ease of implementation of the idea
- Expected impact of the idea on the goal

Example

After using the Brainwriting 6-3-5 tool to generate a large number of ideas on how to develop the best new product development strategy for the department, the team reduced the list using Nominal Group Technique. The team produced two top strategies:

- Work on various aspects of a new product concurrently
- "Back up" to figure out what customers need

The team decided it needed to use another idea selection tool to be sure these were the appropriate strategies to recommend. The team chose the basic Prioritization Matrix to first narrow down the set of alternatives. The team decided that the criteria it wanted to use for making this initial selection were:

- Likelihood of successfully meeting the goal

- Ease of implementation

- Expected impact of the idea on the goal

Step 2. Construct a matrix for rating ideas against the designated criteria.

The team builds a matrix based on the number of criteria to be used in rating the ideas. For example, a team may choose these criteria:

- Likelihood that the idea will help the team successfully achieve the goal

- Ease of implementation of the idea

- Expected impact of the idea on the goal

Variations on these three criteria are at the option of the team. Some other criteria might include:

- Cost of implementation

- Likelihood that the problem will be permanently solved

- Likely to produce the most realistic possibilities

In this case, the matrix should have five columns and one row for each idea. The team should label each column, from left to right, with the following:

- Idea

- Likelihood of successfully reaching the goal

- Ease of implementation

- Expected impact on the problem

- Total

Example

The matrix that the team constructed is shown in Figure 10-1.

Idea	Likelihood of successfully meeting goal	Ease of implementation	Expected Impact on the Goal	Total
A. Work on various aspects of a new product concurrently				
B. Get more young and more experienced people on the team				
C. Get 50 projects' experience into one team				
D. Practice forward thinking, or how to think in the future				
E. Develop a family of products around a core delivery system				
F. Use modular development with defined interfaces				
G. Keep talking to users				
H. "Back up" to figure out what customers need				

Figure 10-1: Basic Prioritization Matrix for Problem Defined as "What is the best new product development strategy for our department?"

"I said that an expert was a fella who was afraid to learn anything new because then he wouldn't be an expert anymore."

Harry S. Truman

Chapter 10

Step 3. Rate each idea statement against the criteria; assign ratings; figure totals.

The team can use the following rating scale:

3 = Good/High

2 = Average/Medium

1 = Poor/ Low

Team members can discuss each idea and decide on a rating for each of the three categories. The ratings are then totaled.

Example

Figure 10-2 shows the team's ratings for the ideas.

Idea	Likelihood of successfully meeting goal	Ease of implementation	Expected Impact on the Goal	Total
A. Work on various aspects of a new product concurrently	2	1	3	6
B. Get more young and more experienced people on the team	2	2	2	6
C. Get 50 projects' experience into one team	3	2	3	8
D. Practice forward thinking, or how to think in the future	3	2	3	8
E. Develop a family of products around a core delivery system	3	1	3	7
F. Use modular development with defined interfaces	2	1	2	5
G. Keep talking to users	3	3	3	9
H. "Back up" to figure out what customers need	3	1	2	6

3 = Good/High
2 = Average/Medium
1 = Poor/Low

Figure 10-2: Team's Ratings of the Ideas

Step 4. Discuss and choose the idea(s) based on the total rating.

The totals provide team members with information to discuss. For example, just because an idea statement scored high on this matrix, it does not mean that it fits into the company's strategy, is within the company's accepted risk level, or is otherwise worth pursuing. The positives and negatives of each approach need to be determined and debated by the team. If team members are working with a small number of ideas, they can choose one or two ideas to explore further.

For more complex or critical problems, which may have generated a large number of ideas, the team can use the Full Analytical Criteria Method for further exploration of five or six ideas.

Example

The team determined there were four ideas that scored well on the basic Prioritization Matrix that made sense for them to pursue. Those ideas were:

C. Get 50 projects' experience into one team, or "develop a best practices manual."

D. Practice forward thinking, or how to think in the future. (The team decided to clarify this strategy as "Develop strategic thinking skills in order to anticipate the future.")

E. Develop a family of products around a core delivery system.

G. Keep talking to users.

The team used the Full Analytical Criteria Method to decide among the four ideas. While in this example the team chose to further explore the ideas using a second matrix, it is not always necessary.

Note how this example differs from the team's conclusion in Chapter 9. There, the team's use of Nominal Group Technique resulted in selecting items A, concurrent work, and H, customer needs. In this case, when ease of implementation is considered, regularly talking to users (G) is more effective.

Full Analytical Criteria Method[3]

Introduction

The second type of Prioritization Matrix, the Full Analytical Criteria Method, is a more detailed and involved tool. This approach encourages full discussion and consensus on critical issues. It tends to be time consuming, but the quality of the results would indicate that the time is well invested.

Definition of the Tool

The Full Analytical Criteria Method uses weighted criteria to prioritize tasks, issues, product/service characteristics or other factors. This tool helps a team decide where to devote scarce resources. By using the Full Analytical Criteria Method to build a Prioritization Matrix, a team is forced to compare each criterion and option to every other criterion and option. This method is superior to a general discussion because it allows the team to make detailed comparisons and conclusions, whereas a general discussion can tend to ramble, lose direction, or go in circles.

Use of the Tool

This tool will help a team quickly identify disagreements so they may be resolved early in the decision-making process. It focuses a team on the best thing(s) to do, thereby dramatically increasing the chances for implementation success.

This tool breaks down a large number of factors and choices into individual decisions. The team can then use the matrix to make thorough decisions by focusing on just one cell at a time. In doing this, the team will uncover very basic assumptions and biases of team members. Because the tool promotes full discussion and consensus on the issues, it fosters open discussion, limits hidden agendas, and thus reduces the chances of selecting a team member's pet project.

Because this tool is complex, rigorous, and somewhat time consuming, it should be used when decisions are critical to the organization or when consensus is vital to success. For example, one team used this tool

---

3. The Full Analytical Criteria Method is a simplified adaptation of an even more rigorous model known as the Analytical Hierarchy Process. It is based on the work of Thomas Saaty, which he describes in his book *Decision Making for Leaders*.

to help decide what software packages should become standard throughout their organization. Another team used it to select a dean for a college.

There must be several criteria that need to be applied in analyzing options. All of the criteria should play a significant role in the decision. For example, if one criterion, such as "implementable in the next 30 days," renders the other criteria unimportant, this method is unnecessary and not very worthwhile.

Overview of the Tool Process

There are three major phases of building a Prioritization Matrix with the Full Analytical Criteria Method. In the first phase, the team defines, prioritizes, and assigns weights to a list of criteria. In the next phase, team members prioritize the list of options based on each criterion. In the final phase, the team selects the best option(s) across all criteria.

Applying the Tool: Full Analytical Criteria Method

Outline of Steps

Step	Activity
1.	Agree on the ultimate goal to be achieved and describe it in a clear, concise sentence.
2.	Create the list of criteria to be applied to the options generated.
3.	Judge the relative importance of each criterion as compared to every other criterion.
4.	Compare all of the options to each other on the basis of the weighted criterion.
5.	Compare each option based on all criteria combined.
6.	Choose the best option(s) across all criteria.

Step-by-Step Instructions

Step 1. Agree on the ultimate goal to be achieved and describe it in a clear, concise sentence.

The team needs to agree on a clear goal statement because it will strongly affect which criteria are used. Therefore, the team needs to take the time necessary to reach consensus on the statement.

If this step has already been accomplished, move on to Step 2.

Step 2. Create the list of criteria to be applied to the options generated.

The team can brainstorm a list of criteria or review previous documents that are available, like corporate goals or budget-related guidelines. It's very important for the team to reach consensus on the final criteria and their meanings.

Example

The team selected the following criteria for deciding on the best new product development strategy for the department:

A. Potential to achieve breakthrough

B. Cost involved

C. Implementation speed

D. Training required

Step 3. Judge the relative importance of each criterion as compared to every other criterion.

After the team has developed a list of criteria, it rates each criterion against the others so that a weighting number can be assigned. The team builds an L-shaped matrix to facilitate this process.

The team lists all the criteria on both the vertical and horizontal sides of the matrix, crossing out cells where one criterion is compared to itself. The team establishes a rating scale, then rates the importance of each criterion against the other criteria. An example of a rating scale is shown in Figure 10–3.

Number	Meaning
1	Equally important/preferred
5	More important/preferred
10	Much more important/preferred
1/5	Less important/preferred
1/10	Much less important/preferred

Figure 10-3: Rating Scale

The team compares each criterion in the rows to those in the columns. Each time a weight (e.g., 1, 5, 10) is recorded in a row cell, its reciprocal value (e.g., 1/5, 1/10) must be recorded in the corresponding column cell. In the example below, the team rates Criterion A significantly more important than Criterion B. Therefore, in the cell where Criterion B is compared to Criterion A, the reciprocal value must be given to be consistent.

The team converts the fractions into decimals and determines the ratings for each criterion across the row. The row totals are then added to reach a grand total. Finally, the team divides each row total by the grand total to convert each row total to a relative decimal value. This relative decimal value becomes the weighting score that will be used as the multiplier in the final matrix that compares all of the options across all of the criteria.

Since the criteria weightings are meant to be indicators of major patterns and differences, the team should carefully review the totals and percentages.

Example

The team constructed an L-shaped matrix for determining the weight of the four criteria. The team followed the instructions for rating each criterion against one another, according to the scale described in Figure 10–3. The relative weightings for each of the criteria are listed below.

Criteria \ Criteria	A	B	C	D	Row Total	Relative Decimal Value (RT÷GT)
A		10	5	5	20	0.49
B	1/10		1/5	1/5	0.5	0.01
C	1/5	5		10	15.2	0.37
D	1/5	5	1/10		5.3	0.13
				Grand Total	41	

Figure 10-4: Rating Criterion Against Criterion

Step 4. Compare all of the options to each other on the basis of the weighted criterion.

Now that the team has determined the relative importance of each criterion, all ideas can be judged on how completely they meet the chosen criterion. The team should create an L-shaped matrix with all of the ideas listed on the vertical and horizontal axes, and the criterion listed in the left-hand corner of the matrix. There will be as many idea matrices as there are criteria to be applied.

The team should use the same rating scale (1, 5, 10) as in Step 3, but the wording for each criterion should be specific. For example, in the example below, instead of "more important/ preferred," the team can use the criterion on which the options are being evaluated to more fully explain the ratings—in this case "more costly."

As in Step 3, the team should total the rows across the matrix. They can then compute a grand total as in the initial criterion matrix. Finally, they compute the relative decimal value for each option, by dividing the row total by the grand total. The relative decimal value is called the "option rating."

This process is repeated for each criterion.

Example

The team's first matrix is shown in Figure 10-5. The team repeated the same process for the other three criteria. (These matrices are not shown.)

A. Potential to Achieve Breakthrough	1.	2.	3.	4.	Row Total	Relative Decimal Value (RT÷GT)
1. Get 50 projects' experience into one team		5	1/5	1/5	5.4	0.17
2. Practice forward thinking, or how to think in the future	1/5		1/5	5	5.4	0.17
3. Develop a family of products around a core delivery system	5	5		1/5	10.2	0.33
4. Keep talking to users	5	1/5	5		10.2	0.33
				Grand Total	31.2	

Figure 10-5: Options Against Criterion A

Step 5. Compare each option based on all criteria combined.

The next step for the team is to compare each option based on all criteria combined. Using another L-shaped summary matrix, the team can list all criteria on the horizontal axis (across the columns) and all options on the vertical axis (down the rows).

In each matrix cell, the team multiplies the "criteria weighting" of each criterion (decimal value from Step 3) by the "option rating" (decimal value from Step 4). This creates an "option score."

Then the teams can add each option score across all criteria for a row total. Each row total is divided by the grand total and converted to the relative decimal value.

Example

The team proceeded to determine the option scores for each one of the four criteria:

Criteria / Options	A (0.49)	B (0.01)	C (0.37)	D (0.13)	Row Total	Relative Decimal Value (RT÷GT)
1. Get 50 projects' experience into one team	0.08	0	0.04	0.01	0.14	0.14
2. Practice forward thinking, or how to think in the future	0.08	0	0.18	0.07	0.34	0.34
3. Develop a family of products around a core delivery system	0.16	0	0	0.02	0.18	0.18
4. Keep talking to users	0.16	0	0.15	0.03	0.34	0.34
				Grand Total	1.00	

Figure 10-6: Options Against All Criteria

Step 6. Choose the best option(s) across all criteria.

The team compares option scores to decide which idea to pursue. When reviewing and discussing the results, the team needs to be aware that this method is more systematic than traditional decision making, but it is not a science. Team members must use common sense and judgment when ideas are rated very closely, but must remain open to non-traditional conclusions. The team should also decide on the next action steps.

Example

The team reviewed the alternative strategies that received the highest ratings through using the Full Analytical Criteria Method.

The alternatives with the highest scores were:

- Practice forward thinking.
- Keep talking with users.

The team was surprised that their analysis using this tool produced these two alternatives. They reviewed the steps and small decisions made throughout the application of the tool to make sure the choices all made sense. The team decided that the resulting two alternatives were indeed appropriate. In looking at the results from the use of the Nominal Group Technique, the team decided that those results reflected current thinking. The use of the Full Analytical Criteria Method produced results that reflected more forward thinking on the part of the team.

Summary of the Tool

The Full Analytical Method forces a discussion of assumptions right from the beginning of the comparison of criteria. Each step of the process gives team members the chance to understand why people may agree or disagree. It is difficult to simply gloss over fundamental disagreements that could later return to block the implementation of the team's decision. In the end, this method is one of the best for encouraging and harvesting the fruits of honest discussion and true consensus.

Enhancing the Process

Helpful Hints

Take the Time to Get the Benefits. One of the key challenges for the team leader and facilitator is to convince team members of the value of this approach. It can be time consuming and tedious. However, it is critical that the team follows the process step by step. If the team has three or four established criteria, which will be applied to six to eight options, the team should plan on at least two hours to complete the matrices (with a quick up-front training before real-time practice on a problem). This estimate depends on the level of complexity of the problem and the degree of controversy around the subject. However, one strength of this method is that fundamental differences of opinion and/or approach are forced to the surface for consideration and reconciliation. In situations where consensus is vital to the success of the effort, this is time well spent.

"I had never been as resigned to ready-made ideas as I was to ready-made clothes, perhaps because although I couldn't sew, I could think."

Jane Rule

Chapter 10

Keep the Numbers Manageable. Since a matrix is required for evaluating ideas relative to each criterion, the number of matrices can multiply rapidly. The recommended number of criteria is three to six.

Make the Criteria Explicit. The team leader or facilitator should make sure that everyone on the team understands the criteria in the same way. The most effective method for doing this is to create an accepted operational definition of each criterion. These definitions should be kept handy and visible.

Frequently Asked Questions

Q. **What is the best method to construct this tool?**

A. The following matrix can help a team to decide which method will be the most useful.

Method	Description	Typically Use When:
Basic Prioritization Matrix	An easy-to-use method for selecting an idea by using criteria based on data.	• Larger teams are involved (8 or more people) • Options are many (20–30 choices) • There are only a few criteria (3 items) • Quick consensus is needed to proceed
Full Analytical Criteria Method	See description above.	• Smaller teams are involved (3–8 people) • Options are few (5–10 choices) • There are relatively few criteria (3–6 items) • Complete consensus is needed • The stakes are high if the plan fails
Consensus Criteria Method	This method follows the same steps as in the Full Analytical Criteria Method except it uses a combination of weighted voting, and ranking is used instead of paired comparisons.	• Larger teams are involved (8 or more people) • Options are many (10–20 choices) • There are a significant number of criteria (6–15 items) • Quick consensus is needed to proceed
Combination ID/Matrix Method	This method is different from the other two because it is based on cause and effect, rather than criteria.	• Interrelationships among options are high, and finding the option with the greatest impact is critical

For additional information, consult any of these GOAL/QPC publications: *The Memory Jogger™ II*, the *Coach's Guide to The Memory Jogger™ II*, and *The Memory Jogger Plus+®*.

Q. How many criteria are too many?

A. If the team is using the process for the first time, three or four criteria are a wise choice. Any fewer than this, and the team may feel that the matrices are too simple to warrant the time spent. Any more criteria than this would probably tax the patience of a team that is likely to be skeptical anyway.

Q. Why use the 1, 5, 10, 1/5, 1/10 rating scale?

A. This computation scheme was chosen by GOAL/QPC for its ease of use and simplicity. This tool has been designed for use without a computer and by a variety of people. While the rating scale may not be as sensitive to small distinctions between ratings as some other rating scales, this scale has proven to lead to the same results.

"It's not the tragedies that kill us, it's the messes."

Dorothy Parker

Pugh New Concept Selection Tool

Introduction

Another tool that helps teams to select a few good ideas from dozens or hundreds of ideas is Stuart Pugh's New Concept Selection, one of the most successful and popular ways of finding the best and strongest idea or concept. This tool was first developed and used in England and is now being used throughout the world for product development applications. Pugh's New Concept Selection Tool is often applied to enhance Quality Function Deployment[1], the process by which a multifunctional team translates the voice of the customer into product and operational decisions. To date, it has been used in a broad range of activities, including organizational development and marketing, as well as product development. It is presented here as an important addition to the set of idea selection tools.

Definition of the Tool

While the Pugh New Concept Selection tool is a structured and disciplined approach to idea selection, in the process of idea selection its use can actually foster creativity. A team uses a criteria matrix to help it evaluate and choose from many concept/idea alternatives. Through application of its disciplined approach, the team will find that the best and strongest concepts emerge. In this process, however, the team often generates new ideas that are a synthesis of the best features of the different alternatives. The final choice of an idea may be one that the team had yet to consider or even know about.

---

1. Bob King, *Better Designs in Half the Time* (Methuen, MA: GOAL/QPC, 1989).

"The idea was fragrant with possibilities."

Jean Ferris

Chapter 11

Use of the Tool

The power of this tool is in helping teams to evaluate concepts and in facilitating creative thinking. It can provide teams with:

- a greater understanding of the problem or opportunity under consideration.

- a greater understanding of potential solutions.

- a thorough, structured analysis of the reasons why one concept or idea is stronger or weaker than other concepts or ideas.

- an understanding of the interactions among the proposed concepts or ideas, which can give rise to a new concept or idea.

The Pugh New Concept Selection tool can be used by itself or can be combined with other tools. A team should consider using this tool after it has identified a number of ideas or concepts. It is an excellent tool for shaping multiple alternatives into the best idea or concept. It can also help individuals and teams break out of old ways of thinking, especially when some of the players are experts in the subject under consideration.

Overview of the Tool Process

To use the Pugh New Concept Selection Tool, a team needs to have a number of ideas or concepts available. The team also needs to have a definition of what constitutes a good idea or concept. When a team is concerned with finding product concepts, the combination of customer requirements, functional requirements, and product specifications define "a good concept." If a team is searching for breakthrough products or services that are beyond the realm of its current understanding of customer needs, the definition of a good idea can be very fuzzy. If the desired breakthrough should perform a function, then a good concept might be one that comes closest to achieving the ideal function, e.g., an electric light will dissipate less energy than a candle or gas lamp. More esoteric idea searches may require more esoteric characterizations of what constitutes a good concept.

The attributes that a team has chosen to define as "a good concept" should be used as the criteria for evaluating the alternative concepts. After this definition of criteria, the team then selects one of the alternatives as the baseline, against which all the other alternatives will be compared. The current product or service is typically chosen as the baseline.

The Idea Edge

Team members first sketch out the alternatives to the same level of detail. Drawings or sketches provide a level of understanding that word descriptions don't always achieve. Then, team members compare each alternative against the baseline and for each of the criteria, judge the alternative on whether it is better than (+), worse than (–), or the same as (s) the baseline. The team totals the "+'s," "–'s," and "s's." The alternative with the most "+'s" is identified as a favored concept. However, it may not be the best possible concept to pursue.

The team analyzes the results of the evaluations. When a team discusses possible ways to remove the negatives and enhance the positives of all the alternatives, the team will often derive an even better alternative, which is a synthesis of the best features of all of the alternatives. Vigorous pursuit of the best alternative can lead to major breakthrough ideas.

Applying the Tool

Outline of Steps

The steps for creating and completing a matrix are listed below. Steps 1–4 are the actions to create the matrix, and steps 5–9 are the actions to derive the best alternative.

Step	Activity
1.	List the ideas or concepts and represent each one with a simple sketch or picture.
2.	Choose the criteria for rating the alternative concepts.
3.	Create an "L-shaped" matrix with the criteria as row headers and the idea/concept sketches as the column headers.
4.	Clarify the concepts.
5.	Choose the baseline.
6.	Rate the alternatives against the baseline.
7.	Total up the ratings.
8.	Discuss how to minimize the negatives and enhance the positives.
9.	Repeat the process until satisfied.
10.	Agree on next steps.

Step-by-Step Instructions

Step 1. List the ideas or concepts and represent each one with a simple sketch or picture.

Team members prepare sketches or other pictorial representations for each concept or idea. The sketches or other pictorial representations should be clear enough for all team members to have an accurate understanding of the concept. Team members can use clay models, working model, schematic drawings or diagrams, artistic renditions, or any other means of visual communication. The different ideas and concepts should be sketched or drawn out to the same level of detail. Otherwise, a breakthrough idea that is not well represented might be dropped in favor of a brilliantly drawn, but more routine idea.

Example

A team has been assembled to develop a new product to meet the needs of high-rise construction crews who work on steel beams several stories above ground level. The product is needed to move bulk materials from the ground up to the steel beam, and along the steel beam. While the basic idea the team has is similar to a wheelbarrow, the wheelbarrow design is not suitable because it lacks maneuverability on a steel beam and this raises safety concerns. The team generated some alternative concepts using several of the creativity tools. These ideas are listed below in Figure 11-1.

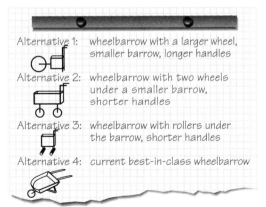

Alternative 1: wheelbarrow with a larger wheel, smaller barrow, longer handles

Alternative 2: wheelbarrow with two wheels under a smaller barrow, shorter handles

Alternative 3: wheelbarrow with rollers under the barrow, shorter handles

Alternative 4: current best-in-class wheelbarrow

Figure 11-1: Ideas for Redesigning the Wheelbarrow to Transport Bulk Materials at High-Rise Construction Sites

"I am not young enough to know everything."

James M. Barrie

Step 2. Choose the criteria for rating the alternative concepts.

If the concepts are product concepts, then the criteria should be derived from customer requirements and technical specifications. On the other hand, if the ideas were generated in search of a product or service that customers did not know they needed or wanted (whom do you ask about light bulbs in a world of candles and lanterns?), the criteria may be best generated by team members practicing creative thinking or finding experts in the subject area. In either case, the team needs to be sure that:

- The criteria have been defined without any ambiguity and are viewed from the customers' perspective.

- All team members have an equal understanding of the criteria.

- Everyone agrees on all the criteria.

For product concepts, the criteria should include clearly articulated levels of customer satisfaction, quality, and costs.

Example

The team, based on preliminary feedback from customers, agreed on the following criteria for rating the alternatives:

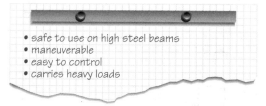

Figure 11-2: Criteria for Evaluating Wheelbarrow Designs

Step 3. Create an "L-shaped" matrix with the criteria as row headers and the idea/concept sketches as the column headers.

The team constructs a matrix to make it easier to compare each concept or idea against the criteria. The sketches, images, models, etc., that were chosen in Step 1 to represent the concepts and ideas should be added to the head column cells in the matrix. The sketches or images should be large enough for all team members to see. The team may need additional information to fully understand all the concepts and ideas, and to put the team at the same level of understanding with each of the concepts as with the baseline. Such information should be located around the room in some arrangement consistent with the order of the columns in the matrix and be identified by the sketches or images. These "display booths" of information should be easily accessible to facilitate comparisons of alternatives. The "booths" might be regarded as extensions of the matrix entries—the explanation of what the sketches and images represent.

Example

	Alt. 1 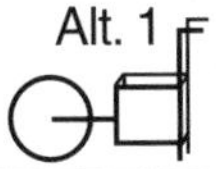	Alt. 2 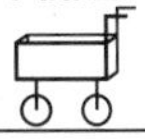	Alt. 3 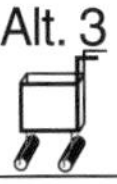	Alt. 4 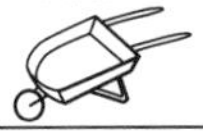
Safe to use on high steel beams				
Maneuverable				
Easy to control				
Carries heavy loads				

Figure 11-3: "L-shaped" Matrix for Comparing Wheelbarrow Designs Against Criteria

Step 4. Clarify the alternatives.

The alternatives are explored one by one until all of the team members reach a common understanding of each of the alternatives. Prior to this discussion team members will have their own perspectives, levels of understanding, and personal opinions about the different concepts and ideas. Discussion helps bring team members to the same levels of understanding. The clarification process is very important because it can bring new understanding of the specifications and requirements of the solution and new insights to the problem itself. In the process of such clarification, team members often generate new solution alternatives.

Step 5. Choose the baseline.

The team examines the alternatives and chooses a baseline (typically an existing product), such as this year's model. (If the team is going through the tool a second time, then the baseline will typically be the favored alternative.)

If a current product is not chosen as the baseline, then the current product should be included in the list of alternatives. For product concepts, the team might also choose as a baseline the best-in-class product or a projection of what product introductions could be best in class.

Example

The team decided to pick the current product as the baseline for their matrix. Their matrix now looks like this:

	Alt. 1	Alt. 2	Alt. 3	Alt. 4
Safe to use on high steel beams				B A
Maneuverable				S E
Easy to control				L I
Carries heavy loads				N E

Figure 11-4: Alternative 4 (Current Best-in-Class Wheelbarrow) Chosen as Baseline

Step 6. Rate the alternatives against the baseline.

The team's goal in this step is to use the criteria agreed to in Step 2, to evaluate each alternative against the baseline. Team members set up a comparison between each alternative and the baseline by inserting each criterion into a question such as: "Is Alternative #1 easier to use (or whatever the criterion is) than the baseline?" Other criteria could be "easier to develop than," "less complex than," "less prone to," and so on.

If the alternative is better than the baseline on that particular criterion, a "+" is marked in the appropriate cell of the matrix. If the alternative is worse than the baseline on that particular criterion (e.g., more expensive than, more difficult to develop than, more complex than the baseline, etc.), then a minus sign "−" is marked in the appropriate cell of the matrix. If the alternative is essentially the same as the baseline— not "more or less than" compared to the baseline on that particular criterion—then the team marks an "s" in the cell.

The specific questions used in this step depend on the criteria in the rows that the team has agreed are important. The questions and the efforts to assign values (+, −, or s) can often lead to revisions or additions to the team's original list of criteria. If this happens, the team should add the criterion or criteria to the matrix and start the evaluation from the beginning.

"The brain has muscles for thinking as the legs have muscles for walking."
J.O. DeLa Mettrie

Chapter 11

The primary benefit of this step is not filling in the matrix. The true benefits are the insights that team members gain in discussing and trying to understand the value of each cell of the matrix. The increased understanding and clarification that result often stimulate thoughts about how to take the best features from, for example, Alternatives #3 and #4, and combine them with the best features of Alternative #2. In this process, often a new idea, superior to any of the current alternatives, will emerge.

Example

The team members ask whether Alternative #1 is better than, worse than, or the same as the baseline on the first criterion: safe to use on high steel beams. They decided that Alternative #1 was the same as the baseline on this criterion and therefore marked an "s" in this cell of the matrix. They decided to go on down the column, comparing Alternative #1 to the baseline on the other three criteria. In each case, they asked whether Alternative #1 was better than, worse than, or the same as the baseline on the each criterion. Their matrix begins to take shape. See Figure 11-5.

	Alt. 1	Alt. 2	Alt. 3	Alt. 4
Safe to use on high steel beams	+			B A
Maneuverable	s			S E
Easy to control	–			L I
Carries heavy loads	–			N E

Figure 11-5: Rating Alternative 1 Against the Baseline

Step 7. Total up the ratings.

After completing the matrix, the team compiles the scores by totaling the number of pluses, minuses, and s's at the bottom of each column. Minuses are not subtracted from the pluses; they are totaled separately. The purpose of this step is to find the best concepts suggested by the pluses, not to numerically rate the alternatives. The team should not let the numbers drive out learnings.

Example

The team continued to ask the same set of questions for each of the other alternatives compared to the baseline on each of the four criteria. Their completed matrix, with the totals of pluses, minuses, and s's is shown in Figure 11-6.

	Alt. 1	Alt. 2	Alt. 3	Alt. 4
Safe to use on high steel beams	+	+	+	B
				A
Maneuverable	s	+	−	S
				E
Easy to control	−	s	−	L
				I
Carries heavy loads	−	−	−	N
				E
Totals	1+ 1s 2−	2+ 1s 1−	1+ 0s 3−	

Figure 11-6: Completed Matrix for Comparing Wheelbarrow Designs to Baseline

Step 8. Discuss how to minimize the negatives and enhance the positives.

A concept can often be revised to minimize a negative value, and conversely, the positives can be enhanced. A team can do this by finding the other alternatives in the matrix that have been marked with pluses for the criterion and exploring how certain features of the alternative concepts might be combined. Any discussions about reducing the negatives and enhancing the positives will usually yield improved insights and ideas.

Example

The team reviewed the different alternatives and saw that the key issue was whether their ideas could be used to improve the baseline wheelbarrow by increasing its capacity for carrying heavy loads. Unfortunately, none of the team's alternatives had improved upon the load-bearing capacity of the current best-in-class wheelbarrow. The team decided to move on to Step 9 and repeat the process.

Step 9. Repeat the process until satisfied.

While the team may be comfortable that it has found a good idea, another round through the matrix is an important next step, particularly if the team has been through the process just once. In some cases, the team may change its perception of the product, the market, or the customer after the first round. In other cases, some team members may not be entirely comfortable with the rating process or with the concept that emerged with the most pluses.

There are several ways for the team to proceed at this point:

- If the team is relatively comfortable with the concept or design that emerged, it should still choose a different baseline and repeat Steps 5–8 to confirm the choice. The new baseline might be the alternative that was rated with the most pluses or it might be a new alternative that emerged in the evaluation process. The "second pass" through the process almost always yields new insights and stronger alternatives. This additional work should result in a greater understanding of the problem and its possible solutions.

- If new criteria have emerged during any pass through the process, the team can refine the criteria and repeat the matrix with the selected alternatives.

- If the team is dissatisfied with the results, the team can generate new ideas and repeat the process with the selected criteria. Team members may find that they missed some ideas during previous idea generation efforts. The team may have come up with some new ideas during the first time through the matrix, possibly as a result of a new combination of alternatives or a new synthesis that emerged. In some cases, the team may have discarded some "crazy ideas" from the first idea generation session, which they may after all decide are quite appropriate to consider.

The alternating idea generation and idea selection steps, which Pugh called Controlled Convergence, provide an orderly process that maximizes the creativity introduced into the narrowing down process. People often find more excitement in creative activities than in analysis and evaluation efforts. The process of alternating steps adds the excitement of creativity to the team's efforts to analyze and evaluate ideas, thereby enhancing both creativity and idea selection. The narrowing down process may stimulate new ideas, or new ideas may be generated by the next idea generation session.

The alternating steps are continued until further effort seems unrewarding, that is, when no new ideas are being generated, and the best idea has clearly emerged. The repetitive sequence of divergent and convergent thinking cycles adds significant creativity to the use of the Pugh New Concept Selection tool and dramatically improves the chances of generating the best ideas and of finding that elusive breakthrough idea.[2]

Whether a team moves ahead with its results or starts the process over to generate new ideas and new criteria depends on the team's level of satisfaction with the results.

Once the team has experienced the iterative applications of the Pugh New Concept Selection tool, team members should feel confident in their final choice, knowing the strengths and weaknesses of the selected alternative. As the work on making refinements proceeds, and depending on the complexity and criticality of the design problem, the team may find that it needs to repeat the

2. Stuart Pugh, *Total Design: Integrated Methods for Successful Product Engineering* (Reading, MA: Addison-Wesley, 1991), 74–5.

steps several times to get to a final, acceptable solution. However, the rewards of mixing idea generation and selection thought processes and tools can be well worth the team's time.

If the team has completed the matrix a second time and is satisfied with its results, it can move on to Step 10.

Example

The wheelbarrow team members determined that they needed to generate new alternatives based on the insight they had gained in their first pass through the matrix. Using the creativity tools and taking several passes through the matrix, they ended up with an idea that they agreed to apply to the development of a prototype.

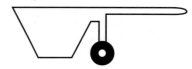

Step 10. Agree on next steps.

The next steps for the team often include more detailed design work on the chosen alternative before implementation can begin. The idea selection session should end on agreement on and assignment of the next steps.

Summary of the Tool

Use of the Pugh New Concept Selection Tool provides a structure for teams to objectively compare alternatives and come up with a solid solution. While the matrix provides the team with a structure for making a decision, this decision remains with the team. Through thorough analysis and comparison, the team can creatively select the strongest and best alternative and will be comfortable in defending their choice. This tool helps team members review new concepts more objectively and helps them avoid being limited in their thinking by present technology or products.

Enhancing the Process

Helpful Hints

Make the Matrix Visible to All. Both the images and the matrix should be large enough to be visible for everyone in the room. The facilitator should consider using a large whiteboard (manual or electronic) for the matrix.

Identify the Sources for the Criteria. There are a variety of sources, which include: customer requirements, quality characteristics, or product or service functions.

Choose a Different Baseline When a Strong Preference Fails to Emerge. If no strong preference has emerged after the team has evaluated all the alternatives in Step 8, then the team should choose a different baseline to compare it with the other alternatives and complete the matrix again.

Frequently Asked Questions

Q. **Can this selection tool be used with service concepts as well as product concepts?**

A. Yes, the Pugh New Concept Selection Tool can be used with any product or service, at any stage of design.

Q. **How much time needs to be allocated for this tool?**

A. The Pugh New Concept Selection Tool can consume several hours of a team's time, depending on the level of training and experience with the tool, and the complexity of the issue. According to Stuart Pugh, ". . . depending upon the complexity of the project, it is not untypical in our experience to carry out five or six evaluations and comparisons before a single concept emerges, which is then carried through to final design, detailing, and manufacture. A single typical matrix run may take up to a whole day to complete."[3]

For Further Study

For additional examples, see *Better Designs in Half the Time*, Bob King, Methuen, MA: GOAL/QPC, 1989; and *Creating Innovative Products Using Total Design*, Stuart Pugh. Reading, MA: Addison-Wesley, 1996.

---

3. Stuart Pugh, *Creating Innovative Products Using Total Design* (Reading, MA: Addison-Wesley, 1996), 172.

Implementing Ideas: Project Management Tools at Work

Introduction

Innovation is about the conversion of creativity into real things . . . products, policies, services, initiatives, organizations, and so on, and so on. Even the most brilliant insight serves little purpose if it's left on the laboratory floor. Especially in these hyper-competitive times, the winners are those who can effectively implement, as well as generate, breakthrough ideas. Winning in this case requires a commercialization process that is both quick AND sure. If it's not, competitors are looking to take immediate advantage of virtually any misstep. There is little, if any, margin for error.

This hard reality coincides with another emerging trend: the increasing use of a structured project management process to get work done.[1] Project management processes and tools fit the competitive environment especially well since they allow organizations to:

- Convene teams that exist only for the life of the project.

- Cross functional lines in order to accomplish the goal of the project.

> "In trying to make something new, half the undertaking lies in discovering whether it can be done. Once it has been established that it can, duplication is inevitable."
>
> Helen Gahagan Douglas

---

1. The *Project Management Memory Jogger*™, a GOAL/QPC publication released in 1997, was written in response to this industry trend. It includes a simplified, standard project management process that applies to situations ranging from small scale process improvement to moderately complex, budgeted projects.

- Change work assignments quickly in response to changing market conditions.

- Provide more and more people with the opportunity to exercise leadership.

In support of this expanded use of project teams, there has also been increased use of project management tools, which help to increase the quality and efficiency of completing important tasks. When used in combination with the creativity tools, project management tools can dramatically improve the implementation of innovative ideas by:

- Fostering agreement among the implementers as to what is actually involved in making the idea a reality. This results in a credible, rather than an incredible action plan.

- Making the entire plan visible both before and during implementation. This allows a team to review the plan for completeness and shows clearly where everyone contributes to the overall success of the plan.

- Serving as documentation that can be used for progress reviews and corrective action planning.

Project Management Processes

Over the last 40 years, a number of project management models have evolved. There are differences among them, but they all share one common purpose: to set and maintain the most efficient course toward accomplishing a clearly stated goal. GOAL/QPC introduced a generic model in the *Project Management Memory Jogger*™ that applies well to a wide variety of project types and scopes. As in most effective planning models, this project management process closely mirrors the Plan-Do-Check-Act (PDCA) cycle of continuous improvement and learning. The project management steps are as follows:

1. Creating the project charter: The "big picture" scope and project limits are defined.

2. Working as a team: Team member commitments and team meeting guidelines are clarified.

3. Developing the project plan: Project scope and boundaries are finalized along with matching schedule, budget and staffing estimates.

4. Doing the project: Project progress is monitored and changes made as required.

5. Closing out the project: Customer satisfaction is evaluated and project lessons are captured.

It should be clear from these steps that they apply to many of the types of breakthrough changes that would be generated using the creativity tools. The process itself is very helpful in clarifying both the purpose and path of any proposed innovation. At the very least, such a simple (but disciplined) process will help to keep an important innovation project on track. In other cases, the process may uncover potentially fatal flaws in the logic of creative ideas. Without such a process at the beginning of the project, it could easily proceed down a very expensive and time-consuming dead end.

Project Management Tools

Tools make the process operate more consistently by helping teams to identify the full range of tasks that are necessary to convert an innovative idea into a real product or service. There are a several tools that have emerged as popular and powerful options that serve to strengthen the process management model described in the *Project Management Memory Jogger*™. These are:

- The Process Decision Program Chart (PDPC) is a simple-to-use variation of the Tree Diagram that helps a team to anticipate potential implementation problems and responses. (The Tree Diagram is briefly described in Appendix A.)

- The Gantt Chart is the simplest of the schedule planning and monitoring tools. It is used to show the sequence in which key tasks are scheduled to occur.

- The Activity Network Diagram (AND) is a variation of the PERT Chart, which is an acronym for Program Evaluation and Review Technique. It has been used for decades in all industries to find the most efficient path to project completion. It graphically shows the interdependencies among all project tasks as well as their impact on the project.

This chapter will briefly describe how each of these tools can be used to take a breakthrough idea that has been generated using the creativity tools and efficiently turn it into a practical reality. Without a standard implementation process and tool kit, innovation can become unpredictable and therefore unmanageable.

Process Decision Program Chart (PDPC): A Tool for Contingency Planning

Asking "what if" questions is often considered counterproductive, especially when dealing with an attempted breakthrough. Such questions often seem to break the "creative momentum" of a team. This can actually be true when people throw down roadblocks and then dare the team to scale them. The PDPC has quite the opposite effect on discussions. It turns potential barriers to success into a platform for even more creative thinking.

Definition of the Tool

The PDPC is a tool that individuals and teams can use to anticipate and respond to problems that may arise during the implementation phase of a plan, anticipates LIKELY problems for each major step, and then helps to generate REASONABLE countermeasures to each anticipated problem. Unlike other approaches, the PDPC helps to move a team beyond simply identifying problems. Think of using this tool as a way to "mistake-proof" a plan.

Use of the Tool

This tool is invaluable when the price of project failure is high. In such projects, teams often stumble upon problems and improvise solutions. Unfortunately, solutions generated in the "heat of the battle" are often expedient, inefficient and expensive. As the cost of failure (real or perceived) increases, the tendency becomes ever stronger to "do something . . . do anything!" The PDPC helps a team to reflect and plan, rather than crash and react.

This tool also helps when a project has many tasks that have never been done before, or that are being done in a very different way from the past. Despite this uncertainty, teams are often expected to create detailed, credible action plans. The PDPC helps the team take into account real risks and intelligent alternatives when creating the plan.

Overview of the Tool Process

The team must first identify the broadest implementation steps needed to achieve a goal and post them in a Tree Diagram format. (For more information on the Tree Diagram, consult Appendix A in this book or other books such as *The Memory Jogger™ II* or *The Memory Jogger Plus+®*.) The project can be broken down into further detail, but in most cases a single list of 5–6 major tasks is sufficient. Identify and post likely and significant problems associated with each of the major implementation steps. Generate one or more creative, but reasonable countermeasures to each identified problem. Finally, the team must evaluate all of the potential countermeasures and select the one(s) that can be adopted to either prevent or react to the identified problems.

Applying the Tool (PDPC)

Outline of Steps

Step	Activity
1.	Assemble a team closest to the implementation.
2.	Determine proposed implementation steps.
3.	Identify likely problems related to each broad implementation step.
4.	Generate possible and reasonable responses for each likely problem.
5.	Choose the most effective countermeasures and build them into a revised implementation plan.

Step-by-Step Instructions

Step 1. Assemble a team closest to the implementation.

Since the major benefit of the PDPC is to surface likely implementation problems, then those people closest to an issue or problem should be in the best position to identify such issues. This

"The power of imagination makes us infinite."

John Muir

limits the "wishful thinking" that was so indispensable in the idea generation phase, but that can become a barrier to successful innovation.

Step 2. Determine proposed implementation steps.

These steps should be stated as broadly as possible and then recorded. (The steps should follow the sequence of implementation.) Don't worry about missing individual steps in the project. The broad steps will be expanded further as needed, based upon the number and severity of the problems connected with each one.

Step 3. Identify likely problems related to each broad implementation step.

This is an opportunity to anticipate problems that have occurred in similar projects or that are easy to imagine given the situation and/or players involved. This is NOT a chance to surface every imaginable project pitfall since the dawn of time. If the team is digging too hard for problems, the problems are probably more trivial than traumatic.

Step 4. Generate possible and reasonable responses for each likely problem.

Brainstorm actions that could be taken to either prevent a problem from occurring or to react intelligently if it does occur. This step requires a balanced approach. Think creatively while considering the practical things that can be accomplished.

Step 5. Choose the most effective countermeasures and build them into a revised implementation plan.

Turn a potential problem into an asset by building selected countermeasures into the plan. This can result in changes ranging from slight to paradigm shaking.

Summary of the Tool

The PDPC is a simple, powerful, and pragmatic tool for effective contingency planning. It takes advantage of the straightforward logic of a Tree Diagram, while allowing a team to expand its thinking to include both problems and creative solutions. By giving team members permission to think "negatively" and the responsibility to respond intelligently, the PDPC can help a team produce a plan that is very likely to work. This is a real contribution in high-risk, low-experience situations.

Enhancing the Process

Helpful Hints

Stay Broad when Listing the Steps. There is a temptation to get very detailed in listing implementation steps when the team is thinking of how to anticipate potential problems. This temptation relates to the assumption that all steps are equally prone to problems. This, of course, is not true. Some activities are simpler than others or have been done many times and are routine.

When starting the PDPC, identify only 5–6 major steps. The steps with the most problems associated with them will naturally be broken down into further detail. This method guarantees that the team will spend the greatest time on the tasks that pose the greatest threat to the success of the overall project. This method also helps the team to focus its creativity on those areas of an implementation plan that truly require a breakthrough.

Do a Quick Pass on the Entire Project Instead of Detailing a Small Piece of It. The PDPC is somewhat unpredictable; it's never clear which step in the implementation plan will spawn a breakthrough. Consider the example of a team that was recruited to develop a company newsletter. The last step of the team's plan was, "distribute the newsletter." The last potential problem the team identified was, "few people read it." This potential problem led the team to the idea of putting the newsletter on the company's internal electronic network.

Having an electronic version of the newsletter would allow each person to print only those articles and features that he or she thought would be interesting. In effect, each person would get a customized newsletter. This approach helps the team eliminate many of the tasks associated with a traditional newsletter. If this team had become trapped in the early steps of the process, then this dramatic change in the plan would never have occurred.

The Idea Edge

Frequently Asked Questions

Q. How do you know when enough "what if's" have been identified?

A. Most activities have 2–3 potential "what if's" that come to mind quickly. Often, these are the activities that happen most frequently or have occurred most recently. These are also the problems that tend to have a significant impact on implementation. As the team adds more potential problems, it's helpful to ask, "What are the chances of this problem occurring? If it did occur, would it have a significant impact on the implementation step?" This will prevent the team from adding unlikely, trivial problems to a sizeable list of very real issues that need to be addressed. More is not always better!

Q. Doesn't the PDPC encourage people to think, "can't do" instead of "can do"?

A. Quite the contrary. Problems can either be seen as gold to be mined or garbage to be buried. Unanticipated problems act as landmines on the path to progress. By identifying and resolving them, we take firmer control of the future. A positive, structured approach to problems can turn "what can you do" fatalism to a "can do" plan for an efficient, effective implementation.

For Further Study

- *The Memory Jogger™ II*, pages 160–162
- *The Memory Jogger Plus+®*, pages 171–199
- *Coach's Guide to The Memory Jogger™ II*, pages 213–216
- *The Memory Jogger™ II Off-the-Shelf Modular Training Materials*, Process Decision Program Chart (PDPC)

Example of Tool Usage

Based upon the work of a team that had brainstormed ideas around the question of how to expand the use of the Web/Internet in the company, a sub-team was asked to create a project plan for starting up a newsletter for Web/Internet users. The sub-team started the project by doing a Process Decision Program Chart (PDPC). The team chose to do a PDPC because several team members had tried to start newsletters for other purposes in the past. They were determined not to repeat history.

The process: The team was a mix of people with no newsletter experience and others who had actually worked on previously unsuccessful attempts. This mix allowed team members to take both a fresh and realistic look at the challenge. The process was very helpful because it kept the team thinking at a high level of detail, but also allowed them to get more detailed in areas in which there were serious implementation problems. It also forced everyone to take responsibility to think creatively about every potential problem that was identified.

Conclusions: There were four major implementation conclusions that came out of the PDPC.

First, the newsletter would work best if it got people to contribute in areas or subjects in which they had a deep interest. This would create a positive interest from the beginning and would help to avoid the type of "hounding" that typically accompanies a newsletter.

Second, the team would need to base the content and design on what users really wanted and needed. Again, this creates a positive starting point.

Third, the team would use subtle (and not so subtle) mechanisms to get people to make and meet commitments to the newsletter. The idea to post "scorecards" on deadlines and the idea to have the CEO do a regular column create a positive pressure to perform.

Finally, and most significantly, the team realized that the major risk connected with the project was that few people would read the final product. They developed the idea of a non-traditional, online newsletter that would enable each person to create his or her own customized version. This not only produced a more useful newsletter, but also eliminated the entire printing and distribution portion of the project. Because the PDPC provided the team with a positive approach to potential problems, the nature and quality of the solution was changed.

"We think too small. Like the frog at the bottom of the well. He thinks the sky is only as big as the top of the well. If he surfaced, he would have an entirely different view."

Mao Tse-Tung

Chapter 12

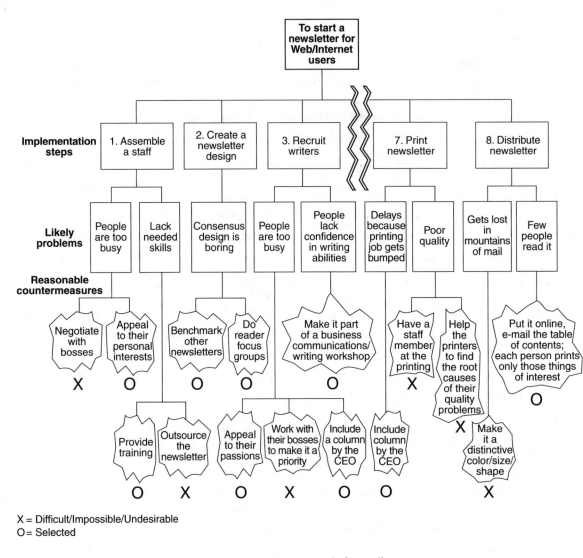

Implementation steps

1. Assemble a staff
2. Create a newsletter design
3. Recruit writers
7. Print newsletter
8. Distribute newsletter

Likely problems

People are too busy | Lack needed skills | Consensus design is boring | People are too busy | People lack confidence in writing abilities | Delays because printing job gets bumped | Poor quality | Gets lost in mountains of mail | Few people read it

Reasonable countermeasures

Negotiate with bosses — X
Appeal to their personal interests — O
Benchmark other newsletters — O
Do reader focus groups — O
Make it part of a business communications/writing workshop — O
Have a staff member at the printing — X
Help the printers to find the root causes of their quality problems — X
Put it online, e-mail the table of contents; each person prints only those things of interest — O

Provide training — O
Outsource the newsletter — X
Appeal to their passions — O
Work with their bosses to make it a priority — X
Include a column by the CEO — O
Include column by the CEO — O
Make it a distinctive color/size/shape — X

X = Difficult/Impossible/Undesirable
O = Selected

Figure 12-1: PDPC Example (Partial)

Gantt Chart: A Tool for Project Scheduling

Just as the PDPC surfaces potential implementation barriers, the Gantt Chart deals with the most pervasive obstacle of all: time. This is particularly true when the project in question involves a major change. Incremental changes can often be accomplished with minimal disruption. A breakthrough normally requires that resources be reallocated. Since time is the scarcest resource of all, any tool that presents both a detailed and overall picture of a project's schedule is invaluable. The Gantt Chart is the simplest and most widely used project-scheduling tool being used today.

Definition of the Tool

The Gantt Chart is a simple scheduling tool that has been widely used since it was developed in 1917 by Henry Gantt, an early expert on scientific management. It is a matrix that shows a time scale on the horizontal axis and the project tasks on the vertical axis. Horizontal bars are used to show the estimated time to complete each task. It is a very user-friendly method for showing which tasks are scheduled to occur simultaneously, staggered or end to end. It can be used to both plan projects as well as monitor their progress against the projected schedule.

Use of the Tool

The Gantt Chart has so many natural and useful applications that it's a challenge to think of occasions in which it would not be helpful. Most often it is used when a team must either create or communicate a high-level overview of the entire project schedule. This helps everyone to understand how his or her assignment or sub-project fits into the overall implementation picture. The Gantt Chart is also invaluable when a team must quickly examine the tasks that are scheduled simultaneously, in order to assess the actual project workload. It is a very visual reality check. Finally, as a project monitoring tool, it is an easy-to-use, highly visible tool that shows an actual implementation schedule of a project versus the planned project schedule.

Overview of the Tool Process

A team that's very close to the implementation process must first create the timeline for the complete project in the top row of a matrix. This must cover the total start-to-finish time of the project. The team identifies and sequences the tasks in the project plan. These can either be very broad or detailed, based on the nature and complexity of the project. These can now be listed on the vertical axis of the chart. The team can now determine how long they estimate that each of tasks will take to complete. These estimates are then drawn on the chart against the project timeline. The team can now easily see which tasks are scheduled simultaneously, in a staggered schedule or completely end to end.

Applying the Tool (Gantt Chart)

Outline of Steps

Step	Activity
1.	Assemble a team closest to the implementation.
2.	Create the timeline in the top row of a matrix. Be sure to cover the total start to finish time of the project.
3.	Brainstorm, sequence, and list all project tasks on the vertical axis of the matrix. Tasks can be at any appropriate level of detail.
4.	Estimate the time to complete each project task. Next to each task draw horizontal bars that show the start and finish times of each task against the project timeline.
5.	Mark milestones on the timeline.

Step-by-Step Instructions

Step 1. Assemble a team closest to the implementation.

The closer a project gets to the actual allocation of resources, the more important it becomes to involve people who have intimate knowledge of the tasks at hand. This applies even in the case of a breakthrough project, since people have often worked on the same tasks but in a different context. Because of the experience of the team, the end result will be both more creative and realistic.

Step 2. Create the timeline in the top row of a matrix.

Start by defining the estimated time to complete the entire project. This determines the time periods into which the chart should be broken. For example, in a one year product development project, it may be appropriate to have a high level Gantt Chart that's divided into monthly increments. But in a one month home renovation, the chart would be divided at least by the week, and in many cases, by the day. This depends entirely on how closely the project must be monitored, based on how tight the schedule is and the cost of deviating from it.

Step 3. Brainstorm, sequence, and list all project tasks on the vertical axis of the matrix.

Typically a team would generate 10–20 tasks that must be scheduled. These can result either from an unstructured brainstorming process or through the use of one of the Management and Planning Tools. For example, a team could use the header cards from an Affinity Diagram to determine the final task list. Ultimately, the team must decide the task level at which project monitoring and control is required. The greater the need for control, the greater the level of detail that should be shown on the Gantt Chart. Finally, list the tasks on the vertical axis in their order of implementation.

Step 4. Estimate the time to complete each project task.

Begin by placing a mark along the timeline that corresponds to the earliest start and finish for each task. These marks must reflect when tasks can be done either:

- Simultaneously (same start and finish times)
- Staggered (some overlapping schedules)
- End to end (cannot start until other tasks are completed)

Next to each task, fill in a horizontal bar that shows the start and finish times for that task.

"No [one] ever made a great discovery without the exercise of the imagination."

George Henry Lewis

Chapter 12

Step 5. Mark milestones on the timeline.

Since a major purpose of the Gantt Chart is to monitor progress against the projected schedule, major review points or "milestones" should be marked on the chart. Generally such milestones are indicated by a diamond shape in place of the horizontal bar.

Summary of the Tool

The Gantt Chart is the most widely used project scheduling tool available today. It's especially useful because it can be used both with and without a formal project management model. Its power comes from the straightforward way it communicates the "big picture" of any project. Its use as an overview tool is particularly helpful in a breakthrough project because it really defines the scope and pace of the effort. This helps to define the investment that the organization is making in the idea. The team can then give a better answer to the questions, "Is it worth it?" and "Can we do it?" The team can assess whether the organization can do what is needed in order to make the innovation a reality. If there is a capacity problem, then a revised Gantt Chart also shows the impact on the overall schedule if certain tasks are extended. Sometimes innovations fail because the organization's resources simply can't move the project forward at the pace required by the marketplace.

Enhancing the Process

Helpful Hints

Add More Columns or Information, If Needed. In addition to timeline information, the Gantt Chart can include virtually any dimension of a project as one of the column headers. Some of these include the duration of each task (as compared to elapsed time), the exact scheduled start date/time, names of leaders/resources, special skills required, etc. Any or all of these items provide a clearer picture of the true nature of the project. Accordingly, the team and the organization understand fully the risks and rewards that are associated with the project.

Track the Team's Progress. In order to simplify the use of the Gantt Chart as a project review tool, many teams leave a blank row between each of the horizontal bars. A second bar (usually a different color or fill pattern) is added to indicate the actual start and finish time for each task. An alternative to this method, which saves space, is the use of distinctive markers to indicate on each bar when the task actually started and finished. Use whatever is most visible and obvious at a glance.

Frequently Asked Questions

Q. **How can you give a time estimate for something you've never done before?**

A. Very few breakthroughs are achieved by entirely unique tasks. They often involve a blend of the new (untested) and the old (proven). For this reason, the composition of the team becomes critical. Especially in areas of breakthrough, this is an opportunity for experienced team members to exercise their judgment. Often such team members can transfer related experience to the new tasks at hand. If this is reflected in the Gantt Chart, then an innovation may become more real and attainable, rather than an illusion that can be dismissed. This is an area in which the PDPC can also be very helpful. As you recall, the PDPC is a contingency planning tool. By anticipating problems and creating countermeasures, it helps a team to get closer to a realistic time estimate.

Q. **What are the advantages and disadvantages of using a Gantt Chart rather than the Activity Network Diagram and PERT (which are more complex project scheduling tools)?**

A. The power of the Gantt Chart lies in its familiarity and simplicity. Gantt Charts occur almost organically whenever schedules are discussed. As a result, Gantt Charts require virtually no explanation and instantly communicate the reality of a project schedule. The same cannot be said for the Activity Network Diagram (AND) and PERT (described in the next section). It takes training and experience to construct and interpret the AND. Even so, the AND is more effective at showing ALL interdependencies and the "critical path" (shortest possible completion time) of the project. In fact, the AND allows a team to mathematically determine the critical path along with the precise impact of any deviation from the schedule. As usual, there is a trade-off between the user friendliness and the analytical power of any tool.

For Further Study

Example of Tool Usage

Based on the results of the PDPC, the Web/Internet newsletter team shifted its focus from a traditional, paper-based newsletter to a customized online version. In order to move the project forward, the team next mapped the major tasks against the calendar using the Gantt Chart.

The process: The experience of those team members who had worked on newsletters in the past became even more valuable when doing the Gantt Chart. They could share that experience when helping the team decide on the time that it would take to complete each major task. The team also identified those tasks that could be done simultaneously.

Conclusions: Based on the Gantt Chart, the team determined that it would take approximately four months to get the newsletter up and running. The PDPC helped the team to realistically scale each of the major tasks. It's tempting to simply "trim" the schedule to fit either the required completion time or the time that everyone feels the project "should take." However, the team was interested in a newsletter that would be designed to succeed over the long haul. The two tools used in combination made it easier to be creative (the online option), while not engaging in wishful thinking (the realistic implementation schedule in the Gantt Chart).

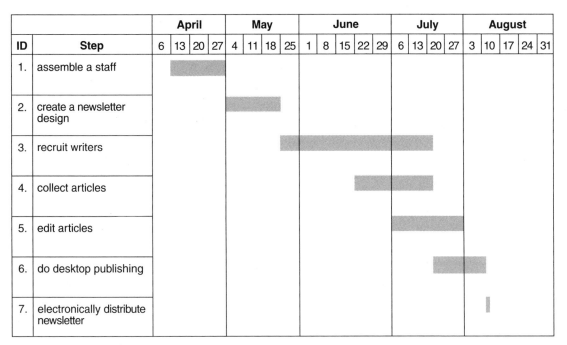

ID	Step	April				May				June					July				August				
		6	13	20	27	4	11	18	25	1	8	15	22	29	6	13	20	27	3	10	17	24	31
1.	assemble a staff		▓	▓																			
2.	create a newsletter design						▓	▓															
3.	recruit writers									▓	▓	▓	▓	▓	▓								
4.	collect articles											▓	▓	▓									
5.	edit articles														▓	▓							
6.	do desktop publishing																▓	▓					
7.	electronically distribute newsletter																			▓			

Figure 12-2: Gantt Chart Example

Activity Network Diagram (AND):
A Tool for Showing Major Tasks of the Project

People are often skeptical about breakthrough proposals because they can't see the path from "here" to "there." What they need is an implementation road map that shows parallel routes, junctions and yes, potential roadblocks. When breakthroughs are left ill defined, they are subject to equally vague objections. When the route to implementation is put on paper, however, reviewers can assess the quality of the logic (or lack thereof) behind the idea. The quality of the input increases with the likelihood of "buy-in." The Activity Network Diagram (AND) is the most effective tool available to show both this general and detailed implementation picture.

"The road was new to me, as roads always are, going back."
Sarah Orne Jewett

Chapter 12

Definition of the Tool

The AND is a simplified version of the Program Evaluation and Review Technique (PERT) and Critical Path Method (CPM). PERT/CPM were developed almost simultaneously in the 1950s in conjunction with the Polaris Missile System project. They are used so often in combination that people think of them as one tool. Like PERT/CPM, the Activity Network Diagram shows the interdependencies among ALL project tasks and reveals the most efficient and realistic path to project completion. It also indicates the NECESSARY sequence among project tasks and the tasks that are most critical to complete as scheduled.

Use of the Tool

The AND can be intimidating at first glance, since it shows the connection between and among all scheduled project tasks. But when the risks of failure are high enough that any slippage in the project schedule will have serious consequences, the AND is more than worth the effort. It is most effective when there are a significant number of tasks that can be done simultaneously in order to make the project more efficient. If this is not the case, the result would be simply a string of dependent events. The AND should be used only when team members have experience with most of the project tasks. This allows them to provide reasonably accurate time estimates. Without this experience, it could be little more than a sketch of a fantasy. Perhaps more intangibly, the AND can be a great tool for uniting a project team behind a common purpose. It lets people see throughout the project how the timely completion of their particular tasks affect the overall project.

Overview of the Tool Process

The AND begins with an experienced team that is as close as possible to the details of implementation. This even applies to breakthrough projects, since they are normally a mix of new tasks with established activities. Having an experienced team lays the groundwork for brainstorming everything that must be done within a project. The diagram begins to take shape when the team finds the very first task that can be done. "Task #1" must be independent from any other task.

The team next identifies any other tasks that can be accomplished simultaneously to "task #1." The question of whether "anything else can be done simultaneously" is repeated until there are no more such tasks.

The team finds the next dependent task and repeats the questioning process until all of the tasks are in place. Lines and arrows are added between all dependent tasks. The team is now ready to estimate and record the amount of time to complete each task. Using basic addition and subtraction, the earliest and latest times at which each tasks must be started and finished are calculated. This reveals the shortest possible time for project completion (the critical path), those places in the schedule where there can be some slippage (slack), and the tasks that must be completed EXACTLY as scheduled.

Applying the Tool (Activity Network Diagram)

Outline of Steps

Step	Activity
1.	Assemble the team closest to project implementation.
2.	Brainstorm all of the tasks necessary to complete the project.
3.	Find the first task that can be completed.
4.	Find tasks that can be done simultaneously with the first task.
5.	Find the next tasks.
6.	Detail the chart by estimating task duration and start/finish times.
7.	Find the critical path.

Step-by-Step Instructions

Step 1. *Assemble the team closest to project implementation.*

When developing an implementation plan for achieving a breakthrough, it's particularly important to pull together a diverse team of planners. The AND can be a bridge between the wide-open thinking of the creativity tools and the detailed orientation of budgets and planning. If each task is an opportunity to ask, "Is this task REALLY necessary?" or "Could it be done in a different way?" then diverse experiences and perspectives on the team can lead to innovative options. This is particularly true when the AND process uncovers roadblocks and/or schedule overruns. When the road to implementation hits those rough spots, necessity can become the mother of invention.

Step 2. *Brainstorm all of the tasks necessary to complete the project.*

Since the AND is a scheduling and resource allocation tool, creativity must be tempered by reality. Brainstormed tasks should end up in the final AND only if they are "necessary and sufficient" for achieving the breakthrough. There are two ways to weed out unnecessary tasks:

- Through discussion, agree on which tasks could be eliminated before constructing the draft diagram.

- Include all brainstormed tasks in a draft diagram, and eliminate unnecessary tasks only during the final editing process.

The second option preserves creativity, but it may also create an unnecessarily cumbersome diagram. In either case, use either Post-it™ Notes or software in order to keep the process flexible. The AND is one tool that requires complete flexibility until the final line is drawn.

Step 3. Find the first task that can be completed.

Especially in a breakthrough project, the first question must be, "Where do you start?" The AND requires that the team identify the first task that CAN be done. "First" is defined as the task that doesn't depend on anything else happening before it. Therefore the question the team must ask is, "What is the most important task that can be carried out independently of all other tasks?" If there is more than one task that fits this description, use common sense to simply choose one as a starting point.

Step 4. Find tasks that can be done simultaneously with the first task.

Next look for tasks that can be done at the same time as the selected "first" task. Such tasks must be completely independent of each other. If there are such tasks, place them above or below task #1. This is the first step in creating an efficient plan. Each of these represents an opportunity to save total project time by reducing the "hurry up and wait" periods that occur in most projects. This step also provides the opportunity to ask whether there are any other needed tasks (not yet identified) that could be done simultaneously. Keep thinking as the process proceeds.

Step 5. Find the next tasks.

This is the step that is repeated for the remainder of the process. These next tasks are identified by asking, "Which task can be done next that cannot be started until one or more of the tasks (in Step 4) is completed?" Once this task is identified, repeat the question from Step 4; "Can any of the remaining tasks be done simultaneously?" These "next" and "simultaneous" questions are alternately asked until all of the tasks are connected in sequence.

Step 6. Detail the chart by estimating task duration and start/finish times.

Once all of the tasks are connected in a way that shows ALL of the interdependencies among them, the team agrees on and records the estimated time that it takes to complete each task. The earliest and latest start and finish times for each task is then calculated. When this is completed, the team will know how much flexibility there is in the scheduled completion of each task.

Step 7. Find the critical path.

Step 6 automatically identifies the "critical path" of the project. This is the shortest possible time in which the project can be completed. Any task that lies on this path must be completed exactly as scheduled, or the entire project schedule slips. When pursuing a breakthrough, this step is particularly critical because it provides the ultimate reality check. Until this level of detailed planning is done, it is never really clear as to what it will take to convert that "great idea" into that "great product or service."

Summary of the Tool

The AND is the most widely used project-scheduling tool for large scale, formal projects. Unfortunately, this tool is often underused by smaller, less formal projects because people perceive the AND as "rocket science." Interestingly enough, this tool really was developed to do rocket science (the Polaris Missile project), and to do it more efficiently. The AND only appears to be complex because of the size of the projects in which it has been used. The underlying questions of this tool are very straightforward:

- What needs to get done?
- What depends on what to be accomplished?
- How long will each task take?
- How long will the entire project take?
- Which tasks are most critical to monitor for adherence to the schedule?

Aren't these the central questions of innovation? If so, then the AND can be an important tool in moving concepts to commercial reality. In addition, the mechanics of the process have been vastly simplified by the many fine AND/PERT software packages that are on the market today.

Enhancing the Process

Helpful Hints

Balance Team Involvement and Efficiency. There are a few simple things that a team can do to increase involvement, while keeping the process workable. First, include a larger group of "doers" for the initial stages of brainstorming the tasks and estimating their duration. This will create a realistic foundation upon which a smaller team can build an AND. Second, include the "doers" early in the process as reviewers. Third, involve more people by breaking the AND into smaller diagrams that can later be combined.

Think "Could Do" Rather than "Have Done." It's important to identify those things that "could be done" simultaneously, rather than those things that "have been done" simultaneously. By focusing on the tasks that are truly independent of each other, team members are challenged to think creatively about when things can actually happen. For example, in a Japanese manufacturing concept known as SMED, (Single Minute Exchange of Dies), machine changeovers have been reduced from hours to minutes by having changeover equipment staged and ready to use. Traditionally, machines were shut down while product lines were changed. Using SMED, much of the changeover activity is done away from the machine while the machine is running. Similarly, the AND can surface opportunities to make incredible gains in project implementation efficiency.

Pay Critical Attention to the Critical Path. Knowing the critical path should help any team do at least these three things: One, to go back to the drawing board whenever the total project time exceeds the available time for completion. Two, closely monitor the tasks on the critical path to make sure that everyone on the team has as much notice as possible about potential delays in the schedule. And three, shift people and resources as needed from tasks that are not on the critical path to those tasks that are on the path and have exceeded their time estimate, or are likely to do so.

Frequently Asked Questions

Q. How can a team ensure that the time estimates are accurate?

A. First, use facts as much as possible. Work records from identical or very similar projects should at least provide a range of completion times. Second, load the team with people as close to the real implementation as possible. This is the most practical way to keep the team's feet on the ground, even when it's shooting for the stars.

Q. Should the process be done manually or should a software program be used?

A. As always, it depends. When the project is rather small (i.e., less than 25–30 tasks) and the end product must reflect a strong consensus, then the manual AND is actually preferable. The use of larger Post it™ Notes makes it possible for a team of up to 10 people to gather around and truly build it together. With this number of tasks, the math is still quite manageable. However, when there are 50–100 tasks, software is indispensable. The software enables the team to focus on the decisions and dependencies rather than on the math and the physical placement of the tasks.

For Further Study

- *The Memory Jogger™ II*, pages 3–11
- *Coach's Guide to The Memory Jogger™ II*, pages 1–10
- *The Memory Jogger™ II Off-the-Shelf Modular Training Materials*, Activity Network Diagram Module
- *The Memory Jogger Plus+®* Videotape Series
- *Integrated Management & Planning Tools* Videotape

Example of Tool Usage

Based on the results of the PDPC and the Gantt Chart, the Web/Internet newsletter team decided to create a more detailed picture of the implementation schedule. They chose to use an AND because it allowed them to identify all of the tasks, their duration, connections, and earliest and latest start/finish times. The diagram ultimately painted a picture of the most efficient path to the completion of the newsletter project

The process: The AND helped to create even more insights into the project than the Gantt Chart, since it allowed the team to incorporate many of the creative ideas from the PDPC. The team could now estimate the time it would take to implement each of these ideas, as well as where they could fit into the overall implementation plan. The AND provided a way to experiment with additions and deletions. Once again, the tools provided a means to be simultaneously creative, expansive, and responsible.

Conclusions: Based on the AND, the team determined that it would take 121 days (about 6 months) to get the newsletter up and running. Coincidentally, the Gantt Chart had "predicted" that it would take almost exactly that amount of time. In the process however, the AND also identified 13 out of a total of 21 tasks that had to be completed exactly as scheduled because they were on the critical path. Perhaps most importantly, the team confirmed that the newsletter was a major undertaking, with major paybacks to the company if it was done well. Otherwise, the old newsletter story would have the same unhappy ending.

"Genius is one percent inspiration and ninety-nine percent perspiration."

Thomas Edison

Chapter 12

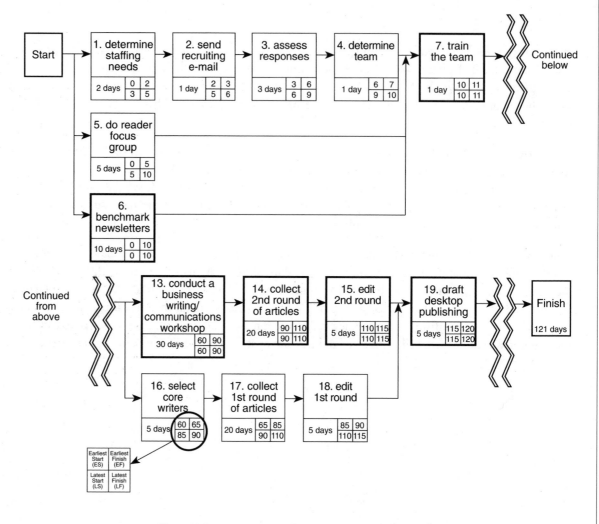

Figure 12-3: Activity Network Diagram Example (Partial)

Section III:
Putting the Tools to Work

The tools for generating and selecting ideas can heighten the creativity and innovation levels in any organization. Where they really achieve their power, however, is when they are applied to business processes such as problem solving and process improvement, planning, and product or service development. This section focuses on how the tools in Sections I and II can be used to create breakthroughs in:

- problem solving, where they can generate multiple ideas for eliminating root causes and help define the real problem.

- process improvement and standardization, where they can help the team break through fixed mental patterns and discover new ways of doing business.

- planning, where they can help planners stop coming up with the same plans.

- new product and service development to meet and exceed customer expectations.

Chapters 13, 14, and 15 focus on how the idea generation and selection tools can be used to achieve the necessary breakthroughs in core business processes. Chapter 16 discusses strategies for implementing the tools. Chapter 17 summarizes the rationale for using tools to stimulate creativity and innovation.

Section III

*"Imagination lit every lamp in this country, produced every article we use,
built every church, made every discovery, performed every act of kindness and progress,
created more and better things for more people.
It is the priceless ingredient for a better day."*

Henry J. Taylor

Using the Tools for Better Problem Solving and Process Improvement

When teams use the creativity tools described in Chapters 1 through 7, they can generate many break-through ideas. Teams can then use the tools described in Chapters 8 through 11 to select the best alternatives from a pool of great ideas and use the hints in Chapter 12 to manage the implementation of the chosen ideas.

Teams will find the creativity tools particularly useful when they integrate the tools into business processes. The tools help teams find new solutions to problems, define inventive process improvements, develop products that delight customers, and foster innovative ideas for future strategies. The tools are especially valuable when:

- The problem is particularly difficult.
- Significant change is required.
- The improvement is required quickly.
- The problem has been unsuccessfully tackled in the past.

Two of the key areas where the creativity and idea selection tools can add value are problem solving and process improvement. The tools contribute to improved problem solving and process improvement in two basic ways:

"Great imaginations are apt to work from hints and suggestions and a single moment of emotion is sometimes sufficient to create a masterpiece."

Margaret Sackville

Chapter 13

- The tools help teams better define how to approach the problem.

- After teams have used Classic Brainstorming and Brainwriting 6-3-5, they can generate more alternatives that represent a wider variety of possible solutions.

Using a standard problem-solving model provides teams with a common language and a common set of repeatable steps to be learned and followed. A standard model can also help team leaders address business issues that are fairly broad, such as product development and planning, as well as more clearly defined problems and process improvement needs. Since there are many standard problem-solving models, teams that are considering the integration of the tools into their own business processes should check to see if the organization already has its own standardized problem-solving model.

A typical problem-solving model includes steps similar to those listed below:

1. Select the problem

2. Define the problem statement

3. Find and analyze data

4. Generate solution ideas and an action plan

5. Select and implement the solution

6. Review and evaluate the results

7. Review and reflect on the process

The rest of this chapter discusses how teams can integrate the creativity tools into a generic, seven-step, problem-solving model. Keep in mind that the steps and/or the tasks and activities for solving problems and improving processes are not necessarily linear. There are often many feedback loops involved, which will require that teams work in a nonlinear way. For example, a team may not always start the problem-solving process at Step 1. One reason for this may be that the team wants to try out a possible solution and then cycle back through the model to explore a different solution. Another reason is that the team is coming into the problem-solving process after the problem has already been well defined by another group and the data needed for working toward a solution has already been collected. The "later team" might then be responsible for generating alternative solutions and then moving the solution through implementation.

Step 1. Select the problem or process that will be addressed first (or next) and describe the improvement opportunity.

Step 1 may be undertaken by a steering committee, a management team, or an improvement team, depending on the organization's formal process structure. Team leaders should be prepared to start with Step 1 or Step 2. The following are the activities usually covered in this step.

- Ask "What's wrong?" and "What's not working?"
- Define the customer's problem or opportunity.
- Look for changes in important business indicators.
- Assemble and support the right team.
- Collect and review customer data.
- Narrow down project focus.
- Develop project purpose statement.
- Identify the customers.

Sometimes in the process of reviewing the data and developing a project purpose statement, the team uncovers an obvious and compelling solution. If this happens and the team is sure that the solution meets the customer's needs, the team can go directly to Step 4, bypassing the next two steps in the problem-solving process.

More often, the team needs to use the fact-finding capabilities of the Basic Quality Control Tools[1] to get at the heart of the problem. In addition, team members need to keep an open mind—one of the hallmarks of creative thinking—in completing the other activities that will improve the likelihood of the team finding innovative solutions.

---

1. A brief description of these tools, and also the Management and Planning Tools, are included in Appendix A.

Step 2. Describe the current process surrounding the improvement opportunity.

In this step the team maps the process flow in order to get a broader understanding of the process and the critical inputs, processing steps, and output. The team needs to focus on completing the following tasks:

- Map out and describe the current process.
- Validate map with process users.
- Collect data on process performance.
- Select the problem process or process segments that must be improved.

In this step, the team can use the creativity tool Heuristic Redefinition to help it see the problem from new angles and to be sure it selects the best direction for solving the problem.

Step 3. Describe all of the possible causes of the problem and agree on the root cause(s).

In this step, the team agrees on the root causes of the problem. Team members should:

- Ask "Why?" five times.
- Identify the cause(s) of the problem.
- Whenever possible, verify the root cause(s) with data.
- Collect more data as necessary.

Example

This example will help illustrate the use of the creativity tools within the first three steps of this problem-solving process. Top management at Stop 'N Go Pizza, a small but growing pizza delivery business with six shops, recently formed a cross-functional team of store managers, kitchen staff, and delivery personnel. The purpose of the team is to find out why, after a period of rapid growth, Stop 'N Go Pizza has experienced a six-month decline in sales volume. The team was also charged with generating an implementation plan to correct the situation.[2]

The team members used a number of fact-finding and analysis tools to define the problem. Their analysis initially revealed a problem with employee training. The team could have pursued this initial direction, however, team members agreed it would be better to use Heuristic Redefinition to be sure this was the problem to focus on. By using Heuristic Redefinition, they could see the problem within the context of the total system. In the process of visually describing the problem and using the matrix to evaluate possible directions to pursue, the team concluded that addressing employee turnover had more potential for reversing the decline in sales.

Step 4. Develop an effective and workable solution and action plan, including targets for improvement.

The team moves from data finding to generating possible alternative solutions. The team's focus in this step is to:

- Generate potential solutions.
- Analyze solutions.
- Define and rank solutions.
- Select the solution that best meets the customer's needs.
- Plan the change process: What? Who? When?
- Do contingency planning when dealing with new and risky plans.
- Define possible resistance and objections.
- Determine what resources are needed to deal with change.
- Set targets for improvement and establish monitoring methods.

---

2. This example is based on a more detailed case study described in *The Memory Jogger™ II: A Pocket Guide of Tools for Continuous Improvement and Effective Planning*, pages 115–131.

"When I can no longer create anything, I'll be done for."

Coco Chanel

Example

In the Stop 'N Go Pizza problem, the team began to fully explore all the possible solutions to reducing employee turnover. The team started out by using Classic Brainstorming to generate initial ideas for reducing employee turnover. The team next used Imaginary Brainstorming, Word-Picture Analogies and Associations, and the Morphological Box to generate more ideas. The team's initial ideas are shown in Figure 13-1.

- have teams of friends
- increase pay
- simplify work
- make work fun
- make work challenging
- make benefits package irresistible
- increase teamwork
- institute flextime
- start job-sharing
- employees set own hours
- let employees take pizzas home after work
- provide fashionable ("cool") uniforms
- start profit sharing

Figure 13-1: Initial Ideas for How to Reduce Employee Turnover

After brainstorming the initial ideas, the team changed one element of the problem ("employees") and developed an imaginary problem: "How do we reduce turnover among professional athletes?" The team's ideas are shown in Figure 13-2.

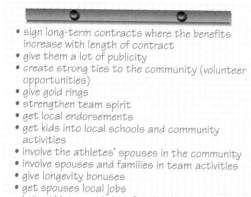

- sign long-term contracts where the benefits increase with length of contract
- give them a lot of publicity
- create strong ties to the community (volunteer opportunities)
- give gold rings
- strengthen team spirit
- get local endorsements
- get kids into local schools and community activities
- involve the athletes' spouses in the community
- involve spouses and families in team activities
- give longevity bonuses
- get spouses local jobs
- help athletes and their families buy homes
- hire personal skills coach
- find medical resources that are difficult to duplicate

Figure 13-2: Ideas for Imaginary Problem of Reducing Turnover Among Professional Athletes

The team then took ideas from the imaginary problem and transferred them to the Stop 'N Go Pizza problem of reducing employee turnover. These ideas are shown in Figure 13-3.

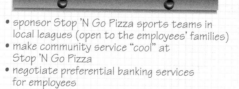

- sponsor Stop 'N Go Pizza sports teams in local leagues (open to the employees' families)
- make community service "cool" at Stop 'N Go Pizza
- negotiate preferential banking services for employees
- establish "buddy/mentoring" system
- hire family members
- get a lot of local media recognition
- set up college scholarships for children of long-term employees

Figure 13-3: Applying Ideas for the Imaginary Problem Back to the Problem of How to Reduce Employee Turnover

Even though the team had generated some great ideas with Imaginary Brainstorming, some team members felt they had stayed too close to the original problem. Team members agreed that, to be sure of breaking out of fixed thinking patterns, they would try using Word-Picture Associations and Analogies. At the next meeting, team members showed up with their own collections of pictures, selected a few of them, and began listing associations for each picture. The solutions that developed out of their associations with two of the pictures are shown on the flipcharts in Figures 13-4 and 13-5.

- add stretch goals
- look at what motivates each employee
- get outside
- reward employees for sticking out their necks
- develop a job rotation where employees could pick their own jobs
- help employees adapt to the challenges of work

Figure 13-4: Solutions Generated from a Picture of a Giraffe Reaching to the Top of a Tree for Food

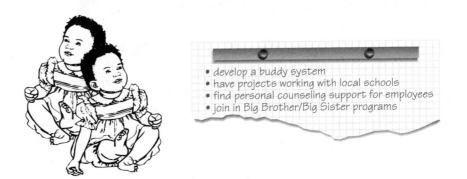

- develop a buddy system
- have projects working with local schools
- find personal counseling support for employees
- join in Big Brother/Big Sister programs

Figure 13-5: Solutions Generated from a Picture of Twin Babies

The team members, who were excited about the ideas they had generated, agreed that they would next focus their attention on narrowing down the options to select one idea, or a combination of several ideas. The team decided to use Nominal Group Technique (Chapter 8) to select an area for further focus. Using this idea selection tool, they narrowed down their options based on the following criteria:

- Most widespread impact

- Most realistic for implementation within the next six months

- Most interesting

Based on these criteria, the team selected "getting Stop 'N Go Pizza more involved in the community" as a strategy for reducing employee turnover. The team settled on finding programs for fundraising for local charities. To generate ideas for these programs, the team built a Morphological Box with the following parameters:

- Source of funding

- Participants

- Beneficiaries

- Type of activities

- Schedule

- Frequency

- Means of recognition

Next the team generated options for each parameter and listed the options within the cells of the Morphological Box. What followed was a team review and discussion of the many possible options and how they could be combined to create an innovative and workable solution.

The Morphological Box presented the team with many potential solutions so team members had to work through a series of different options before they agreed on the best solution. They decided that Stop 'N Go Pizza would find a community organization that would be willing to sponsor employees and their families in a 10K (6 mile) walk. This walk would raise money for

"Genius is only a superior power of seeing."

John Ruskin

Chapter 13

a local program that helped physically challenged children, which had helped one employee's child significantly. The walk would be announced in the local newspaper several times, and it would take place on the weekend.

The team's chosen solution, marked by a string of triangles, is shown in Figure 13-6.

Parameters	Options					
Source of funding	Stop 'N Go Pizza	employees	grants	community	other companies	shared company and employees
Participants	employees	employees and families	local school athletes	paid participants	local community groups	regional sports stars
Beneficiaries	local schools	local service centers	programs for the physically challenged	hospitals	arts programs	basketball
Type of activities	bowling	softball	pledge activities (walks/runs)	soccer	fund raisers	
Schedule	during work hours	after work	weekends			
Frequency	weekly	monthly	quarterly	annually	as scheduled	
Means of recognition	local newspaper	state newspaper	company newletter	trophies	mayor/ governor on hand	special rewards programs

Figure 13-6: Morphological Box for Ways to Implement a Fundraising Program at Stop 'N Go Pizza

Step 5. Implement the solution or process change.

In this step, the team implements the chosen alternative, either on a small scale or in its full-blown version. During implementation, the team monitors the action plan to ensure the key objectives are being met. In addition, the team collects more data to be sure that the solution meets the customer's needs. The steps include:

- Implement.

- Collect more data for subsequent assessment.

- Follow the plan and monitor the milestones and measures.

Example

The team used the appropriate project management tools (see Chapter 12) to help them develop an implementation plan. The team recognized that this was just one program in a longer term strategy that needed to be developed for reducing employee turnover. However, they decided to pilot this program before proceeding with developing a longer-term strategy and before setting targets for employee turnover.

Step 6. Review and evaluate the result of the change.

After the change has been implemented, the team reviews and evaluates its results:

- Review the results of the change. Is the solution having the intended effect? Any unintended consequences?

- Revise the process, as necessary.

- Standardize the improvement to hold the gain.

- Establish measures for monitoring the process for changes.

Example

The team developed the implementation plan in April, with the walk planned for early September. The walk was a great success. Employees talked about it for weeks afterward. While it was too early to tell if this one event would have long-term impact on employee turnover, the top management team of Stop 'N Go Pizza was so impressed with the success that they urged the team to continue with its work.

As part of their responsibilities, the team members also decided that some of their suggestions needed to be documented and developed into policies, and that some current policies needed revision. For example, the team had generated ideas about changing the processes for employee recruiting and performance review and the processes for employee training and development. In addition, a team member had suggested that a "buddy system" be implemented.

To make the necessary changes, the team decided to follow the requirements of the ISO 9001 Standard. Team members were all in agreement that they didn't want to just document their current processes; they wanted to take a look at their current processes and suggest changes that would make them more efficient and innovative.

The team reviewed the 20 clauses within the ISO 9001 Standard. While the team knew that the clauses referred to routine procedures, it seemed that in their review, they would find many opportunities where the idea generation and idea selection tools could be applied. These were:

- Identifying requirements
- Identifying critical elements or factors, such as control points or factors affecting controls
- Documenting current processes, workflows, and procedures
- Defining more efficient processes and systems
- Designing outputs of the systems and processes
- Implementing the processes and systems
- Reviewing and improving procedures, processes, and systems
- Defining plans

For any of these areas, the team could use the creativity tools, such as Heuristic Redefinition (to review the current processes and workflows, and to define more efficient processes and systems) or any of the other creativity tools to generate ideas about improvements in procedures, processes, and systems. The Morphological Box could help the team generate new ways to implement changes.

Example

The team looked specifically at hiring and performance review policies and practices. They used several of the creativity tools, such as Word-Picture Associations and Analogies and TILMAG, to make significant improvements in these processes.

Step 7. Reflect and act on learnings.

Finally, the team takes time to reflect and learn from its experience. To accomplish this, the team:

- Assesses the results of the problem-solving process, assesses the process, and recommends changes.
- Continues the improvement process where needed; standardizes it where possible.
- Seeks other opportunities for improvement.
- Evaluates lessons learned from the experience: what can be improved?
- Celebrates success.

Example

In a meeting two weeks after the event, the team evaluated its results and the process. Team members were also pleased that they had been able to use most of the creativity and idea selection tools and that their ideas were so successful.

When the team reviewed its progress with top management, there was general agreement that many of the ideas the team had generated were very innovative and could help the company resolve a historically tough problem not only for Stop 'N Go Pizza, but also for the pizza industry in general. In fact, management was so pleased with the ideas that they decided they should begin to roll them out over the next several months. Top management, working with the team, developed a strategy and some targets. This time the team set very ambitious targets for their strategy: reduce the turnover rate from 62% to 30%.

Over the next year, as the team continued to meet and to successfully implement many of the ideas, turnover began to decrease. The CEO was so impressed with the team's success, that she decided to form a team, keeping some of the original members, provide training, and use the idea generation and selection tools for more than just the routine issues. The team met to discuss its new scope and decided that the new challenges extended beyond problem solving. This new team has been charged with learning more about integrating the new tools with Strategic Planning and New Product Development processes. (See the next two chapters for a discussion of the power of the tools in these two core business processes.)

"The rewards in business go to the [person] who does something with an idea."

William Benton

*"Almost all really new ideas have a
certain aspect of foolishness
when they are first produced, and almost any idea
which jogs you out of your current abstractions
may be better than nothing."*

Alfred North Whitehead

Using the Tools
for Strategic Planning

While Chapter 13 dealt with how teams can use the creativity tools in problem solving and process improvement, this chapter discusses the creativity tools in the context of improved planning. At the strategic level, it is important that teams have a wide range of choices in selecting the best plans and targets. At the tactical level, each area of the company strives to contribute to the strategic goal. How this can happen is not always readily apparent. The creativity tools create options from which to make good tactical choices. And when the plan doesn't work, the creativity tools create the brainpower to come up with alternative approaches.

"If one cares about ideas, one wants to gather them from every available source and test them in every way possible."

Mary I. Bunting

Introduction to Strategic Planning

There are many approaches to strategic planning and each one can be improved with the creativity tools. The approach discussed in this chapter has been referred to by a host of names, several of which are: hoshin, hoshin planning, policy management, and Breakthrough Strategic Planning™. (Breakthrough Strategic Planning is the name that GOAL/QPC uses in the market to describe its approach to participative strategic planning.)

Strategic Planning has established processes that help teams select the most highly leveraged breakthrough objectives, and it involves all employees at all levels in identifying and aligning breakthroughs throughout the organization. Strategic Planning has been used successfully by many organizations such as Hewlett-Packard, Xerox, Motorola, and the soap division of Procter & Gamble, to dramatically improve quality, cost, and competitive position. It is beyond the scope of this chapter to cover the

Chapter 14

Strategic Planning process in depth. What this chapter will focus on is how teams can use the creativity tools in each of the four phases of Breakthrough Strategic Planning. These four phases are:

1. Selecting the Breakthrough

2. Aligning and Deploying the Plan

3. Implementing the Plan

4. Reviewing and Improving the Plan

Phase 1: Selecting the Breakthrough

A woman who runs an exclusive dress shop in Boston reported, "We spend a considerable amount of time on planning each year, but we always come up with the same plan." What the creativity tools do is help teams to break out of this routine.

To be sure, many aspects of the initial phases of strategic planning are very analytical. For example, a company needs to analyze its past successes and failures; its strengths, weaknesses, opportunities, and threats; its position in the marketplace; the particular life-cycle stages of its products; its market growth rate; and the relative market share of its products. A company needs to be very analytical on the one hand, but there is also a need for a company to expand its thinking on strategic possibilities.

Use of the Creativity Tools
The Morphological Box is a helpful way for teams to consider the strategic possibilities. A team can map out all the possible products in a specific area and show its company's products with their relative strength, the competition's product with its relative strength, and the products that no one has addressed yet. For an example, see Figure 14-1.

Portfolio Categories	Options			
Customer company size	Small	Medium	Large	X-Large
Average profit level	10%	20%	30%	40%
Product/service mix	50/50	80/20	60/40	20/80
Average product/service age	1 year	2 years	3 years	4 years

Figure 14-1: Critical Characteristics of a Product/Service Portfolio and Possible Options

A more free-wheeling generation of ideas for new products and services and other organizational strategies can come from Brainstorming, Brainwriting 6-3-5, Imaginary Brainstorming, Word-Picture Associations and Analogies, and TILMAG.

Use of the TRIZ Method

Another approach is to use the lines of evolution of TRIZ, which is described in Appendix B of this book. Altshuller, in his study of inventive products, identified several patterns of evolution. By examining these patterns of evolution, it is possible to identify the one pattern that is most applicable to the company's products and services. Some companies are using this information to identify future evolutions and tie them up with patents. Gillette for example, moved from the one-blade razor to the two-blade razor, to various devices to raise the whiskers. The German company Bosch has also used TRIZ to design a car radio that doubles as a phone.

Use of the Idea Selection Tools

The Prioritization Matrix is often used for selecting the key strategic breakthrough. The combination of the Affinity Diagram and the Interrelationship Digraph is also in wide use.

Phase 2: Aligning and Deploying the Plan

Once the breakthrough has been defined, it is necessary to identify the means to carry it out, at every level of the organization. "Catchball" is a term for the process in which ideas of how to carry out the breakthrough are formulated, revised, and aligned, both vertically and horizontally in the organization. If someone throws a ball and another person catches it, that is not a game of catch. Catchball implies that "the ball" is thrown back and forth several times among the players.

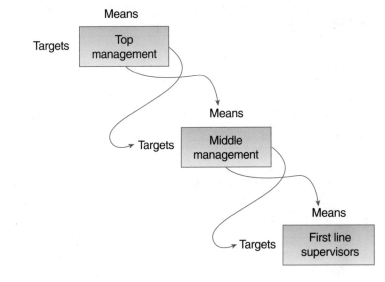

Figure 14-2: Playing Catchball

Use of the Creativity Tools

It may not be immediately apparent how each level of the organization can support the breakthrough. The creativity tools can be used to generate new implementation ideas and the selection tools can be used to find the best choices.

Phase 3: Implementing the Plan

Implementing the plan includes clarity of the measurable. What are the targets for each manager? How will each manager know if the targets (control items) have been achieved? What are the means that managers will use to reach the targets? What are the measures (check items)? The Flag Chart, shown in Figure 14-3, is a easy way to visualize this concept.

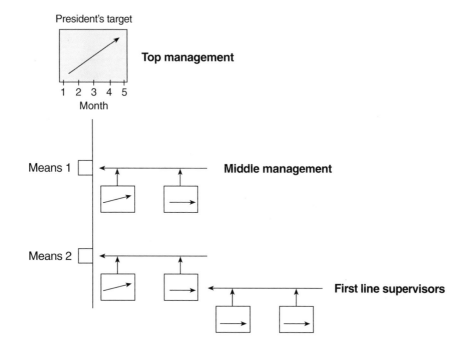

Figure 14-3: Flag Chart Showing the President's Target and the Means for Achieving It

The key to implementation is to check the planned targets and means against the actual progression of events, and to work on the gaps. As a team works on these gaps, the creativity tools can be used on a daily basis. For example, the president's target depicted in Figure 14-3 above represents the planned target and the means to achieve it. Figure 14-4 below shows the gaps in implementation.

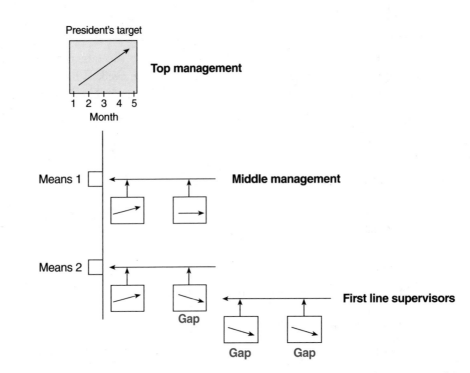

Figure 14-4: Flag Chart Showing the President's Target and the Gaps in the Implementation of the Means

Use of the Creativity Tools

To correct the gaps will require a breakthrough. Enter the creativity tools. If the gaps are not major, using Brainstorming, Brainwriting 6-3-5, Imaginary Brainstorming, or Word-Picture Associations and Analogies may be enough. If the gaps are more serious or continue for two months in a row, the Heuristic Redefinition tool or the Morphological Box may be needed to find the breakthrough. Selecting the best idea here is easier because there probably are not a lot of new ideas.

Phase 4: Reviewing and Improving the Plan

Each month, quarter, and year, the plan is reviewed on an organization-wide basis to see if the plan is being met. The Flag Chart (shown in Figures 14-3 and 14-4) is one mechanism for reviewing the plan, however, the Tree Diagram is more widely used in the United States.

Each month the actual numbers can be posted on a Tree Diagram to show the variation between the plan and the actual implementation of it. An example is shown in Figure 14-5 below.

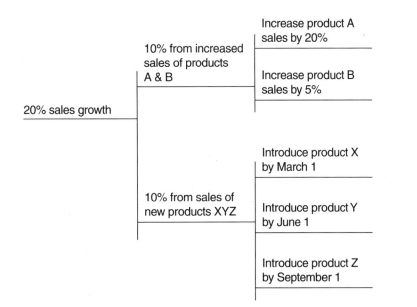

Figure 14-5: Using the Tree Diagram to Review and Improve the Plan

Use of the Creativity Tools

Where progress has been shown to be better than expected, there may be some important learnings to share with other parts of the organization. Where there are negative gaps between the plan and actual events, changes will most likely need to be implemented. A facilitator should meet with each manager where there is a problem. The creativity tools provide the opportunity for one or two individuals, or a team, to develop some alternative plans that will reduce the shortfall. If the shortfall is minimal, then

Brainstorming, Brainwriting 6-3-5, Imaginary Brainstorming, or Word-Picture Associations and Analogies may be sufficient. If there are any gaps that are beyond minimal, it may be important for a team to use TILMAG, Heuristic Redefinition, or the Morphological Box.

At the end of the year, the team reviews the progress made toward achieving the targets and the quality of the planning process. The analysis of the learnings should lead to more fundamental ideas for the breakthrough, back to the beginning of the cycle where the team first used the creativity tools to clarify that breakthrough.

Using the Tools for New Product Development

Introduction

New product development and strategic planning are often intertwined, so some of the discussion from Chapter 14 also applies to this chapter. For example, new product development needs to include an analysis of a company's past successes and failures, an analysis of its position in the marketplace, the life-cycle stages of its products, its market growth rate, and the relative market share of its products.

Creativity tools can help a team to study and analyze these data. For example, a Morphological Box that shows areas where a company has products, where competitors have products, and areas that are as yet undeveloped can contribute to a team's considerations for new product development. In addition, using the lines of evolution (mentioned in Chapter 14), which are part of Altshuller's TRIZ system, can be beneficial when a team is trying to develop new products.

New product development processes have recently been greatly enhanced by the processes of Quality Function Deployment (QFD). QFD was initially developed in Japan in the 1970s and has since been used by many companies in the United States, including Ford, General Motors, Hughes Satellite Division, Hewlett-Packard, and Citibank. QFD provides a team with a structured, efficient approach to capture the "voices" of the customer, company engineers, and other technical specialists, and to prioritize the most important design improvements.

There are numerous applications of the creativity tools to enhance the QFD process. It is beyond the scope of this book to fully explain these applications. (For a detailed presentation and examples, see the Web site "www.goalqpc.com/ideaedge.") Several themes will be briefly mentioned here:

"You can never plan the future by the past."

Edmund Burke

1. Gather the voice of the customer

2. Identify and prioritize quality characteristics

3. Improve a design concept

4. Remove engineering bottlenecks

5. Improve product and process reliability

These five aspects of a new product development process are outlined in Figure 15-1.

QFD Steps	Step 1	Step 2	Step 3	Step 4	Step 5
Step name	Gather the voice of the customer	Identify and prioritize quality characteristics	Improve a design concept	Eliminate engineering bottlenecks	Improve product and process reliability
Process	Gather customers' needs through focus groups, surveys, Kano model, etc.	Identify what quality characteristics (measures, not features) will ensure meeting customer needs. Prioritize these needs.	Identify what new concepts will help achieve a breakthrough in key quality characteristics.	Design the new product or service. First solve those improvements that are key to top quality characteristics.	Use FMEA (Failure Mode Effect Analysis) to make sure that new product or service will rarely if ever fail.
Creativity tools	*Expected & One-Dimensional Quality* •Brainstorming •Brainwriting 6-3-5 *Exciting Quality* •Imaginary Brainstorming •Word-Picture Associations & Analogies •TILMAG •Morphological Box	•Brainstorming •TILMAG	•Pugh New Concept Selection •TILMAG •Morphological Box	•Heuristic Redefinition •TRIZ •Other creativity tools, depending on the problem.	•Brainstorming •Morphological Box

Figure 15-1: Application of the Creativity Tools to the Basic Steps of New Product Development

1. Gather the Voice of the Customer

Many valuable new products start with new insights into what the customer needs. The Japanese have an expression, "go to the *gemba*," which means visiting the customer to see firsthand how the customer is using a product or service. Noriaki Kano, a noted Japanese quality expert, has developed a model that helps explain different aspects of customer needs. Figure 15-2 is an illustration of Kano's model.

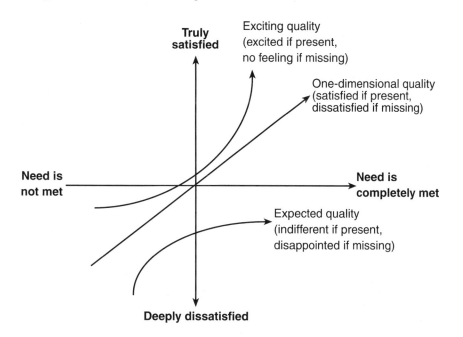

Figure 15-2: Kano Model of Customer Needs and Levels of Satisfaction

In Kano's model, the horizontal line represents specific customer requirements and the vertical line represents customer satisfaction. The three lines that cut cross the horizontal and vertical lines represent three different kinds of customer demands, i.e., expected quality, one-dimensional quality, and exciting quality.

An example of expected quality is a car that has seat belts in the front and back seats. If a car lacks seat belts, the customer will be dissatisfied because having seat belts is an expected feature.

An example of one-dimensional quality is the amount of saturated fat in a food product. In today's world, "no fat" and "low-fat" foods are preferable to foods that don't have this feature. So if the fat content in a food product is high, the customer will be dissatisfied; if the fat content is low, the customer will be satisfied.

An example of exciting quality is self-stick note pads, such as 3M's Post-it™ Notes. This product was not requested by customers, but when a new adhesive was developed and applied to note paper, a new market and customer need was created.

Application of the Creativity Tools

Expected quality and one-dimensional quality are dimensions of known customer demands, i.e., these are established areas for knowing how to meet customer needs. If the right individuals are brought together who represent the best mix of knowledge and experience, the group will develop many worthwhile and appropriate ideas to meet these customer needs. Brainstorming and Brainwriting 6-3-5 are helpful on these occasions.

Exciting quality, on the other hand, is not a known dimension. Exciting quality involves the creation of a new product, service, or method. To take this leap of thought to find a breakthrough, teams can use Imaginary Brainstorming, Word-Picture Associations and Analogies, TILMAG, and the Morphological Box.

2. Identify and Prioritize Quality Characteristics

After the voice of the customer has been gathered, it is important to identify how this voice will be measured. These measures are called quality characteristics. They are not product features or tests; they are what is measured to make sure that key customer needs are met.

A typical way to show customer needs and quality characteristics is to use a matrix. It is important that there is a quality characterisitic for each customer need, otherwise, it isn't clear that all customer needs will be met. It is also important to identify which quality characteristics are the most critical for meeting customer needs. These key characteristics will be the priority focus of new product development. A simple example is shown in Figure 15-3.

Quality Characteristics

Product: Car	Looks	Purchase price	Comfort level	Repair cost
Attractive	X			
Affordable		X		X
Comfortable			X	
Low repair frequency				X
Total	1X	1X	1X	2X

Customer Needs

Figure 15-3: The Basic Matrix that Starts the QFD Process

A key quality characteristic is the repair cost because it relates to the customers' needs for affordability and low frequency of repair.

Application of the Creativity Tools

Many times engineers have not thought about customer needs in this way, so it takes some creativity to understand what to measure to meet a customer need. Each customer need must have at least one measure. Brainstorming is usually sufficient to identify this measure, but if not, some of the other creativity tools can be used.

During the 1980s, a team at Ford Motor Company was addressing a customer need of reduced tire wear on light trucks. The team used the QFD process to identify new measures related to reduced tire wear and eventually solved a long-standing problem.

3. Improve a Design Concept

The next step in the new product development process is to generate new concepts for a product or service that not only meets key customer needs, but also surpasses all competitor's products.

"Obvious thinking commonly leads to wrong judgments and wrong conclusions."

Humphrey B. Neil

Chapter 15

Application of the Creativity Tools

Chapter 11 looked at Stuart Pugh's process for new concept selection. Sometimes the new concepts are not satisfactory. When it is unclear how to approach the breakthrough, the Heuristic Redefinition tool can be helpful. TILMAG is particularly useful because the criteria for new concepts can be used as the ideal solution elements (ISEs) in generating new ideas. The Morphological Box is also a good choice for generating a number of new concepts.

4. Eliminate Engineering Bottlenecks

One of the key benefits of QFD is that it can dramatically reduce design time. By addressing key engineering bottlenecks up front, many engineering changes are eliminated down the road, saving time and cost. Figure 15-4[1] shows the difference in the number of engineering/product changes between two manufacturing companies in the 1980s.

Japanese/U.S. Engineering Change Comparison

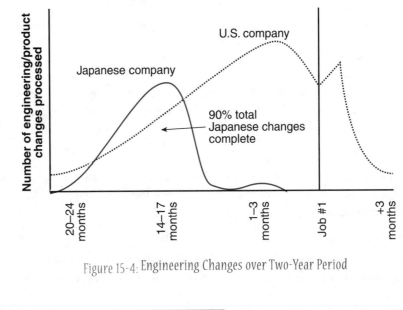

Figure 15-4: Engineering Changes over Two-Year Period

---

1. © 1986 American Society for Quality. Reprinted with permission. "Quality Function Deployment," *Quality Progress* (June 1986).

Reducing bottlenecks sounds like a fine idea in theory, but what if the engineering group cannot figure out how to meet the breakthrough objective?

Application of the Creativity Tools

More than one company has been held back by the inability to commercialize a new product concept. The creativity tools, especially when they are coupled with the TRIZ tools described in Appendix B, are eliminating, in days or weeks, engineering bottlenecks that persisted for years.

5. Improve Product and Process Reliability

Reliability is the process for determining what causes a product or process to fail and makes the changes to reduce the frequency and severity of the failure.

Application of the Creativity Tools

The Failure Mode Effects Analysis (FMEA) chart is one of the reliability improvement tools. It identifies the cause of failure (frequency, detectability, and severity), and creates an index of these three items to prioritize areas for improvement. The FMEA chart enhances new product development by developing products that will rarely fail. Some companies do too little reliability design, which results in products that always have to be repaired. Other companies do too much reliability design, which results in delays in time to market and a higher purchase price for the customer.

The use of the Morphological Box in conjunction with the reliability tools makes it possible to efficiently achieve the most reliable design. In the Morphological Box, each realistic option is identified, so it is possible to select those options that will result in the most reliable product.

Conclusion

This brief overview should demonstrate to a team the power and value of the creativity tools for several aspects of product design. Using the tools also helps a team to open up its thinking, explore ideas more positively, find new connections, and create breakthrough products that excite customers.

'Failure to use such an abundant inherent treasure as creativity,
whether it be because of unawareness that it exists, indifference,
or deliberate stultification is more than a waste; it is self-betrayal.'

Masathoshi Yoshimura

Strategies for Implementing the Tools

A team leader should be aware of some important factors that can influence the successful application of the creativity and idea selection tools to an organization's business processes. The enhanced ability to innovate through the use of the tools described in this book will be achieved if:

- Sufficient numbers of employees throughout the organization are skilled in using these methods.

- The tools are used frequently in practical applications.

- The tools are integrated into normal business processes.

- The tools are practiced with appropriate levels of support.

These requirements may appear obvious, however, many organizations make attempts to promote more creative thinking with insufficient preparation and support. Some of the critical success factors that will ensure organizations achieve tremendous results with the tools are described in this chapter.

Critical Success Factors for Using the Tools

A. Adequate knowledge and training in how the tools work
B. Adequate facilitation resources
C. Demonstrated and widespread organizational support for creativity and innovation
D. Realistic expectations
E. Effective management of personal resistance

"These people who are always briskly doing something and as busy as waltzing mice, they have little, sharp, staccato ideas, such as: 'I see where I can make an annual cut of $3.47 in my meat budget.' But they have no slow, big ideas."

Brenda Ueland

Chapter 16

A. Adequate Knowledge and Training in How the Tools Work

Unless there is sufficient training and practice in the use of the tools, they can be dismissed as either too easy, too hard, or useless. They can be seen as silly and not worth the team's time. Lack of sufficient knowledge about the use and value of the tools can lead to misunderstandings about their application and the results to be obtained.

Studies have shown that creative thinking can be improved through training. Yet, improved results through the use of tools will not happen automatically. The development of creativity and innovation is necessarily tied to learning processes. Time and practice are critical success factors. The tools and techniques for generating and selecting ideas that are provided in this book are excellent training aids to support the learning process.

In some ways, mental activities can be compared with physical movements. If we watch people who are learning to play tennis, we notice how often they practice their serve until it is good enough for a match. Learning the right serve does not happen on a theoretical level. People need practice to get used to the movements that have to be performed. It's the same with any creativity tool. The tools are not hard to understand or use, but successful application needs a lot of practice until the "mental movements" perform as they should.

One important issue of training is whether people will be able to use their new skills back in the workplace to enhance their team's ability for creative thinking. The factors that support an individual's ability to transfer this knowledge include:

- Sufficient opportunities and/or an adequate level of new knowledge for the trained person to pass on the newly acquired skills to others.

- The right degree of readiness on the part of colleagues to adopt this knowledge.

- Frequent opportunities for immediate application and practice.

A well thought-out training and implementation strategy is one way to successfully deal with these challenges. This strategy should include the approach of "just-in-time" training, in which training is tied to real-world problems that need immediate attention. In this case, the participants will have a chance to practice the tools both in the training session and on the job. The strategy should also address the availability of opportunities for further application and practice.

B. Adequate Facilitation Resources

A training strategy should address the development of appropriate individuals to support the use of the tools after training workshops have been held. One way to do this during the training period is to have experienced facilitators available to create and support a stimulating and relaxed environment that favors creativity and innovation. Experienced facilitators can also serve as role models, can help others overcome insecurity with the new methods, and can help break through deadlocks.

Such facilitators can be trained employees. Another alternative is to engage experienced external facilitators during the training period. The external facilitators can help with the training in the idea generation and selection tools and support the development of in-house facilitators.

C. Demonstrated and Widespread Organizational Support for Creativity and Innovation

The idea generation and selection tools are new to most people. It takes time to learn and practice them. Having opportunities to put the learning into practice soon after the training is also critical for preventing the new knowledge from rapidly fading away. Often, people who have been individually trained may be hesitant about organizing tool sessions because:

- They feel unsure about how to correctly apply the tools.

- They fear their colleagues might assume they are unable to cope with their problems by themselves.

- They don't have authority to make their colleagues come to a tool session.

- They think their efforts will be met with reluctance and excuses.

An organization can keep creative thinking alive by:

- Convening regularly held training sessions that address actual business problems and situations.

- Establishing creativity or innovation teams whose members are focused on developing new ideas for defined projects and services.

- Developing "creativity experts" who have specific responsibilities for providing support to others by planning and facilitating the creativity tool sessions.

Organizational leaders also need to address the issues of top management support, reward and recognition systems, as well as organizational design and development. These issues are discussed in more detail in several of the books listed under Recommended Resources in Appendix C.

The Idea Edge

D. Realistic Expectations

Articles with overstated accounts about the results of creativity and innovation techniques, reports about extraordinary inventions produced with the help of such techniques, myths attached to creativity and innovation, or expensive training with creativity specialists may all inflate the expectations for spectacular results. These unrealistic expectations will inevitably lead to disappointment with the outcomes of the first applications of creativity and innovation tools. Therefore, building fair and appropriate expectations is critical to getting successful results.

E. Effective Management of Personal Resistance

A training and implementation strategy also needs to take into account personal resistance to new approaches. In almost all companies, the demands of daily business tend to prevail over strategic projects and initiatives. Tactical, day-to-day pressures are the reasons for lack of support of the new techniques. New ways of thinking about and approaching problems can be stressful, so many people avoid conceptual work, preferring to deal with the more tangible, tried and true routines. Thus, there can be both open and covert resistance to trying out the new approaches.

Leaders who are attempting to implement these tools and any other new ways of doing business need to address this resistance in their plans for implementation. One strategy is to include the people with the greatest resistance on the project team; another strategy is to plan on frequent and consistent, formal and informal communication about the tools and their benefits.

Summary

If team leaders want to convince employees to use creativity and innovation tools, then they need to carefully plan and implement communications and training that will support the use of these tools. The training should never be seen as corrective action. Team leaders need to market the training as an opportunity for team members to get to know some new methods and tools that can promote creativity and innovation. These new skills can also enhance the individual team member's own job and a sense of market value. Such skills, in turn, will improve the team's ability to find better solutions to problems and processes, create breakthrough products and services, and attract and delight customers.

Conclusion: Making a Case for Creativity

Why should anyone spend time and effort understanding creativity and innovation and learning these tools and their application? The contributions of creativity and innovation have been evident throughout human history. In more recent years, however, the importance of creative ability has increased exponentially. Only a few generations ago, workers would rarely need to change their products or their methods of producing and selling them. Those processes remained stable throughout one's whole life. A cooper, for example, would produce the wooden barrels and tubs again and again, in the very same way as had been done for generations.

In this century, the life cycles of innovations have shortened dramatically. Continuous improvement and innovation have become an everyday necessity for every organization. Many factors have fueled the accelerated drive for creativity and innovation:

- A continuous stream of new products has led to a shorter life cycle and more pressure to be first to market.

- New technological advances become the "seeds" of new product applications.

- Process technologies change at an accelerating speed—what is state-of-the art today is obsolete tomorrow.

- New products must be sensitive to the environment in their manufacturing, use, and disposal.

- Products need to be customized to meet the expanding needs of diverse international markets.

- Global competition has broadened the set of economic challenges.

"This is not the end. It is not even the beginning of the end. But it is, perhaps, the end of the beginning."

Winston Churchill

- Cost containment pressures are leading to unprecedented downsizing, reengineering of processes, and changes in organizational structures.

- The increasing complexity and associated chaos facing organizations today require new thinking skills and flexibility to deal with ambiguity and uncertainty.

Never before have creativity and innovation been so essential to every aspect of an organization. The power of creative thinking is evidenced by the growth of companies such as Microsoft, Intel, Rubbermaid, Xerox, Wal-Mart, The Home Depot, and others. These and many other companies around the world have shown that success depends on the collective sum of the creative minds in an organization. In this regard, every organization has immense potential but an organization can only be as successful as the quality of the collective thinking of its employees.

Most companies work continuously to improve their processes and reduce costs. However, comparable efforts to improve creative activities are very often neglected. The advantages of harnessing the creative potential of employees are many, including:

- new product generation

- market share growth

- expansion of a competitive advantage

- maintenance and development of the company's intellectual capital

- cost savings

- organizational survival

Introducing and supporting more creativity in the workplace can also have a positive impact on employee productivity and morale. Any organization will succeed in the long run when its people can deploy their full creative potential. The spirit of innovation is not only a motivator for current employees, but also a critical strategy for attracting and retaining personnel for the future.

Examples of the benefits of releasing the creative potential and improving the morale of employees are many. In the early 1980s Frito-Lay's sales began to level off. Instead of using short-term budget cutting to face the problem, the company brought in a creativity consultant to find new ways to solve problems. During the next six years, the company saved over $500 million. According to a Frito-Lay spokesman,

"Creative problem solving is one way to tap employees' thinking. It also sends a strong signal that they're valued."

DuPont, a company with many business divisions and mature products, began to emphasize creativity training as part of its renewal process several years ago. DuPont has reaped the benefits because "when people are allowed to exercise their creative talents, they're happier, have higher self-esteem, and are more productive."

In addition, studies have shown that "one of the fastest ways to achieve stock price appreciation is to launch a steady stream of competitive, successful, new products and services. . . . [These results are] evidenced by the stock appreciation track record of companies like 3M, Motorola, Amgen, Owens-Corning, Rubbermaid, and Pfizer."

The tools described in this book provide many different approaches to developing new products and services, improving business processes, and bringing out individual and group creativity for all employees. Creativity tools, no matter how powerful, can neither replace knowledge nor substitute for individual thinking. They bring out productive ways of thinking and help in processing knowledge through specific operations that have a higher probability for producing creative and innovative results. Individuals must be ready to adopt new ways of thinking and to change their problem-solving behaviors. Only those who are capable of doing so will realize the full benefit of these creativity tools.

Enhancing the creative thinking skills of all employees can indeed improve organizational outcomes and profitability. Within an environment of freedom and openness, where effective teamwork is encouraged and supported, where appropriate processes, tools, techniques, and training are provided, organizations can gain a major competitive advantage and thereby ensure their long-term survival. Future organizational success is closely tied to the ability to make full use of everyone's creative talents, to find new solutions to problems, and to create new products and services. By understanding the tools and putting them to use to harness that creativity, organizations will find a major competitive advantage—the sustained capacity to create and innovate.

*"At first people refuse to believe that a strange new thing
can't be done, then they begin to hope it can be done,
then they see if can't be done
—then it is done and all the world wonders
why it was not done centuries ago."*

Frances Hodgson Burnett

Tools for Quality Control and Management & Planning

This appendix briefly summarizes the purpose and uses of 14 tools. Seven of the 14 tools are appropriate for Quality Control (QC) activities, and the other half are appropriate for Management and Planning (MP) activities. These tools and instructions on how to use them are described in more detail in GOAL/QPC's pocket guide *The Memory Jogger™ II*. The Management and Planning Tools are discussed at length in the book *The Memory Jogger Plus+®*, also a GOAL/QPC publication.

Tools for Quality Control

These tools include: Cause & Effect Diagram, Control Chart, Flowchart, Histogram, Pareto Chart, Run Chart, and Scatter Diagram.

"Contemplation is necessary to generate an object, but action must propagate it."

Owen Feltham

Appendix A

Cause & Effect Diagram

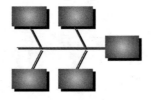

Definition: The Cause and Effect Diagram is a tool that helps a team to identify, explore, and graphically display in increasing detail, all of the possible causes related to a problem or condition in order to discover its root cause(s). This tool:

- helps a team develop a snapshot of the collective knowledge and consensus of a team around a problem.
- usually looks like a skeleton of a fish, with the problem statement (the effect) as the "head," and all of the causes displayed on the "bones."
- is often referred to as a Fishbone Diagram or Ishikawa Diagram.

Control Chart

Definition: The Control Chart is a tool that helps a team identify sources of variation in a process over time, and to monitor, control, and improve process performance.

- Visual images help a team to conceptualize, or "see" something. The Control Chart helps a

team see the performance of its work and answer the questions of how is the team doing? How much variation is there in the output? What is the source of that variation?

- The Control Chart graphically helps a team to focus attention on detecting and monitoring process variation over time.
- The Control Chart also helps point a team to the source of the variation: Is it some unique event that can be traced to an element of the process and corrected locally? Or, is it always present, part of the random variation inherent to the process itself and corrected more globally?
- There are different types of Control Charts based on the type of data available. They generally fall into two categories: Variable Control Charts for continuous, measurable data (e.g., time, length, weight, volume, etc.), and Attribute Control Charts for discrete, countable data (e.g., number of customer complaints, percent defects, number of flaws per unit of fabric, etc.).

Flowchart

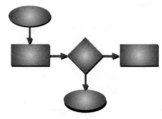

Definition: The Flowchart allows a team to identify the actual flow or sequence of events in a process that any product or service follows.

- The Flowchart graphically shows the logical flow of a process. A process is a series of steps, actions, operations, or decision points involved in accomplishing an end product or service.
- Flowcharts usually look like a series of boxes, diamonds, circles, ovals, etc., that are connected with directional arrows. These symbols help a team to quickly pick out activities in the Flowchart: ovals signify the starting or ending point of the process flow; boxes represent actions or tasks being performed; while diamonds represent a decision point..
- The Flowchart is a roadmap, indicating what to do first and next, who's involved, where to go, and what to do if some criteria are met or not met.

Histogram

Definition: The Histogram helps a team summarize data that has been collected over a period of time, by graphically presenting its frequency distribution in bar form. The Histogram:

- shows the relative frequency of occurrence of various data values.

- displays a profile of the performance of a process and the degree of variation in a process.
- displays large amounts of data that are difficult to interpret in tabular form.

Pareto Chart

Definition: The Pareto Chart is a bar chart that ranks problems or causes of problems. It helps a team to focus efforts on the problems that offer the greatest potential for improvement by showing their relative frequency or size in a descending order from left to right on a horizontal axis.

- A simple but powerful visual tool, the Pareto Chart helps a team build consensus on which problems to attack first, second, and so on.
- The Pareto Chart provides data on how problems stack up "before" and "after" problem-solving or process-improvement teams do their work.
- Pareto Charts usually look like stairs descending in height from left to right. The most frequent or significant factor (the tallest bar) is on the left.

Appendix A

- Named for Vilfredo Pareto, this tool illustrates the proven Pareto Principle or 80-20 principle: 20% of the sources cause 80% of any problem. This principle holds that teams should spend their time addressing the few critical problems, which are the high impact, driving forces in a process or system, and not waste their time and resources on many trivial problems, i.e., things that make little impact on improving a process or system.

Run Chart

Definition: The Run Chart is a tool that helps a person or team to study observed data (a performance measure of a process) for trends or patterns over a specified period of time. The Run Chart:

- is by far the most commonly used tool for tracking data over time. Newspapers, magazines, and textbooks are filled with them, covering everything from the unemployment rate to the sales of peanut butter in North America.
- helps to track the performance of a process over time to detect trends, shifts, or cycles.
- allows the comparison of a performance measure before and after an important

change is made to a process in order to determine the impact of that change.
- helps the team focus on the vital changes in the process.

Scatter Diagram

Definition: The Scatter Diagram helps a team to study and identify the possible relationship between the changes observed in two different sets of variables.

- The Scatter Diagram always looks at the relationship between TWO variables. For example, variable 1 could be height, measured in inches and variable 2 could be weight, measured in pounds.
- Each dot on the Scatter Diagram is a data point that represents both variables.
- The relationship between the two variables is represented by the dispersion of the dots—anything from a random buckshot pattern (no relationship) to a very straight line (potential positive or negative relationship).

Tools for Management & Planning

These tools include: Activity Network Diagram, Affinity Diagram, Interrelationship Digraph (ID), Matrix Diagram, Prioritization Matrices, Process Decision Program Chart, Tree Diagram.

Activity Network Diagram

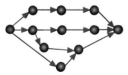

Definition: The Activity Network Diagram allows a team or individual to plan the most efficient schedule for the completion of complex projects and identifies key subtasks to monitor. This tool:

- enables teams to name and sequence the tasks necessary to complete a goal.
- helps the team to determine completion times of individual tasks and the project as a whole.
- helps a team to coordinate parallel tasks and find the critical path.

Affinity Diagram

Definition: The Affinity Diagram is a tool that helps a team gather large amounts of language data (ideas, opinions, issues, etc.), organize it into groupings based on the natural relationship between each item, and define groups of items. The Affinity Diagram:

- encourages non-traditional connections among ideas/issues.
- usually looks like a wall of Post-it™ Notes, which then get arranged into columns. Each column supports a "header card" that summarizes the characteristics of the items in that column.
- allows breakthroughs to emerge naturally, even on long-standing issues.

Interrelationship Digraph (ID)

Definition: The Interrelationship Digraph (ID) allows a team to identify, analyze, and classify the cause-and-effect relationships that exist among a set of issues. The ID:

- enables teams to identify the key drivers of a complex system.

"I never worry about action, but only about inaction."

Winston Churchill

- helps define relationships among large numbers of issues.
- permits the effective deployment of limited resources to reach an objective.

Matrix Diagram

Definition: The Matrix Diagram allows a team or individual to systematically identify, analyze, and rate the presence and strength of relationships between two or more sets of information. The Matrix:

- enables teams to get consensus on small decisions, enhancing the quality and support for the final decision.
- improves a team's discipline in systematically analyzing relationships among a large number of important factors.
- makes patterns of responsibilities visible and clear so that there is an even and appropriate distribution of tasks.

Prioritization Matrices

Definition: The Prioritization Matrices tool allows a team to systematically compare a number of options by selecting, weighing, and applying criteria to them. This tool:

- helps a team to identify and select key action items among several options.
- creates consensus on decision-making criteria and their relative importance.
- helps teams to get the best results with limited resources.

Process Decision Program Chart (PDPC)

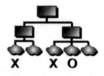

Definition: The PDPC maps out conceivable and likely implementation problems along with appropriate and reasonable counter-measures. This tool:

- encourages teams to consider likely problems that could happen in a given situation.
- enables teams to brainstorm 1) counter-measures to prevent these problems from happening and (2) contingency plans in the event that problems cannot be prevented.

Tree Diagram

Definition: The Tree Diagram breaks any broad goal into detailed actions that must or could be done to achieve the stated broad goal and each related subgoal. The Tree Diagram:

- breaks down a broad goal into activities to accomplish the goal.
- graphically shows the complexity of accomplishing a stated goal.
- allows team members and outsiders to review the team's thinking for completeness and logical flow.

"There is no problem of human nature which is insoluble."
Ralph J. Bunche

Systematic Innovation:

Inventing on Purpose Instead of Waiting for the Lightning to Strike

This appendix is a reprint of an article that appeared in Journal of Innovative Management, Winter 1995–1996, on pages 65–70. The article was written by Ellen Domb, Ph.D., President of the PQR Group; Bob King, CEO of GOAL/QPC; and Karen Tate, President of The Griffin Tate Group.

"Neither a wise man nor a brave man lies down on the tracks of history to wait for the train of the future to run over him."

Dwight D. Eisenhower

Preface

Some people espouse the idea that creativity and innovation happen by accident. Others say you cannot force it or predict it. In the vernacular, not true!

True, you can invent by running thousands of experiments, trying various ideas. Thomas Edison did just that when he invented the light bulb. He had a large staff just running experiments. But there are methods for systematic creativity and systematic innovation. GOAL/QPC has organized the methods for systematic creativity in the Seven Creativity Tool Boxes course.

Systematic Innovation is a disciplined way of focusing thought for efficient solving of technical problems and for the forecasting of technological evolution. This article is a brief overview of Systematic Innovation, and future issues of the *Journal* will amplify specific aspects of Systematic Innovation. (In-house demonstration courses are available for those who can't wait.)

Appendix B

Introduction

Systematic Innovation (SI) is a set of methods and principles for examining technical problems and quickly developing many possible solutions. It is especially useful for new product development, service delivery, or solving production problems. Spectacular results tend to be the norm:

- In two hours an automotive supplier came up with 60 patentable ideas for improving a component that had been inadequate for five years.

- In two days, a powder metallurgy problem that had persisted for 10 years was solved, in eight different ways.

- A new design concept for a hydraulic hammer that had a four year history of field failure was developed in the first half-day of analysis.

- As part of a homework assignment, a Norwegian graduate student developed a prototype 3-D model maker that is 10 times faster than stereo lithography.

A Tool for Generating Solutions

The methods of SI acquaint an individual or a team with an array of problem solutions from a variety of industries and other sciences. Dozens of principles are provided for modeling any kind of problem, then matching it to "standard solutions" that have a proven history of solving that kind of problem.

Begin with Analysis

Systematic Innovation starts with a thorough analysis of a problem or perceived opportunity:

- Why is it a problem or opportunity?
- For whom?
- Under what circumstances?
- Is there a contradiction in the problem?

Examples of Using Contradictions

Contradictions, rather than being a problem, are very important and useful in SI. Here are two examples:

1. Airplanes are required to have wheels to maneuver on the ground, but to not have wheels to be streamlined in the air. In SI, the requirement that something have two opposite properties is called a "physical contradiction." For this class of contradiction, SI recommends separating the properties of the system in time, which leads to the idea of landing gear that can be present on the ground and absent in flight.

2. A razor is required to be sharp to cut hair, but the sharper it gets, the more likely it is to cut the skin. An SI analysis would lead to phrasing this contradiction as: increasing the capacity to do work causes an increase in the harm done by the system. When improving one parameter causes another to degrade, we have a "technical contradiction." Conventional engineering frequently tries to compromise the solution when a technical contradiction arises; that is, a trade-off is made based on how much good will result versus how much harm. SI uses the contradiction as a springboard for breakthrough—to remove the contradiction, rather than compromise the design by accepting the harm with the good. To facilitate this work, the SI tools include a special matrix. (After presenting this tool, we'll tell you the solution to the razor example.)

Contradiction Matrix

The SI tools include the Contradiction Matrix, a 39x39 matrix of characteristics of general technical systems that could be in conflict. Figure 1 is an excerpt of the matrix; it's only a partial, constructed for an example, as the full matrix would be too large to show here.

The row elements are the characteristics to be improved, and the columns are the characteristics that could be adversely affected. The numbers at the intersection guide the user to some of the 40 principles that might be of help in resolving the contradiction. (The shaded cells mean there is no conflict or contradiction; strength does not contradict strength, for example.)

Each cell of the matrix contains up to five of the 40 principles of problem solving that are possible solutions to the contradiction. The problem solving team reads the recommended principles, and the case studies that illustrate them, then uses advanced analogy to generate solutions to their problem.

	Characteristic which is Deteriorating	14	21	32	39
Characteristic to be Improved		Strength	Power	Convenience to Manufacture	Capacity
14	Strength		10, 26, 35, 28	11,3,10,32	29, 35,10,14
21	Power	26,10,28		26, 10, 34	28, 35, 34
32	Convenience to Manufacture	1, 3, 10, 32	27, 12, 1, 24		35, 1, 10, 28
39	Capacity	29, 28, 10, 18	35, 20, 10	35, 28, 2, 24	

Figure 1: Contradiction Matrix (Excerpt)

Now back to the razor example. One of the recommended principles was "Localization of Quality" which states that different parts of the system should be optimized to do specific functions. In the case of the razor, the product team decided that they should make the blade very sharp to optimize cutting, and then design the blade holder to push the skin aside and position the skin properly to cut the hair without cutting the skin; thus, the razor can cut very close without harming the skin. Many different designs are now on the market that apply this principle.

This is a type of advanced problem solving that requires the taking of different views—one looks at the system level, the supersystem, and any subsystem of the problem. The reason for this is that what looks like a technical contradiction at one level may look like a physical contradiction at another level. Having several views enriches the set of available solutions and leads to the generation of better options.

Technology Forecasting for Competitive Advantage

SI can also be used to forecast technological change. The technology forecasting methods of SI multiply your ability to understand where your designs are going, and where your competitors are going, so you can plan development investments now to get the right products to market at the right time. This is a good way to leapfrog the competition, rather than just catch up.

You can also use these same methods to predict where your suppliers' technologies are headed and avoid the problems of having great products that require unavailable parts and processes. In like manner, predicting your customers' technologies will help prevent you from being in the wrong market at the wrong time.

The U.S. Air Force is an enthusiastic user of SI's technology forecasting methods. The Air University is engaged in a future forecasting project for the year 2025. They recently began applying SI's technology forecasting tools to this work of creating concepts for Air Force systems in the year 2025. Within two hours of first seeing examples of the SI methods, 13 cross-disciplinary teams (including other services, civilians, and non-U.S. military) had applied the techniques to four different technology areas and developed scenarios that have accelerated their research.

Where Did SI Come From?

Systematic Innovation is relatively new to the United States. SI is based on decades of patent study by the Russian researcher G.S. Altshuller and his colleagues. It is known as The Theory of the Solution of Inventive Problems (TRIZ, from the Russian acronym) or TIPS, from the English paraphrase: Theory of Inventive Problem Solving.

Altshuller's study of patents began in the USSR in 1946 and has since spread to Germany, Sweden, Norway, Israel, and North America. From this research, standard problems and standard solutions were derived and formulated into algorithms, principles, and standard approaches to solving technical problems (see Figure 2).

"Make your plans as fantastic as you like, because 25 years from now, they will seem mediocre. Make your plans ten times as great as you first planned, and 25 years from now you will wonder why you did not make them 50 times as great."

Henry Curtis

Appendix B

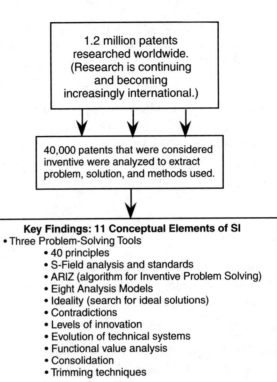

Figure 2: G. S. Altshuller and his colleagues found research data in the patent literature, initially in the USSR, then worldwide.

From this research, standard problems and standard solutions were derived and formulated into algorithms, principles, and standard approaches to solving technical problems.

Where is it Being Used?

Many U.S. companies are discovering SI and rapidly using it to solve significant problems in design and production. Xerox, Ford, General Motors, Procter & Gamble, Motorola, Kodak, McDonnell Douglas, Hughes, AT&T, and dozens of smaller, fast-moving creative companies are starting to use SI.

How Does SI Fit In with Other Tools and Methods?

What about all the other "new" quality tools? Robust Design? Design for manufacturability? Quality Function Deployment? Voice of the Customer? Concurrent (or Simultaneous) Engineering? Integrated product and process development? Customer intimate service? Agile production?

Figure 3 (shown on the next page) shows the opportunities for use of just the problem-solving side of SI in a QFD approach to product design. Different aspects of SI can be used at each of the possible points of contradiction. Many QFD practitioners have been frustrated by QFD's power to point out contradictions between customers' needs and the capability to fulfill them. SI now gives them tools to solve those problems, not just find compromises.

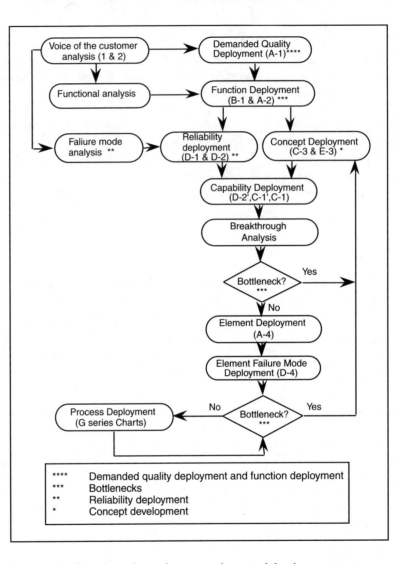

Figure 3: This flow chart shows the stages of a typical development process.
The asterisks show where SI may be needed.

Conclusion

Systematic Innovation is not a replacement for other tools or methods, nor is it a substitute for the conventional product development disciplines. In future issues of the *Journal* we'll show specific examples of the principles of SI, and how they enhance the other techniques of product and service development.

References

Altov, H. *And Suddenly the Inventor Appeared*. Translation by Lev Shulyak. Worcester, MA. Technical Innovation Center, 1994.

Altshuller, G. S. *Creativity as an Exact Science*. Gordon and Breach,1988.

King, Bob. *Better Designs In Half The Time: Implementing QFD in America*. Methuen, MA. GOAL/QPC, 1989.

Kowalik, James; Domb, Ellen. Tutorial on QFD & Systematic Innovation, QFDI Symposium, Novi, Michigan, June 1995.

Marsh, Stan, et. al. *Facilitating and Training in Quality Function Deployment*. Methuen, MA. GOAL/QPC, 1991.

Nadler, Gerald and Hibino, Shozo. *Breakthrough Thinking*. Rocklin, CA. Prima Publishing, 1994.

Tsourikov, Valery M. *Inventive Machine: Second Generation*. Artificial Intelligence & Society, 1993, #7, pp. 62-77, Springer-Verlag London Ltd.

"The trouble with our times is that the future is not what it used to be."

Paul Valery

Appendix B

Author Information

Dr. Ellen Domb is President of the PQR Group in Upland, California, a consulting firm specializing in the application of Total Quality Management. She has a B.S. from MIT and a Ph.D. in Physics from Temple University. She has been a director of the Aerojet Electronics Systems Division with specific responsibility for TQM implementation.

Bob King is Chairman and CEO of GOAL/QPC in Methuen, Massachusetts, a not-for-profit management research, training, and publishing organization. He is the author of two books: *Better Designs in Half the Time: Implementing QFD in America*, and *Hoshin Planning: the Developmental Approach*. He has a master's degree in education from Boston University.

Karen Tate is principal of the Griffin-Tate Group in Cincinnati, Ohio. Prior to that she was a Senior Project Manager and a Director of Continuous Improvement with Belcan Engineering Group and Senior Construction Engineer with Bechtel Power Corporation. She has an MBA degree from Xavier University and a B.S. degree in Finance from Bloomsburg University of Pennsylvania.

Recommended Resources

Books

Creativity

Adams, James. *Conceptual Blockbusting*. Reading, MA: Addison-Wesley, 1986.

Altshuller, G. (H. Altov). *And Suddenly the Inventor Appeared*. Translated by Lev Shulyak. 1996.

Altshuller, G.S. *Creativity as an Exact Science*. Translated by Anthony Williams. Luxembourg: Gordon and Breach Publishers, 1984.

Amabile, Teresa M. *Creativity in Context*. Boulder, CO: Westview Press, 1996.

Arieti, Silvano. *Creativity, the Magic Synthesis*. New York: Basic Books, Inc., 1976.

Burns, T. and G.M. Stalker. *The Management of Innovation*. London: Tavistock, 1961.

Buzan, Tony. *Use Both Sides of Your Brain*. New York: Dutton, 1983.

Cameron, Julia. *The Artist's Way*. Los Angeles: Jeremy P. Tarcher/Perigee. 1992.

Csikszentmihalyi, Mihaly. *Creativity*. New York: HarperCollins, 1996.

DeBono, Edward. *Serious Creativity*. New York: HarperCollins, 1993.

DeBono, Edward. *Six Thinking Hats*. Toronto: Key Porter Books, Ltd., 1985.

Ford, Cameron M. and Dennis A. Gioia. *Creative Actions in Organizations*. Thousand Oaks, CA: Sage Publications, 1995.

Fritz, Robert. *The Path of Least Resistance*. New York: Ballantine Books, 1989.

Gardner, Howard. *Creating Minds*. New York: Basic Books, Inc., 1993.

Gardner, Howard. *Leading Minds*. New York: Basic Books, Inc., 1995.

Glover, John A., R.R. Ronning, C. R. Reynolds, eds. *Handbook of Creativity*. New York: Plenum Press, 1989.

Gordon, William J., *Synectics*. New York: Harper & Row, 1961.

Gronhaug, K. and Geir Kaufmann, eds. *Innovation: A Cross-Disciplinary Perspective*. Oslo: Norwegian University Press, 1988.

Isaksen, Scott G., Mary C. Murdock, Roger Firestien, Donald J. Treffinger, eds. *Nurturing and Developing Creativity: The Emergence of a Discipline*, Norwood, NJ: Ablex, 1993.

Isaksen, Scott G., Mary C. Murdock, Roger Firestien, Donald J. Treffinger, eds., *Understanding and Recognizing Creativity: The Emergence of a Discipline*. Norwood, NJ: Ablex, 1993.

Isaksen, Scott, ed. *Frontiers of Creativity Research: Beyond the Basics*. Buffalo, NY: Bearly Limited, 1987.

Kao, John. *Jamming: The Art and Discipline of Business Creativity*. New York: HarperCollins, 1996.

Kuczmarski, Thomas D. *Innovation*. Chicago: NTC Business Books, 1996.

Leonard-Barton, Dorothy. *Wellsprings of Knowledge*. Boston: Harvard Business School Press, 1995.

Mattimore, Bryan. *99% Inspiration*. New York: American Management Association, 1994.

Michalko, Michael. *Thinkertoys: A Handbook of Business Creativity for the 90s*. Berkeley, CA: Ten Speed Press, 1991.

Miller, William C. *The Creative Edge*. Reading, MA: Addison-Wesley, 1987.

Morgan, Gareth. *Creative Organization Theory*. Newbury Park, CA: Sage Publications, 1989.

Morgan, Gareth. *Images of Organization*. 2nd edition. Newbury Park, CA: Sage Publications, 1997.

Morgan, Gareth. *Imaginization: The Art of Creative Management*. Newbury Park, CA: Sage Publications, 1997.

Nadler, Gerald and Shigeru Hibino. *Breakthrough Thinking*. 2nd edition. Rocklin, CA: Primo Publishing, 1994.

Osborn, Alex F. *Applied Imagination*. 3rd edition. Buffalo, NY: Creative Education Foundation Press, 1993.

Parnes, Sidney J. and H.F. Harding, eds. *A Source Book for Creative Thinking*. New York: Charles Scribner and Sons, 1962.

Pugh, Stuart. *Creating Innovative Products Using Total Design*. Reading, MA: Addison-Wesley, 1996.

Ray, Michael and Rochelle Myers. *Creativity in Business*. New York: Doubleday, 1986.

Schlicksupp, Helmut. *Führung zu Kreativität*. A. a. O. Renningen-Malmsheim: Expert Verlag. 1995.

Schlicksupp, Helmut. *Innovation, Kreativität und Ideenfindung*. Würzburg, 1992.

Schlicksupp, Helmut. *Kreative Ideenfindung in der Unternehmung*. Berlin: DeGruyter, 1977.

Schlicksupp, Helmut. *Produktinnovation*. Würzburg, 1988.

Schlicksupp, Helmut and Roland Fahle. *Morphos: Methoden systematischer Problemlösung*. Würzburg: Vogel, 1988 (handbook of the software program *Morphos*).

Stein, Morris I. *Stimulating Creativity. Vol. 1: Individual Procedures*. New York: Academic Press, 1974.

Stein, Morris I. *Stimulating Creativity. Vol. 2: Group Procedures*. New York: Academic Press, 1975.

Sternberg, Robert J., ed. *The Nature of Creativity*. Cambridge, MA: Cambridge University Press, 1988.

Tanner, David. *Total Creativity in Business & Industry*. Des Moines, IA: Advanced Practice Thinking Training, Inc., 1997.

West, Michael A. and James L. Farr, eds. *Innovation and Creativity at Work*. Chichester, England: John Wiley & Sons, Ltd., 1990.

Wujec, Tom. *Pumping Ions*. Toronto: Doubleday Canada Ltd., 1988.

Wycoff, Joyce. *Mind Mapping: Your Personal Guide to Exploring Creativity and Problem Solving*. New York: Berkley Publishing Group, 1991.

Project Management

Duncan, William R. *A Guide to the Project Management Body of Knowledge*. 1996.

Martin, Paula and Karen Tate. *Project Management Memory Jogger™*. Methuen, MA: GOAL/QPC, 1997.

Wysocki, Robert W., Robert Beck Jr., and David B. Crane. *Effective Project Management*. 1995.

Teambuilding

GOAL/QPC and Joiner Associates. *The Team Memory Jogger™*. Methuen, MA: GOAL/QPC, 1995.

Katzenbach, Jon R. and Douglas K. Smith. *The Wisdom of Teams*. New York: HarperCollins, 1993.

Total Quality Management

Brassard, Michael. *The Memory Jogger Plus+®*. Methuen, MA: GOAL/QPC,1989.

Brassard, Michael, Diane Ritter, et al. *Coach's Guide to The Memory Jogger™ II: The Easy-to-Use, Complete Reference for Working with Improvement and Planning Tools in Teams*. Methuen, MA: GOAL/QPC, 1995.

Brassard, Michael and Diane Ritter. *The Memory Jogger™ II*. Methuen, MA: GOAL/QPC, 1994.

Clausing, Don. *Total Quality Development: A Step-by-Step Guide to World-Class Concurrent Engineering*. American Society of Mechanical Engineers. 1994.

Deming, W. Edwards. *Out of the Crisis*. Cambridge, MA: MIT Center for Advanced Engineering Study, 1986.

Deming, W. Edwards. *The New Economics: For Industry, Government, Education*. Cambridge, MA: MIT Center for Advanced Engineering Study, 1993.

King, Bob. *Better Designs in Half the Time: Implementing Quality Function Deployment in America*. Methuen, MA: GOAL/QPC, 1989.

Articles on Creativity

Amabile, Teresa M. "Within You, Without You: The Social Psychology of Creativity, and Beyond." In Mark A. Runco & Robert S. Albert (eds.), *Theories of Creativity*, Newbury Park, CA: Sage Publications, 1990, 61–91.

Amabile, Teresa M. and Elizabeth Tighe. "Questions of Creativity." In John Brockman (ed.), *Creativity*. New York: Simon & Shuster, 1993, 7–27.

Damanpour, Fariborz. "Organizational Innovation: A Meta-Analysis of Effects of Determinants and Moderators." *Academy of Management Journal* 34 (March 1991): 555–590.

Gardner, Howard. "Creative Lives and Creative Works: A Synthetic Scientific Approach." In Robert Sternberg (ed.), *The Nature of Creativity*, 1988. Cambridge, MA: Cambridge University Press, (pp. 298–321).

Guilford, J. P. "Creativity: A Quarter Century of Progress." In I. A. Taylor & J. W. Getzels (eds.), *Perspectives in Creativity*, 1975. Chicago: Aldine Publishing Company, (pp. 37–59).

Harrington, Donald M. "The Ecology of Human Creativity: A Psychological Perspective." In Mark A. Runco & Robert S. Albert (eds.), *Theories of Creativity*. Newbury Park, CA: Sage Publications, 1990, 143–169.

Isaksen, Scott G., Gerard J. Puccio, and Donald J. Treffinger. "An Ecological Approach to Creativity Research: Profiling for Creative Problem Solving." *The Journal of Creative Behavior* 27 (March 1993): 149–170.

Kanter, Rosabeth M. "When a Thousand Flowers Bloom: Structural, Collective, and Social Conditions for Innovation in Organization." In Barry M. Staw & Larry L. Cummings (eds.), *Research in Organizational Behavior*, 10 (1988): 169–211.

Puccio, Gerard J. "An Overview of Creativity Assessment." *The Assessment of Creativity: An Occasional Paper from the Creativity Based Information Resources Project*, 1994, 5–20.

Quinn, James B. "Managing Innovation: Controlled Chaos." *Harvard Business Review* (May/June 1985): 73–85.

Tushman, Michael and David Nadler. "Organizing for Innovation." *California Management Review* 28 (March 1986): 74–92.

Woodman, Richard W., John E. Sawyer, and Ricky W. Griffin. "Toward a Theory of Organizational Creativity." *Academy of Management Review* 18 (February 1993): 293–321.

"A writer didn't need 'an idea' for a book; she needed at least forty. And 'get' was the wrong word, implying that you received an idea as you would a gift. You didn't get ideas. You smelled them out, tracked them down, wrestled them into submission; you pursued them with forks and hope, and if you were lucky enough to catch one you impaled it, with the forks, before the sneaky little devil could get away."

Elizabeth Peters

Index

The Idea Edge

Order Form

Code	Item Name/Title	Unit Price	Qty	Total

Subtotal	
Sales Tax MA, GA, PA, & Canada Only	
Shipping & Handling (see column to the right)	
Total	

Payment Method (choose one)

❑ Check or Money Order attached $ _____
   (Make payable to GOAL/QPC)

❑ Purchase Order # _____
   (Attach a hard copy for all federal government orders)

❑ AMEX   ❑ Discover   ❑ Diners Club   ❑ MasterCard   ❑ VISA

Exp. Date: _____/_____

Cardholder's Name _____
(please print)

Cardholder's Signature _____

Card Number

| | | | | | | | | | | | | | | | |
|1|2|3|4|5|6|7|8|9|10|11|12|13|14|15|16|

Payment Methods

We accept payment by check, money order, credit card, or purchase order. **If you are paying by purchase order:** 1) Provide the name and address of the person to be billed, or 2) Send a copy of the P.O. when order is payable by an agency of the federal government.

Bill To: (If different from "Ship To")

Name _____
Title _____
Company _____
Division/Dept. _____
Address _____
City _____ State/Province _____
Zip/Postal Code _____ Country _____
Phone _____ Fax _____
E-mail _____

Ship To: (Please use street address. We cannot ship to a P.O. Box.)

Name _____
Title _____
Company _____
Division/Dept. _____
Address _____
City _____ State/Province _____
Zip/Postal Code _____ Country _____
Phone _____ Fax _____
E-mail _____
GOAL/QPC Member Number _____
(needed for member discount)

Visit our web site at www.goalqpc.com

Ordering Information

☎

Call Toll Free

1-800-643-4316
(or 978-685-6370)
8:30 AM – 5:00 PM EST

✉

Mail

GOAL/QPC
13 Branch Street
Methuen, MA
01844-1953

☎

Fax

978-685-6151
Any Day, Any Time

Shipping & Handling

Continental US:
Orders up to $10 = $2 (US Mail).
Orders $10 or more = $4 + 4% of the total order (guaranteed Ground Delivery). Call for Overnight, 2 & 3 day delivery.
For Alaska, Hawaii, Canada, Puerto Rico and other countries, please call.

Sales Tax

Canada	7% of order
Georgia	Applicable county tax
Massachusetts	5% of order
Pennsylvania	6% of order

Additional Products from GOAL/QPC

"Only people who have actually experienced the pain of projects failing and the bliss of difficult projects succeeding could have formulated this little beauty."

Bea Glenn, Organizational Development Consultant, Chiquita Banana International, Cincinnati, OH

GOAL/QPC

Manage Your Projects on Time and Within Budget

The Project Management Memory Jogger™

A Pocket Guide for Project Teams

Paula Martin and Karen Tate

Fits in your pocket

- Meet critical deadlines
- Stay within budget limits
- Allocate scarce resources
- Meet or exceed customer requirements

The *Project Management Memory Jogger*™ is the most cost-effective way to ensure that your project teams achieve high-quality results. It provides every member of your organization with an easy-to-use roadmap for managing all types of projects. Whether your team is planning the construction of a new facility or implementing a customer feedback system, this pocket guide helps you avoid typical problems and pitfalls and create successful project outcomes every time. It is packed with useful information on everything from project concept to completion.

The method described in the *Project Management Memory Jogger*™ is consistent with industry standard approaches such as PMBOK, with an emphasis on participation, empowerment, individual accountability, and bottom line project results. It utilizes tools and concepts from continuous process improvement and applies those to making project management something that is accessible to all teams working on projects. Spiral-bound pocket guide measures 3.5" x 5.5". 1997. 164 pages. ISBN 1-57681-001-1. Code 1035E. $7.95 per copy. Quantity discounts available.

Give Your Team the Edge it Needs to Succeed

The Team Memory Jogger™

A Pocket Guide for Team Members

A GOAL/QPC-Joiner Publication

Fits in your pocket

- Learn how to be an effective team member

- Identify key issues that your teams need to address

- Get work done more efficiently in teams

- Know when and how to end a project

- Manage conflict more effectively

Both The Team Memory Jogger™ *and* The Memory Jogger™ II *have played an important role in Inco's Ontario Division over the last six months. We have included these pocket guides with our own training material for a 'Quality Overview' course, and attendees have said they are both instructive and good references for facilitating groups, which they do back in the workplace.*

Bill Dopson,
Divisional TQ Coordinator,
Inco Limited (Ontario Division)

Additional Products from GOAL/QPC

The Team Memory Jogger™ is perfect for every member of your team. Each topic is discussed from the viewpoint of a team member and what one can contribute to the team. This friendly pocket guide is relevant to all kinds of teams; project, process improvement, self-directed or intact work teams, task forces and so on.

Written in collaboration with Joiner Associates, this new pocket guide has become a phenomenal hit for one simple reason—it contains teamwork strategies that really work. Since its introduction in 1995, many organizations have incorporated *The Team Memory Jogger*™ as their standard reference in courses on team effectiveness.

The Team Memory Jogger™ goes beyond theory to provide you with practical, nuts-and-bolts action steps on how to be an effective team member. It is a perfect complement to *The Memory Jogger*™ *II*. Spiral-bound pocket guide measures 3.5" x 5.5". 1995. 164 pages. ISBN 1-879364-51-4. Code 1050E. $7.95 per copy. Quantity discounts available.

GOAL/QPC

Additional Products from GOAL/QPC

"The ISO/QS-9000 quality game is somewhat new to everybody and a complete, reader-friendly pocket guide is a perfect companion to anyone in the field. This new Memory Jogger™ 9000 *is a perfect concept tool to help you implement the ISO 9000 Quality Systems Standard and the Automotive QS-9000 Quality System Requirement."*

Lloyd D. Brumfield,
Quality Assurance
Engineering Specialist,
ASQC Automotive Division
Michigan Quality Council
APX International
Ford Motor Company

GOAL/QPC

Everyone Contributes to Your ISO/QS-9000 Efforts

The Memory Jogger™ 9000

A Pocket Guide to Implementing the ISO 9000 Quality Systems Standard and QS-9000 Requirements
Robert Peach and Diane Ritter

Fits in your pocket

- Communicate the what, why, and how of ISO 9000
- Learn how to meet the ISO 9000 Standards and the QS-9000 Requirements
- Learn how to achieve and maintain ISO 9000/QS-9000 registration

The Memory Jogger™ 9000, an easy-to-use reference, is your everyday guide to the ISO 9000 Quality Systems Standards and QS-9000 Requirements. This is the first publication of its size to address a broad audience, not just the implementation team. It is packed with tips and potential pitfalls; flowcharts, figures, and checklists; documentation examples; definitions of key terms; and other illustrative and supplemental information that will be vital to your understanding of how to comply with the ISO 9000 Standard and QS-9000 Requirements.

The Memory Jogger™ 9000 is the product of a collaboration between GOAL/QPC and Robert Peach, of Peach and Associates, who is a world-renowned consultant for ISO 9000 and editor of *The ISO 9000 Handbook*. Spiral-bound pocket guide measures 3.5" x 5.5". 1996. 164 pages. ISBN 1-879364-82-4. Code 1060E. $7.95 per copy. Quantity discounts available.